To KATHY and Don,

The New Circlemakers

WITH BEST WISHOV

10/8/09.

The New Circlemakers

Insights into the Crop Circle Mystery

Andrew Collins

4th Dimension Press ■ Virginia Beach ■ Virginia

4th Dimension Press
215 67th Street
Virginia Beach, VA 23451-2061

ISBN 13: 978-0-87604-549-7

Photo Credits

Illustrations: 2, 35 George Wingfield; 4, 32, 33 Calyx Photo Agency;
5, 8 Orgone Institute; 8 Busty Taylor; 12 Claire Noble; 13 MUFON, 14,
15 Robin Collyns; 16, 17 M Hermann Chermanne; 18 Tony Beddow; 27,
29 Dr. Greg Little; 29 American Museum of Natural History; 34 Benoit
Mandelbrot; 40 John Day; 41 Brian Froud; 42 Rod Dickinson; 45 V. N.
Tsytovich *et al*, *New Journal of Physics*; 45 V. N. Tsytovich *et al*, *New Journal
of Physics*.

Plates: 1, 7-26 Steven Alexander and Karen Douglas
(temporarytemples.co.uk); 3, 4, 6 Pete Glastonbury, 28 German
Archaeological Institute (DAI), 29 NASA/SRON/MPE.

All other pictures are copyright Andrew Collins.

Cover photo: Steve Alexander Photography
Cover design by Richard Boyle

*This book is dedicated to John Day,
someone who put me on the path of understanding
and enlightenment over 30 years ago.*

Contents

PART FOUR—The Jump

Acknowledgments

I would like to thank John and Doris Van Auken, Greg and Lora Little, Cassie McQuagge, and all at the A.R.E. Press for everything they have done to make this book possible; Steven and Karen Alexander, Pete Glastonbury and Busty Taylor for the use of their photographic images; Adam Crowl, Eileen Buchanan and Denis Montgomery for their correspondence; Matt Kyd for reading the new manuscript; Rodney and Joan Hale for their help and support in all the Orgone projects; John Wilding, Esther Smith, and all at the Henge Shop, along with Charles Mallett of the Silent Circle, for their continued support and promotion of the new book; Amanda and Geoff Baker, Karl Dawkins, Rod Dickinson, Heather Peak Garland, Yuri Leitch, John Lundberg, Lynn and Carl McCoy, Julian Richardson, Ann Smith, Kallista and Chet Snow, Michael Staley and Caroline Wise, Whitley and Anne Strieber, Buster and Abbie Todd, Richard Ward, Paul Weston, Maria Wheatley, Matt Williams, Terry and Jack, Renn, and Raphiem for their continued help and support. Finally, I wish to thank my wife Sue for the love, help, and support she gives on a daily basis.

Preface
2009

Since the publication of *The Circlemakers* in 1992, so much
has happened in the crop circle world that it would be impossible to
sum it all up in just a few brief pages. So I won't try. For me the progression from then on was interesting. Inspired by the book's success, I
initiated a scientific project to investigate the possible relationship between UFOs, crop circles, and the human mind. Orgone 93, as it was
called, found a tentative link between registrable electromagnetic
anomalies recorded during a two-week period in the Alton Barnes area
and the appearance both of crop circles and mysterious lights. The
project was continued the following year under the name Orgone 94,
with the fruits of both years' labors being published in a new book
entitled *Alien Energy* (1994). It looked in much greater detail at many of
the theories proposed in its predecessor and should be sought out by
anyone seriously interested in the findings of this new, remastered edition of *The Circlemakers*.

My personal views on the crop circle phenomenon have evolved
since the publication of *Alien Energy* and so have the crop formations
appearing in the fields of southern England. At the end, there is now
only one pressing question that really matters, and that is whether or not

the crop circles and formations that grace the fields of southern England are "genuine," i.e. of supernatural manufacture, or "hoaxes," i.e. manmade.

Whatever one thinks of the modern circles phenomenon there is insurmountable evidence that swirled or flattened circles of grass and cultivated crop have been occurring for hundreds of years. In the book I cite various examples recalled from the early part of the twentieth century, while British folklore abounds with stories of so-called "fairy rings," a term used both for rings of dark discoloration in grassy meadows caused by fungi *and* swirled circles of wheat and barley. In addition to this, there is the classic account of the mowing devil that creates a flattened circle of crop in a Hertfordshire field in 1678 (see Chapter 12).

More importantly, it has recently come to light that Robert Plot, the seventeenth century naturalist, Professor of Chemistry at Oxford University, and the first keeper of the Ashmolean Museum, can be seen as Britain's first crop circle researcher. In his 1686 work *The Natural History of Staffordshire*, Plot cites appearances of what can only be described as flattened circles of flora as well as other geometric ground patterns.[1] These patterns he investigates and concludes were created by downward bursts of lightning, preempting Terence Meaden's plasma vortex theory for crop circles by 300 years.

Beyond this British tradition of crop circles are accounts of swirled circles in wild and cultivated flora worldwide. Over the years they have appeared in so many different countries and in so many different types of crop, including the rice fields of China, that it hardly seems likely that they can all be put down to the nocturnal actions of crop artists, human "circlemakers," as they like to be called. Moreover, there is evidence from indigenous folklore outside of Britain that crop circles are real. For instance, among the Chippeways, an Algonquian tribe from Michigan and parts of Canada, is an age-old legend concerning their culture hero Algon and how he won a Star-maiden as his bride.

The account appears in Lewis Spence's *Myths of the North American Indians*, published in 1916. The story goes that Algon was out walking among the prairies when he came across a "circular pathway, worn as if by the tread of many feet, though there were no foot-marks visible outside its bounds." Never before, Spence tells us, had the young hunter come upon one of these "fairy rings," and so much did it fill him with surprise that he returned to the long grass in order to try and discover if he might learn of its origin. I'll take up Spence's own words so that nothing is lost:

In a little while he heard the sound of music, so faint and sweet that it surpassed anything he had ever dreamed of. The strains grew fuller and richer, and as they seemed to come from above he turned his eyes toward the sky. Far in the blue he could see a tiny white speck like a floating cloud. Nearer and nearer it came, and the astonished hunter saw that it was no cloud, but a dainty osier car, in which were seated twelve beautiful maidens. The music he had heard was the sound of their voices as they sang strange and magical songs. Descending into the charmed ring, they danced round and round with such exquisite grace and abandon that it was a sheer delight to watch them.[2]

Yet Algon has eyes for only one of the Star-maidens whom he attempts to seize, although she is too quick and eludes his grasp. He tries but fails to capture her on a further occasion, and it is only on a third visit by the Star-maidens on their osier that he is able to grab hold of his love and take her back to the village after having first changed into a mouse and hiding in a hollow tree. She becomes his wife, and they have a son, but she always yearns to return to the "Star-country," and one day this happens. She leaves, taking with her their young son. Algon is heartbroken and spends most of his life at the magic circle on the prairie hoping that she will return with their child. Eventually, when his son has grown to manhood, he returns from the Star-country and meets his father. They then go to the Star-country together, and Algon is finally reunited with his Star-maiden wife.

Even if we accept that Lewis Spence (1874–1955), a noted Scottish folklorist, poet, journalist, and occultist, may have altered the story slightly to conform to British fairy lore (for he describes the Star-maidens as fairies), there are too many elements of this account that figure both in archaic fairy encounters and the modern phenomenon of crop circles and their antecedents, the "saucer nests" of UFO lore, for it to be dismissed as mere fantasy. There is the unidentified aerial craft, the strange noises that accompany it, the manner it settles down on the prairie—a meadow or grassland—to create a swirled ring or circle of grass, and the specific fact that there are no signs of any foot-prints outside the circle to indicate that it might have been of human manufacture.

I believe it would be foolish not to see in this account an age-old

1. Algon, the culture hero of the Chippeways, an Algonquian tribe, carries away the Star-maiden from the flattened circle of long grass.

memory of a "saucer nest" or crop circle caused by some kind of descending aerial phenomenon, interpreted by the ancestors of the Chippeways as a celestial vehicle from a "Star-country" able to carry "Star-maidens." If correct, then this folklore account preempts our modern belief in UFOs as evidence of extraterrestrial contact with human kind by perhaps hundreds of years.

So whatever one might think of modern day crop circles and formations, there is independent evidence from British and American folklore to demonstrate that the circles phenomenon is age-old and has always been associated with entities from other worlds as well as ethereal music and unearthly aerial objects.

This said, there is compelling evidence to show that the greater majority of crop formations found in the fields of southern Britain today are of human manufacture. In fact, many would argue that the more complex the formation, the more likely it is to have been made by human hands. Clearly, such opinions do not sit well with crop circle believers worldwide. They might counter argue that the complexity of the formations, the strange phenomena associated with them, and the odd properties they display, all "prove" that they are the product of supernatural intervention and/or alien intelligences. They would also insist that those who claim to make the formations, the "hoaxers," are liars, and so could not possibly have made them. The human "circlemakers," of course, insist that they do make them, and I am inclined to accept their word, even though I have no *proof* that these individuals can explain everything that happens in the fields of southern England.

In the end it comes down to what you want to believe, for in reality no one can "prove" one way or another who was responsible for *all* the circles or formations. In many ways, this is the nature of the beast. It is like the famous thought experiment proposed in 1935 by Austrian physicist Erwin Schrödinger (1887–1961) and known as Schrödinger's Cat.

The suggestion is to put a live cat in a hermetically sealed box in which is placed a slow release poison triggered by a radioactive substance. The question becomes: when is the cat dead, and when is it alive? Does it even exist once it has been placed in the box? It is a conundrum that creates fierce debate for which there is no single answer, as on a quantum level particles are said to take all possible routes from A to B, creating an infinite number of linear possibilities, of which all are possible yet only the most stable become important in the physical world, i.e. the ones you measure. Yet in doing so, they create all likely outcomes at the same time, and this is a good way to see reality from an individual perspective. All answers are correct—it's just that only some are meaningful to you.

In my mind the subject of crop circles is just such a conundrum, for no one can rightly be said to possess the whole answer, and perhaps this is the way we are meant to perceive them. If so, then it really doesn't matter who, or what, made them—they are here to serve the same purpose, whatever that is.

One crop artist, when asked why he created crop circles year after year, was heard to say: "What would happen if I *didn't* make them?" On the surface this answer might be put down to an inner fear that their handiwork would no longer grace the pages of books, magazines, or online sites, or that Wiltshire would no longer attract tourists from all over the world, but I'd like to see more in it than simply that. Almost all of the human circlemakers believe in aliens and UFOs. Often they see strange lights or feel presences as they do what they do. Often they experience energy effects in the circles they make and can even enter into altered states of consciousness as they get more and more into the circle–making process. In some cases strange symbols, glyphs, and sigils enter their minds as they begin constructing the formation, persuading them to change key elements of the overall design midway into the night. Only afterwards do they find that crop circle enthusiasts have interpreted the formation as, say, encoding important information on the Mayan calendar or something similar. Some of them truly believe they are fulfilling a kind of higher purpose and that the crop art they create is "real," in the same way that the crop circle believers pronounce certain formations to be "genuine."

The English fields full of wheat, oats, barley, or rapeseed are like virgin parchment, just waiting to be defaced by the actions of groups and individuals who, in some cases, can be compared to the surrealist painters of the 1940s and 1950s. These people learned the art of automatic writing and drawing as part of their genre. Some, such as the genius–like Austin Osman Spare (1886–1956), were quite obviously inspired to create what they did either by unseen forces or the higher mind. The same can be said for the human "circlemakers," who see themselves as open channels for the "intelligence" behind both the UFO phenomenon and the message of the crop circles.

Clearly, there are those who create crop formations purely to make fools out of the believers in order to discredit a subject they loath (as was witnessed in 1996 with the creation of a very smart video claiming to show a "snowflake" formation appearing in a matter of seconds beneath Oliver's Castle, near Devizes, Wiltshire, as balls of light circle wildly over the crop), and this type of activity has led the believers to malign *all* "hoaxers." However, it could well be that the nonhuman intelligence behind their actions, the *real* Circlemakers, *need* those who are open–minded and willing to help fulfill its agenda. Thus the human circlemakers, as agents of fate, are as much a part of the phenomenon as the mysterious lights that appear in our skies and the hidden symbolism so often associated with these incredible landscape designs.

Modern crop formations can be seen as an integral part of an ancient art in which land glyphs were created to be seen properly only from the air. This might include such monuments as the White Horse of Uffington, the Avebury stone circle and avenues, and the Nasca lines of Peru. Such creations encourage us to look towards the skies for inspiration and knowledge, for we feel they act as interfaces between heaven and earth, and perhaps that is what crop formations are—places of communication, able to assist us in receiving messages from the stars. This view was expressed perfectly in 2001 with the formation that appeared in a field next to the Chilbolton radio telescope in Hampshire. It was a replica, albeit it with a few subtle changes, of the famous message sent out into space in 1974 from the Arecibo radio telescope in Puerto Rico. The formation was taken to be a direct response to humanity's own message into space, and in many ways this is exactly what it was, whether created by human hands or supernatural forces.

If such an approach to crop circles is valid, then the hidden meaning of the pictograms should be examined in greater depth, for maybe they really are signs of transformation—there to be observed and understood, and not dissected and torn apart during fierce and ugly debates over whether or not they are created by alien intelligences or human hands. For in the end both answers are correct—it is just a matter of personal belief that divides the two camps. My advice is see them for what they truly are—divine creations of beauty and meaning, and as temporary temples to be experienced and interacted with on a personal basis.

The original book entitled *The Circlemakers* captures some of the great moments in crop circle history (the earliest formations at Alton Barnes and the appearance in 1991 of the now legendary Barbury Castle formation), and arguably its lowest ever point (the week that crop circle hoaxers Doug Bower and Dave Chorley came out of the woodwork to reveal what they had done). It was a time of great revelation, theorizing, and debate untainted by the bitter arguments over whether this formation or that was manmade. Lastly it was a time of personal transformation, whereby I suddenly started to realize the nebulous state of some UFOs as plasma constructs, and how they and crop circles related to prehistoric sites, earth energies, and the close encounter experience.

In *The New Circlemakers* I have left untouched that original spirit of discovery back in 1991. Yet, at the same time, I have added towards the end of the book vital new material that vindicates much of what I suspected back then about the fifth-dimensional nature of missing time abduction scenarios and the sentient life existing in plasma environments—something I have long felt was the key to understanding the intelligent nature of some UFOs.

Rereading the old book during its editing stages was itself a revelation, refreshing my memory of just how much evidence there was back then for supernatural occurrences in connection with the appearance of some of the more classic formations. Strange lights, weird noises, animals acting oddly, two or more major formations appearing the same night, and remarkable psychic predictions about upcoming UFO sightings and new formations, all abounded during this incredible period of activity.

Back then I firmly believed in the supernatural reality of the Circlemakers, and in rewriting this book that same spirit has been invoked again. It is something I now wish to share with the reader, for there is a freshness and naivety about what I wrote back then that I feel has been lost from circles research in the post Doug and Dave years. Of course, there is much good work going on out there in an attempt to better understand the nature of the circles, but it is vexed by people's inner fears that they might be caught out—made to pronounce a hoaxed formation as meaningful. Perhaps it is time now to revisit what made the crop circle subject so innovative and inspirational back then. From this review we can draw new strength to tackle the future of crop circles, whatever merry dance they may wish to lead us in the years to come.

Andrew Collins, Marlborough, July 17, 2008.

Prelude

On Wednesday, June 1, 1977, I entered a sea of low, green barley in a field called Black's Meadow, upon Windsor Hill, close to Wooburn Green in the county of Buckinghamshire. Accompanying me on this early evening trek was fellow UFO investigator Barry King, a large camera case slung over his shoulder and cigarette in hand. We were heading towards the power lines some distance away, for beneath them we would find two curious circular depressions discovered in the field two days earlier by Ken Phillips, National Investigations Coordinator for BUFORA—the British UFO Research Association.

He had visited the area on Monday, May 30 to see if he could interview any of the three youngsters who had initiated a local furor following an alleged UFO they had witnessed on several occasions in the past few weeks. Although Britain was in the throes of its biggest UFO "flap" in ten years, these particular sightings were not that inspiring—a few strange lights in the sky, that sort of thing.

Ken Phillips had decided to survey the general area where, on one occasion, the UFO had supposedly projected a beam of light towards the ground, and in Black's Meadow he had stumbled upon two perfectly circular depressions in the green barley. As a consequence, he had called in Barry and me to reinterview the boys and carry out an on-site investigation of the disturbed crop.

Two of the three teenagers who had sparked the UFO furor were found and interviewed. After due consideration we decided they had misidentified the landing lights of aircraft descending into nearby Heathrow Airport. Other recent sightings from independent sources were more difficult to dismiss, but the witnesses were proving hard to track down.

Now it was the turn of the circular depressions in the field. What would we find here? One was indeed placed beneath a power line, eliminating the possibility of it being a UFO landing trace. It measured 16 yards in diameter, while the other example, 11 yards away, was only 9 yards across. The actual depressions were the result of the early season barley being swirled to a lower level. In each were slight depressions in the soil, and one revealed a wet patch, indicating an underground water source of some kind. I had never seen anything like them before but knew that so-called "saucer nests" had frequently appeared on the other side of the globe in places such as Australia and New Zealand.

Both circles were studied in detail for some while. An ex-army Geiger counter indicated no radioactive anomalies present, and a standard compass showed no evidence of geo-magnetic anomalies. Soil samples were collected from the centers and edges of the circles, while controls were taken from a 20-yard distance of each one.

The boy's testimonies had not impressed us, so these circles made little sense. Even the local farmer thought he recognized the depressions as places where rubbish had been discarded into pits long ago. For this reason we concluded that the circular marks were the result of a weaker crop more susceptible to wind damage. Matter closed.

The only point that did seem a trifle odd was the fact that each depression was a perfect swirled circle. Soil subsidence or not, this was something I had never encountered before, and it intrigued me.

In the weeks that followed, a comprehensive report was compiled and lodged with BUFORA, and the subject of the curious swirled circles was forgotten. The results of the soil analysis never reached us, and no more was heard of such phenomena until three years later, when on Friday, August 15, 1980, the *Wiltshire Times* ran a story concerning the appearance of three flattened circles of oats found in a field beneath the

Westbury white horse figure. A photograph accompanying the report showed a perfect circle of beautifully laid crop, swirled into a majestic floor pattern.

Quick off the mark to investigate the newly reported crop circles was Ian Mrzyglod, then editor of UFO journal *The Probe Report*, and Dr. Terence Meaden, a Wiltshire–based meteorologist running the influential *Journal of Meteorology* and the Tornado and Storm Research Organization (TORRO). These two researchers quickly established that the circles had formed in the oats at different dates in July and that others had been appearing in the same area for a number of years.

The crop circle enigma had been born, and within a few short years, circles, both singularly and in unique groupings, started appearing across Wiltshire as well as in the neighboring county of Hampshire. Both Ian Mrzyglod and Terence Meaden became the early pioneers of this phenomenon, believing them to be the product of stationary whirlwinds. As the configurations of circles increased and unexpected electromagnetic effects began to be reported in association with circle appearances, Dr. Meaden was forced to update his theories. He devised the so-called plasma vortex theory to explain their creation in meteorological terms.

The sheer perfection of the circles, which often included some extraordinary features, caught the attention of the national media and the world as a whole. UFOs seen in the area of forming circles added to the mystery but also attracted believers in alien contact and other New Age ideas.

In the summer of 1986, the ground designs took a quantum leap when a ring of flattened crop was discovered around a freshly formed circle at Bratton in Wiltshire. Circles with two rings followed, then three rings, then four. Then came linear spurs, circles with connecting corridors to form dumbbells, and finally, in 1990, the advent of the pictogram—dramatic patterns often hundreds of feet long that have continued to appear in the fields of southern England.

Up until this point, I had followed the subject's rise to fame with mild interest, occasionally giving space to Ian Mrzyglod's excellent work in my journal *Earthquest News*. Despite the addition of these articles in my journal, crop circles did not inspire me. That was until one day in late August 1990 when I first saw photographs of the extraordinary crop pictogram that had appeared in the by now famous "East Field" in Alton Barnes, just a few miles from Avebury in Wiltshire. It consisted of

2. Crop pictogram that appeared in East Field,
Alton Barnes, Wiltshire, on July 12, 1990.

circles and rings with keys, boxes, and spurs, all linked together by a long corridor of flattened crop. For me, seeing this image meant that the crop circle phenomenon had now moved out of the realms of pure meteorology and into the grip of either hoaxing on a grand scale or something awesome in implications.

A few weeks later an excellent introductory book entitled *The Crop Circle Enigma*, edited by Ralph Noyes and Busty Taylor, turned up in a local bookshop, and its contents were eagerly digested. I subscribed to *The Cerealogist*, the premier forum for crop circle studies, edited by earth mysteries visionary and author John Michell, and after reading this forum, there was no turning back. When the 1991 summer season finally came around, a weekend was set aside for searching out the circles in the hope that a few simple truths might reveal themselves and that I would begin to understand the nature of this wonder of our times.

PART ONE
A Crash Course

1

Constable's Clue

Friday, July 19, 1991. The idea would be to spend some time in the fields of Wiltshire, wandering from one crop formation to the next, attempting a little observation, evaluation, and meditation. This was the plan at least, but fate was about to deal me an unexpected hand that was to change the course of the whole game.

Although I accepted the possible reality of crop circles, I felt a little experimentation was in order. As I understood it, psychics had already been employed in crop circle research to foretell new circle locations and offer their own inspired thoughts on the nature of the phenomenon. It also seemed that they had become a central focus around which other allied paranormal anomalies had occurred in association with the formation of the circles, such as the appearance of mysterious lights and the hearing of strange sounds.

In view of these promising results, I decided that the best plan of action was to take along a few friends and try to attune not just to the circles but also to the assumed source behind their construction, the so-called Circlemakers, as they were being called. This attunement we would do through the use of visualization—the art of imagining mentally created pictures for mystical purposes. The most obvious imagery to employ was, I decided, the majestic designs of the crop formations. So, with this in mind, I enlarged pen and ink drawings of some 40 representations, commencing with the most simple circle patterns and ending with the extraordinary pictograms of the 1990 season. Each was photocopied on to manageable-sized white card to display a stark black image. These images we would take into the crop circles and use in turn while sitting in a relaxed, meditative state.

Nothing more was needed for our experiment as any other form of ritualistic activity might invoke belief-orientated conceptions of everything from spacemen to gods, goddesses, nature spirits, or mowing devils. This was especially important, as not one of these notions was likely to hold the true solution to the crop circle enigma. We would then see what occurred, and perhaps project a rather tongue-in-cheek message of "Okay, here we are. Whoever you are, why don't you come on down and say hello?" Something was bound to happen; it usually did.

So the plan of action was set in motion and a date chosen for our weekend of crop circle exploration. Unfortunately, I was unable to make the first anniversary of the appearance of the breathtaking Alton Barnes pictogram on July 12, so the following weekend was decided upon. Our party would gather first thing and then journey in convoy around every circle we could find both in Wiltshire and neighboring Hampshire to see what transpired.

That evening, the night before our departure, I sat putting the finishing touches to the deck of crop circle cards. A short while later I noticed the spine of a book half yanked out of a bookshelf nearby. I had definitely not touched it and so wondered what title it was. Perhaps it was an omen for the weekend. Did it contain the key to the crop circle enigma?

Examining its cover, I saw it was a paperback copy of Andrew Tomas's *Atlantis: From Legend to Discovery*, published in 1972. Quickly browsing through its pages, I saw it contained the normal catalog of history's great question marks, everything from the mystery of the Nasca lines to cave paintings of supposed spacemen and Atlantean records beneath the Great Pyramid. Maybe Atlantis was some kind of clue? Perhaps the Atlanteans were making the crop circles?

I hardly thought so.

Slotting the rejected book back into the open gap on the shelf, I realized its somewhat energetic withdrawal had dislodged another paperback that had lain horizontally on top of it, completely out of sight. Its bottom corner was now exposed, tempting further removal, so I let it fall into my hands before scanning the cover. It turned out to be a book I thought I had lost many years before entitled *Sky Creatures: Living UFOs*, by American UFO pioneer Trevor James Constable, originally published in 1976 under the title *The Cosmic Pulse of Life*.

In the book, Constable had expounded his belief that UFOs were not "nuts and bolts" spacecraft but amoeba-like life forms that inhabit the upper atmosphere. He referred to them as "critters," or "sky creatures," and considered them to be intelligent "bioforms" of calcium and fluids, held in a plasma state and existing usually within the invisible ranges of the electromagnetic spectrum.

More intriguing was the author's view that the core of these unknown aerial forms was a biologically produced radiation called "orgone," first discovered and recorded in the late 1930s by an exiled Austrian scientist living in the United States named Wilhelm Reich. He saw this orgone as a natural energy produced by sunlight and detectable within all living things. For him, it was the very force that animated and regulated life on earth.

Wilhelm Reich (1897–1957) worked for many years with this "organic" radiation and had even designed a special box in which to contain it. Known simply as the "orgone energy accumulator," it consisted of various layers of organic and inorganic materials that were said to produce and concentrate the orgone within its interior. This orgone he utilized to heal the human body and develop the idea of mass-free energy with a view to creating alternative sources of power.

Reich had also decided that orgone radiation could be drawn to earth using a device referred to as a cloudbuster, a scientific instrument consisting of hollow metal tubes mounted on a swiveling tripod and carriage. With this device he found he could drain away the orgone potential held in the atmosphere and, in doing so, disperse clouds and create rainfall. These experiments worked not just once, but on every occasion the device was used. Reich's cloudbuster was popularized in the promo video for Kate Bush's 1985 hit "Cloudbusting." During the 1950s UFOs were consistently seen in the skies above the Reich Institute named Orgonon at Rangeley, Maine. Reich linked their appearance with his orgone experiments, as did Trevor James Constable. So was orgone radiation connected in some way with the formation of crop circles?

It was an interesting thought.

I replaced the copy of Constable's *Sky Creatures* and quickly lost interest in it, as I gathered together the crop circle cards and pondered over other more pressing matters, such as attempting to track down where exactly we might find any decent crop formations when we did finally reach Wiltshire.

2
Girl on a White Horse

Saturday, July 20, 1991. So far, news of crop circles that summer had been surprisingly scant. *The Daily Star* had run a feature on how psychic Isabelle Kingston had accurately predicted the arrival of a crop formation near her home at Ogbourne St. Andrew in Wiltshire. The newspaper also carried reader's theories on how crop circles were formed, although these details need not be repeated. Only the previous day a friend from Norway had advised me that the BBC World Service had run a news story, announcing the discovery of strange new formations in the Wiltshire landscape. Other than this, it had been left to self-acclaimed "Son of God" David Icke to cast the kiss of death on any open-mindedness the general public might have held in respect to the circles phenomenon. For two weeks straight he and his aquamarine-clad followers had been seen running rings around a fresh pictogram that had appeared at Alton Barnes.

Armed with these few snippets of information, the journey began. By lunchtime we had reached the Membury Service Station on the M4 motorway, just before the border into Wiltshire. It was here I pulled out a copy of *The Cerealogist* and, as a layman, dialed the number of Busty Taylor, the southern England coordinator for the CCCS—the Center for

5

Crop Circle Studies. They were the national body for circles research, and he, if anyone, would be able to direct our party to the crop formations I could only assume had already appeared this summer season.

Busty was helpful and obliging, directing us to a newly arrived pictogram with a triangular ground-plan, lying beyond the northerly slope of an ancient camp named Barbury Castle. He said that a sign saying "crop circles" pointed the way and that "you'll not have seen anything like it before." He added that there were further examples we could "play with" in the Alton Barnes area.

Thanking him, I carefully followed Busty's suggested route until the elevated treeline marking the location of Barbury Castle's prehistoric summit grew ever more apparent. In archaeological terms it is a hill fort of ditches and banks classified as Iron Age in origin (meaning it could date back to anything between 500 BC and AD 60). To its east lay the "Celtic" field system of Burderop Down, unchanged for nearly 3,000 years, and clearly emphasizing the great age of this agricultural landscape.

The handwritten sign directed those interested in seeing the "crop circles" westwards along the Ridgeway, one of the oldest surviving ancient trackways in Britain. Along its 85-mile course from Beacon Fort, near Leighton Buzzard in Buckinghamshire, to Alton Barnes, south of Marlborough in Wiltshire, this prehistoric right of way passes such ancient monuments as the Uffington white horse, the Avebury stone circle complex, and the East Kennet long barrow. Needless to say, many researchers more worthy than I had already noted the recurring proximity of crop circles to prehistoric monuments.

Taking photographs of this unique sign, which would have caused complete bafflement and dismay to local inhabitants a few years before, we contemplated whether or not to leave the cars where they were and walk to our destination. At that moment a teenage girl on a white horse approached before slowing to a halt and speaking to our enthusiastic party. "Oh, the circles are down there," she was heard to say, steadying the animal.

Were there any others locally?

"I only know of the one that's appeared at Hackpen Hill," she replied.

Hackpen Hill? This was synchronistic—a girl on a white horse speaking of another, quite separate crop circle at Hackpen Hill. A *hackpen* is a circular enclosure where horses are trained to trot around and around in circles. It was certainly a good omen for the day, and it would be here that we would go after visiting Barbury Castle's own formation.

We made the decision to drive along the pitted course of the Ridgeway, and after just a brief distance, the tranquil setting was rudely broken. In front of us now were some two dozen cars haphazardly parked upon the grass verge on both sides. Crowds of people in bright summer wear were either on their way into or just emerging from a ripened field of corn. A farmhand stood by an open gate collecting a £1 admission fee in front of a horsebox that doubled as a makeshift office. Upon its display board were leaflets advertising the Center for Crop Circle Studies (CCCS), next to a news cutting relating to the crop formation apparently present in this field.

Pinned-up pictures of the formation showed the extraordinary nature of what we were about to enter and experience. It consisted of a gigantic triangular frame enclosing a double-ringed circle with unique and individual features at each of its three corners—one was a circle with a radial line, a second showed a ratchet spiral of broken lines, and the third consisted of a ring encircling six curved lines, in the style of a solar wheel. To complete the picture were lines radiating out from the central circle to the corners of the triangle. It was an unbelievable sight and undoubtedly a feat of great artistic merit, whatever its origin. To my knowledge it was the most extraordinary pictogram to date.

3. Line drawing of the Barbury Castle formation of July 17, 1991.

At that moment the owner of the field, John White of nearby Overtown Farm, turned up to oversee the visitors entering on to his land, and I was able to exchange a few words with him on this new addition to his yearly income.

It had arrived, he said, during the dark early hours of Wednesday, July 17, just three days earlier. Apparently, it had not been there at 9:30 the previous evening as he had been in the field. However, a telephone call early the next morning notified him of its presence, for it had been spotted from the air by a professional photographer named Richard Wintle, who was on his way back from photographing another crop formation at Stonehenge.

4. Photograph of the Barbury Castle formation of 1991.

The bemused farmer could give no logical explanation for its presence, adding only that the Ministry of Defense police attached to nearby Wroughton airfield, some half a mile away, regularly patrolled the Ridgeway and would have investigated any light source or disturbance seen in the fields that night. It is in their interests to do so for national security reasons. If it was a hoax, then whoever was responsible for this work of art would have needed to be a mastermind in landscape engineering and group coordination.

He also pointed out that it was the only incident of its kind to have occurred on his farmland and mentioned that the field in question was known as The Flat, eliminating any possible relevance in the place name.

More intriguing were reports of strange lights being seen in the sky the same night as its appearance. Five miles away at Beckhampton, crop watcher Brian Grist and his two friends observed a series of strange, pulsating lights from midnight onwards, some of which appeared to be in the direction of Barbury Castle. By one o'clock that morning they had become so unnerved by the sightings that the watch was abandoned. Independent witnesses reported other lights, and the warden of Barbury Castle, who lives in a bungalow on the hill itself, reported hearing a great roar accompanied by a low humming sound at 3:30 that same morning. He was said to have been quite shaken by the experience.[1]

So, all in all it had been an eventful night. But there was more to come. Within 24 hours of its appearance, a tremendous storm had hit that part of Wiltshire, and so forceful was the wind and rain that much of the standing crop directly beyond the formation had been completely flattened.

Thanking Mr. White for his time, we entered the field via the tramlines—the parallel tracks, 80 feet apart, used by tractors to gain easy access to crops—and followed the other visitors into my first ever crop formation. In just moments it became only too clear how difficult it would have been to have constructed such a unique pattern in the tall standing wheat. Being completely flat made it impossible to see where you were in the design, which I estimated to be over 60 yards in length and breadth. The careful combing of the fallen corn and the sudden changes of direction, leaving many stalks turning at right angles, made it seem as if a giant stamp had descended upon the field and punched out its mark. If it was a hoax, well, then these people were certainly not messing about.

Some two dozen or so visitors were inside the flattened features, with many more following the tramlines, paying their entry fee, or simply picnicking by their vehicles. Some people held angled divining rods and walked back and forth watching for reactions. Others spoke of their genuine interest in crop circles and offered explanations and opinions when asked. In just a few minutes of careful observation, it seemed clear that a relatively aware and intuitive kind of person was now spending weekends visiting crop circles. It simply amazed me how they were openly and quite sensibly talking about such topics as strange noises, mysterious lights, earth energies, and dowsing, when such subjects had been completely taboo only a few years previously. Whatever the source behind the crop circles, it was undoubtedly doing a remarkable job in pushing some very diverse fields of study into the realms of popular consciousness. Even respected meteorologists, such as Terence Meaden, were plainly accepting strange light phenomena, paranormal sounds, and dowsing traces as if they had always been disciplines worthy of study by academics such as him and his Japanese colleagues.

The man, who had taken our money, alerted us to the fact that a member of the CCCS was on-site—someone named Richard Andrews. So, identifying him as the tall figure with angle rods and a small audience around him, I decided to grab a little of his time.

Having just completed his dowsing survey of the formation, Mr. Andrews announced that he was satisfied that this one had, tentatively at least, passed the authenticity test. Taking time away from his duties, he answered my prying questions and pinpointed the positions on an Ordnance Survey map of several further crop circles in the vicinity of Marlborough, Beckhampton, and Alton Barnes.

Our party of six explored and studied every feature within the formation, before settling down to face each other. For everyone the bright July sun and the idyllic, if absurd, setting combined to make it a perfect day. After a period of sufficient relaxation, the preplanned meditation got under way. It began with the visualization of a swirling cone of blue-white light, building up like a wall around the central circle, as if activating its inherent energies, whatever they might be.

I then brought into view the 40 or so crop circle cards, each with its different representation of the design and pattern seen in the fields of southern England since the first single circles were discovered beneath the gaze of the Westbury white horse in 1980. Doublets, triplets, quintuplets, a bead cross, Celtic cross, single ringer, double ringer, and upwards to the more complicated pictograms of summer 1990 were all visualized in turn, helped by the deep orange afterimage temporarily burned into the retinas of our eyes by the bright sun.

The whole thing took some 40 minutes to complete, and, after seeing the electric-blue cone of power gradually slowing down and dispersing, we opened our eyes.

The results were not immediately apparent, although everyone felt

completely spaced out in a manner quite unusual for an outdoor meditation of this sort. It was like having your mind scrambled. One member found he could not visualize what was on the cards and instead saw
new designs that appeared in his head. Others said that, while many of
the patterns were fixed clearly in their minds, certain ones of the designs would not compute, leaving only part of the image and suggesting that certain elements of the patterns had been added separately.
One or two patterns could not be visualized at all. Yet, somehow, beyond the mists of uncertainty, ideas did begin to form, which would
soon transform everything I had ever believed concerning the nature,
not just of the crop circles, but of UFOs and their relationship to human
experience.

3

Diminishing Health

Leaving the awesome pictogram, the group crossed over the Ridgeway and entered the field that climbed the steep slope to Barbury Castle. From the edge of the Iron Age hill fort's ramparts there was a commanding view of the crop formation, and yet the hill's proximity as a viewing platform would have left some in doubt as to the design's supernatural origin.

Moving back to the cars, we began the particularly bumpy journey along the Ridgeway to the other side of the Marlborough Downs. Helpful directions from hikers enabled us to take our vehicles off the pitted track and down a slope towards the wheat field at the base of Hackpen Hill. Nestling into the hedgerow below was what appeared to be a three-circled pictogram with a concentric halo beyond each end. The only additional feature was a small, single circle joined irregularly to the western crescent.

People were milling about and approaching the field in question, where we found another makeshift office–cum–shop and a pleasant lady taking an admission fee of £1 for adults and 50p for children. Some people would call this a rip–off, but, for me, it was the best policy, as it put a stop to mindless trespass and unnecessary crop damage, while at

12

the same time adding a convivial social atmosphere to the proceedings. It also gave a handful of volunteers a temporary job for a few months of the year.

CCCS material was in evidence again, and this time there was a little table selling copies of Ralph Noyes and Busty Taylor's *Crop Circle Enigma* as well as picture postcards and posters of crop circles from the previous summer season. This really was becoming a thriving cottage industry.

Paying our admission fees, we readied ourselves for the journey across the earthen mounds, covered with concrete and discarded tires, before noticing something of significance. Upon the adjacent hill, overlooking the crop formation, no more than 200 yards away, was a small, carved white horse, making me recall the lady on the white horse who had alerted us to the existence of the formation.

The association between carved hill figures and crop circles had also been noted before. Since their appearance beneath the Westbury white horse in 1980, circles had been found below the Long Man of Wilmington, near Eastbourne in Sussex; the Cerne Abbas Giant in Dorset, the Gog Magog figures in Cambridgeshire as well as other white horses scattered throughout the Wiltshire countryside. All such chalk images were situated close to other ancient monuments such as barrows, hill forts, and tumuli, so it was believed that such monuments were first carved either during the Iron Age or Bronze Age periods.

We noticed the farmer overseeing the operation and found that he was quite happy to chat about what had happened on the night the formation arrived. His name was John Hussey, and the first he learned of its presence was on Friday, July 12 when members of the CCCS contacted him. Strangely, at around 4:30 that same morning, his son, who lives just beyond the field where the formation was found, had been awakened by the din being made by his guinea fowl, which were quite literally "going berserk." At the same time his cocker spaniel dog had ripped off the paintwork on the doors in the house, something he had never done in the four long years of his life.

The farmer was in no doubt that the animals had reacted to the appearance of the crop formation and were, therefore, aware of something, most likely some form of sound, arguably either infrasound or ultrasound, which is inaudible to the human ear.

It was the same story at Alton Barnes on the night that the first pictogram had arrived exactly one year beforehand. All the dogs in the nearby villages of Alton Barnes and Alton Priors had gone wild in the early hours, not ceasing their howling and barking until first light. Similar incidents had been reported in association with the formation of other crop circles.

Mr. Hussey went on to say that, during the early hours of Wednesday, July 17 (the same time that the Barbury Castle formation arrived), a further, smaller circle had appeared beyond the rim of the Hackpen Hill formation's western halo. Such "additions," if genuine (and many were clearly not), suggested that crop circles were not merely the remnants of a single past event but the product of an evolving process that takes on a life of its own. This ability of crop formations to transmute was first noticed on June 12, 1990, when circles researcher George Wingfield realized that a huge triple-ring circle near Devizes in Wiltshire, had "grown" a fourth, outer ring of depressed crop only six to eight inches in width and yet with a circumference of nearly 1,000 feet. The original circle and concentric rings had been photographed on May 22, and at that time there had been no sign of a fourth ring.[1]

The final anecdote thrown at us by the farmer was the one about the local arts master named Ian Pillinger. Apparently, "a year ago to the day" before the Hackpen pictogram was found, he had seen "fluorescent lights up towards this way" —this was the night that the first Alton Barnes pictogram had turned up. What neither Mr. Hussey nor we knew at the time was that mysterious lights had been spotted in the area on the night that the Hackpen Hill formation had appeared.[2]

As at Barbury Castle, the swathed wheat in this new formation was beautifully combed and where a corridor met a circle, an immediate change of direction was noted, even though some stalks had bent to flow with the new intrusion. What exactly this meant I couldn't rightly say, but the same picture of a huge stamp coming down and flattening the corn was in our minds once more.

Some of the group now complained of a growing fuzziness in their heads, preventing them from even thinking logically. Each felt lethargic and were in no doubt that it was connected with the "heady" atmosphere present at the two formations we had visited so far. Still others were now feeling quite nauseous, making them unhappy about continuing our journey on to further crop circle sites.

I recalled Wilhelm Reich's orgone radiation. There were many accounts of people becoming nauseous and ill after coming into contact with high doses of this invisible life force. I recalled also the strange manner in which Trevor James Constable's book *Sky Creatures* had presented itself the previous evening. Was that something to do with all this? Remember that he saw UFOs as "critters"—living creatures of the upper atmosphere composed of condensed orgone radiation.

Looking around, I saw a big fellow sporting a beard with divining rods in his hands. He was leading a group of some dozen or so people through the circles. Upon departing they crossed the tramline where good corn was still standing. I decided this did not reflect the spirit of the thing.

Taking leave of the formation ourselves, we passed the dozen or so vehicles parked in the makeshift car park and ascended the gentle slope up to the chalk horse on the side of the hill. The animal needed recutting, I observed, although the view from its elevated position could be described as invigorating, especially as its head was directed straight towards the crop formation below.

We moved on, having already been told that no less than three separate formations could be viewed on field slopes next to the Marlborough Road. The first of these appeared after a drive of some ten minutes. It was an enormous multi-circled pictogram, ending in a three-pronged key, lying on a west-facing field belonging to Temple Farm, some half a mile from the road. We had been warned by Mr. Hussey that the farmer in question did not permit visitors to his fields, which cut both ways really. On the one hand, it prevented people from experiencing, investigating, and sampling a remarkable formation, and on the other, it carefully preserved the pictogram, allowing people from a distance to study its precision-cut circles, rings, and lines. It was a powerful image, and its sheer grandiosity lessened the possibility of it being a hoax.

A small group of circle watchers and hangers-on had gathered in a lay-by further along the road. They gazed with bewilderment at the massive pictogram and thankfully adhered to the prominent "private land—keep out" signs dominating the spot. By all accounts, this one had been discovered at first light on Wednesday, July 17, meaning it had arrived the very same night as both the Barbury Castle pictogram and the additional circle that had been appended to the formation at Hackpen Hill. I shook my head in amazement—it must have been quite a night, what with all the crop circles, strange lights, and peculiar noises.

A glance at the Ordnance Survey map showed that the Temple Farm formation was situated close to a tumulus on Preshute Down and that, if I were not mistaken, its axis was aligned on Barbury Castle, which lay just a mile or so to the north. Also close by was a Bronze Age enclosure and a further Celtic field system of slightly later date.

After stops for photographs, we carried on.

Almost into Marlborough, on a sloping field belonging to Maisey Farm, Ogbourne Maizey, two further formations came into view a quarter of a mile east of the main road. On the left was a large flattened circle with a linear spur and two smaller circles inside, looking like two eggs in a frying pan! I noticed that it could easily be accessed from a track lying just 200 yards behind it, thus not a point in its favor.

A few hundred yards further on, in front of a line of trees, was a more complicated pictogram made up of a long stem linking a circle, a ringed circle, and a smaller ring. Both formations had been found on the morning of Thursday, July 11. We stopped by the entrance gates of Manton House Farm to take photographs and consult the map. It showed that to the southwest, no more than a quarter of a mile away, were two tumuli on Marlborough Common.

By now it was getting near teatime, and stomachs were rumbling in certain quarters, so, following a bag of less-than-wholesome chips at a Chinese take-away in Marlborough, we headed out towards Alton Barnes, the crop circle capital of Wessex, the ancient name for this region of southern England.

4

An Evening at Alton Barnes

A gently sloping barley field south of Lockeridge Dene contained another huge pictogram, this one composed of two different-sized circles linked to a ring of flattened crop by a long axis stem. Although it was virtually impossible to see from the road, it appeared to be identical to the one at Ogbourne Maizey. A stroll through the ancient woodland lying directly behind it would bring the visitor to a ruined long barrow and then, on the edge of the tree line, to the course of an ancient ditch–and–bank earthwork known as the Wansdyke.

Next stop was Alton Barnes, approached through the gap in a brooding ridge of hills, each capped with prehistoric sites. These sites included Adam's Grave long barrow and Knap Hill causewayed camp, both of Neolithic origin, c. 3500 BC, as well as an assortment of earthworks and, as we were about to find out, a south–facing white horse below Milk Hill.

Passing between this wall–like ridge of ancient defense, the road slopes to the right and runs parallel with the Ridgeway, before the earthen track splits away and heads across East Field towards Alton Priors' church, a quarter of a mile east of Alton Barnes. Here the Ridgeway comes to an abrupt halt, having crossed 85 miles of rural England.

It was below in East Field that our eyes now espied two separate pictograms. The nearest was a dumbbell of two interlinked circles of different sizes. Some 200 yards further south was a second formation seemingly identical to the ones at Ogbourne Maizey and Lockeridge Dene. To complete the picture was a third enormous pictogram, almost identical to the one on Preshute Down, located in a sloping field beyond the easterly running Alton Priors to Wilcot road.

Once the Wiltshire Police's "no parking" cones had petered out, we pulled our cars up behind others already abandoned by their owners for the same reason. We scurried through the undergrowth, down to the level of the field below, leaving behind some members of the party who still felt unwell. After climbing over a barbed wire fence and a locked gate, we reached a caravan manned by a farmhand charging £1 admission for adults and 50p for children. We also noticed that everyone else was entering the field through a conveniently placed trackway further along the road!

In front of the man was a trestle table bearing an assortment of crop circle paraphernalia, including books, posters, cards, and plastic key rings containing tiny photographs of this year's main formation on one side and last year's design on the reverse. I had to smile at this blatant, but enterprising, capitalization of the crop circle phenomenon.

A steady stream of visitors strolled down the gentle slope and passed the admission kiosk, where they paid the £1 admission fee. This seemed to be normal behavior for them, and I wondered what they would have been doing had crop circles not taken on such a high profile—enjoying a village fete, visiting a garden center, or watching a cricket match? I just couldn't imagine what.

It seemed that East Field's main formation was found on the morning of Tuesday, July 2, having appeared overnight, which meant that the key rings were on sale within 19 days of its arrival, which was not bad going, really. The dumbbell formation a few hundred yards to its north had been found three days later on Friday, July 5. The other great pictogram in the sloping field beyond the Alton Priors–Wilcot road had only been noticed at first light the previous morning.

Incidentally, this third pictogram was on land owned by Tim Carson, the same farmer responsible for the two in East Field. An admission fee of £1 was being charged for entry into that field as well, and there was a special reduction if you visited the formations in both fields—£1.50 for adults and 75p for children! Yet the farmhand taking the money did want to stress that last year the farmer had given much of the proceeds to a charity for underprivileged children as well as to a local church fund.

Eager to move on, we identified the correct tramline at the edge of the field and followed its course out to the larger of the two formations—the "middle" one as it was being referred to by the farmhand. Its familiar swathed and combed wheat, and its elliptical, off-centered circles showed a marked similarity to those we had already encountered at Barbury Castle and Hackpen Hill. According to our group, this one was slightly less "heady" than the others.

Leaving East Field I purchased a couple of key rings and postcards from the farmhand, who warmed to our interest and began reciting a few anecdotes concerning the nightly vigils kept here by crop watchers. Apparently, just a week before at around three o'clock one morning, a gathered group had witnessed a luminous column descend upon nearby Knap Hill. It had emanated from the base of a dark cloud, and, upon making contact with the summit of the Neolithic camp, the solid tube had broken into rays of light, which then dissipated into the hill. This unique event was said to have completely freaked out those in attendance, and their eyewitness accounts had been eagerly sought by Terence Meaden, who saw it as a prime example of a "plasma vortex." The most immediate point of interest about this incident was the date it took place—July 12—the same night that the Hackpen Hill formation was under construction seven or so miles to the north. So with the guinea fowl and dog disturbances reported by John Hussey's son that same morning, it seemed that, like Wednesday, July 17, the dark early hours of Friday, July 12 had been equally spectacular in crop circle terms.

The farmhand went on to say that Ralph Noyes, one of the editors of *The Crop Circle Enigma*, had recently visited the site. Upon leaving he had explained to some ladies how the glands on his neck would sometimes swell up upon entering a circle. However, he had assured them that the effect lasts only for a couple of hours.

On a lighter note the man spoke of a recent visit by "messiah" David Icke. Apparently, he had arrived with a woman but hung around in a car for some while before eventually paying his respects to East Field's "middle" formation during the early evening. He had muttered something about them being portents of catastrophe, suggesting that everyone should run around their circumference in the direction of the fallen crop. He was later seen doing just this, while his lady friend meditated in one of the small satellite circles just off the main stem.

Evenings at Alton Barnes must just fly by!

5
Rita's Return

It had been agreed by everyone that Alton Barnes was the most obvious location for our proposed crop watch that night, what with columns of light descending on to Neolithic camps and a new formation turning up less than 48 hours beforehand. We could park the cars, conduct our meditation using the black and white cards, and just see what happened. So permission would have to be sought from either Tim Carson or his brother, who also ran the farm. To this end another helpful local, who spent time each day on the East Field entrance, was on hand to lead us to the homes of each of the two brothers. Neither was available, so the man obligingly led us to the door of a local hostelry called The Seven Stars, saying he would return later.

When "later" came, it was dark, and he had still not been able to speak to either brother. Despite this he saw no problem in us entering the field, really.

So in the darkness of the late evening, our party made a brief excursion to the "middle" formation and struck a short sword to create tonal sounds. We wanted to set up a lingering resonance for our intended meditation, and, with this over, we moved back along the tramline to the position of the caravan. Unexpectedly, I saw a frizzy-haired woman coming straight towards me.

The female face took shape, and I realized it was Rita Goold, the well-known physical medium and psychic from Leicester in the Midlands. I had worked with her on various projects during the early 1980s and had been witness to some mystifying events in her presence. She, I knew, had been taking a keen interest in crop circles, following the appearance of a formation at Oadby, Leicestershire, in 1988. I remember her ringing me late one evening to say that she had just returned from visiting the circles in question.

I had read with interest her attempts to communicate with the Circlemakers at Cheesefoot Head (pronounced Chez-foot), just outside Winchester in Hampshire, during Operation White Crow in 1989.[1] In the early hours of Sunday, June 18, she had settled down inside a crop circle with cerealogists Colin Andrews, Pat Delgado, Busty Taylor, George Wingfield, and her husband Steve. They encouraged Rita to seek psychic communication with the source behind the circles, and, after some 20 minutes or so, the assembled party had become aware of a "trilling" noise, which George Wingfield had felt was coming from the circle itself. It then moved out to some 50 yards distance and remained there for a while. Those present described it as possessing an "intense . . . whirring, chattering quality," that was not loud.

Rita then attempted contact with the eerie sound by giving it a verbal command to stop. There was no response, but, on the second time of asking, it did cease for a short while. Upon restarting, it approached the circle once more. Some of the group stood up and advanced towards whatever was lurking out of sight among the sea of crop. Standing just a few yards from the apparent source of the trilling noise, George Wingfield then asked it to make them a circle.

Unbeknown to the group was that, on a nearby road, three other watchers could also hear the trilling noise, and on deciding to investigate, the watchers found that the hypnotic sound had ceased once more. Upon their arrival at the circle, a man named Ron Jones had spoken of a luminous object shaped like a pair of horns seen high above the field, which had not been observed by those inside the circle.

After Rita and Steve had returned to their Leicester home, George Wingfield and Colin Andrews had heard the trilling noise again, but this time it was distant. They attempted to follow its source and eventually gave up as dawn approached. Later that morning they were to find that George Wingfield's request had been granted, for in the direction that the trilling noise had finally been lost, they discovered the only circle to have appeared in the whole of Britain in the past eight days. It was almost as if the strange noise had been leading them to the location of the new circle.[2]

Colin Andrews identified the trilling noise as similar to the "electronic sparrow" sound he had briefly encountered while investigating crop circles at Kimpton, Hampshire, on June 30, 1987.[3] On that occasion he had likened the eerie sound to the chattering of electrodes on an electric arc. The same noise was finally recorded on Thursday, August 10, 1989, at a large single circle at Beckhampton by a BBC camera crew filming Colin Andrews and Pat Delgado for a *Daytime Live* program.[4]

Circles skeptic Ken Brown had demonstrated to his satisfaction that the strange noise captured on camera was, in fact, the song of a bird named the grasshopper warbler.[5] However, those who originally heard the sound were unconvinced by this theory.

It was probably inspiration drawn from the psychic results of Rita Goold as well as the intriguing work of another crop circle psychic named Isabelle Kingston, that had drawn me into actively pursuing my newfound interest in the subject. The idea of communicating with whatever lay behind the phenomenon particularly appealed to me. So it was yet another synchronicity chancing across Rita Goold here in East Field, Alton Barnes, at the dead of night.

After our initial greetings, the Leicester medium explained that she was part of a small group, some local and connected with the farmer, who had been watching East Field for the past month or so. Indeed, it was Rita and her colleagues who had witnessed the luminous column descend upon Knap Hill the previous week.

"Right, who's in charge here?" an almost regimental male voice suddenly demanded out of the darkness. I looked and saw a tall male figure, who had just emerged from an old army jeep. "Have you got permission to be here?"

Well, er, no actually. Quickly, I explained our situation, which was not seen as justification for our presence in the field. Only Rita's intervention on our behalf enabled us to stay. Still, it was not our land and the sentinel figure—who gave his name as "Tom" and said he worked for the farmer—did explain that a great many people turn up with the sole purpose of making life difficult for those on an official crop watch.

By one o'clock that morning, a party of some 15 individuals had gathered around the caravan. Other silhouetted figures gradually joined in small bands, and then the metal gate gave way and crashed to the ground. Shortly afterwards, Tom evicted all unwanted parties in no uncertain terms.

"We'll go to the Westbury white horse. They're more welcoming over there," one disgruntled figure was heard to shout, before he and his girlfriend rose to their feet and sauntered off.

We, too, felt it was time to move on, as we had hoped to be alone to conduct our meditations. So we said our goodbyes to Rita, Tom, and some other guy—who was still kicking himself for having sheltered inside the caravan when the luminous column had descended upon Knap Hill—and journeyed into the night. We passed through Marlborough at 2 a.m. and found the road out on to the Marlborough Downs. Perhaps we could sleep beneath the Hackpen white horse and keep a watch on the fields below.

Upon our arrival we found everywhere locked up and out of bounds, and, in no mood to conquer the problem, we left Hackpen Hill and journeyed back along the Marlborough Road. The two formations at Ogbourne Maizey were reached, and through a little intuition and good judgment, we found the field in question and followed the tramlines. Eventually we came upon the smaller of the two formations—the two eggs in a frying pan as it was described by most cerealogists.

The time was now 2:30 a.m.

Shaking my head, I decided to leave. There was no way we could stay here, as the owners of nearby Maisey Farm would no doubt rise at four o'clock, see our cars, and throw us off their land. Frustrated and lethargic enough not to argue, I accepted the suggestion that we sleep in the car park adjacent to Silbury Hill, which was some eight miles west of Marlborough.

And here day one of our crop circle excursion came to a welcoming end.

6

Why Warminster?

Sunday, July 21, 1991. The eerie drone of the night-flight helicopters and the roar of cars speeding past on the nearby A4 trunk road ensured a restless slumber inside a sweaty, German Army sleeping bag. I was the last to rise and did not feel very well at all—a fact confirmed to the others by my apparently unhealthy appearance. Not even the evocative image of nearby Silbury Hill, the largest man-made mound in Europe, built c. 2500 BC, could raise my spirits. The only heartening plus point was that, despite the cold air, it looked as if it would be another clear summer's day.

There were no visible crop formations in the fields adjacent to Silbury Hill, unusual in itself as in previous years a number of quintuplet sets and single circles had appeared in full view of the gigantic Neolithic structure. There had even been a rumor that one had been found on the hill's truncated grass summit, a matter quietly swept under the carpet by more sober circles researchers!

Zombie-like, the crop quest continued with a cleanup in the toilets at nearby Avebury and half an hour of mellowing out, before the rather unpopular decision was made to survey the final three crop formations pinpointed on the OS map by Richard Andrews the previous day. I think some of our party had had enough of crop formations and wanted simply to go home, my unerring enthusiasm not helping the situation.

Each formation lay close to Beckhampton, a mile or so to the south-west of Avebury, and the first of these was reached in no time at all. It was a simple dumbbell formation, composed of a large circle and a small circle linked together by a line of fallen crop. It lay upon a sloping field of barley to the east–southeast of a farm named The Firs. From our vantage point beside three grass–knolled tumuli, it looked a little weather beaten, so we assumed it had appeared some weeks before (June 6, in fact). The formation was not visible from the main road—indeed its only access was via The Firs farm itself, which was certainly a point in favor of its authenticity. We did not venture through the shallow valley to the formation as my colleagues were now thinking more of their empty bellies than of crop circles.

On the road out to Calne, near the village of Avebury Trusloe, we found and ventured down a trackway that took us north towards the fortified summit of Windmill Hill, home to the Beaker People some 4,500 years ago. Here, it seemed, we would find another formation. "Unsuitable for cars" its entry sign advised, but, once you've navigated the pitted course of the Ridgeway in a Ford Orion, you can take on anything!

To the right of the trackway, I looked towards the sea of ripened corn in the hope of glimpsing any obvious alteration. Eventually in the bright, early morning sunlight my eyes caught sight of another, slightly longer dumbbell formation. Running parallel to its stem, between each circle, were two short boxes of depressed wheat looking like open coffins. It had appeared, it seems, on June 14, and its position upon a gentle incline, invisible to the nearby road, or from anywhere with any clarity, was certainly a point in its favor. We made no attempt to enter the field, just snapped away merrily from the roof of the cars.

At the base of the same field was one more source of mystery. Some 200 yards from the first formation were three fair–sized circles, adjoined to a long stem and orientated east–west. They were virtually impossible to see, and their presence bypassed the group's gradually diminishing interest.

Unfortunately for them, I had contracted the infectious crop circle bug that leaves you wanting more and more, and there was now no way that I was going to leave the area without hunting out every conceivable circle, no matter where it may lie. Past seasons had seen a number of formations appear beneath the powerful presence of the Westbury white horse, just eight miles south-southwest of Devizes, so I made this our next port of call after a welcome break for breakfast at a Little Chef roadside restaurant.

Beyond the village of Bratton, a slip road took us up a steady gradient towards the top of Westbury Hill. To our left was a vast valley that looked decidedly like the deeply carved out basin known as the Cradle, situated beneath that more famous white horse at Uffington in Berkshire. Also similar to Whitehorse Hill, Uffington, Westbury Hill is capped by a ditch and bank hill fort of alleged Iron Age origin. Known as Bratton Castle, it contains a third millennium BC Neolithic long barrow that predates the construction of the camp by some 2,000 years.

On the cupped slope below the earthen castle, we came upon the enormous white horse, first mentioned in local records of 1778 when it was recut to give it the appearance of a more conventional-looking mare. Before this it had almost certainly been similar in design to the Uffington white horse and is likely to be just as old. Today the beast is encased in concrete to preserve and protect its outline.

It had been here that, during the high profile Operation Blackbird the previous summer, Colin Andrews and half the world's news media had been fooled when, on the second night of monitoring the fields below, a hoax crop formation was constructed right under their noses. It was an unfortunate and rather uncomfortable incident that greatly set back the progression of the crop circle debate.

From the elevated position of the white horse, I made a slow scan of the cultivated lands below but could see no artificial indentations, only acre after acre of lodging—the term used to describe crop flattened by the wind, something I had noticed many times during our exploration of the ancient Wessex countryside. It had been particularly in evidence in the fields to the south of Silbury Hill, where crop circles had invariably appeared in past years.

The extraordinary similarity between the terrain surrounding both the Westbury white horse and its counterpart at Uffington remained fixed in my mind, and it made me wonder why so few circles had appeared in the Vale of the White Horse in Berkshire.

Nobody we asked on Bratton Castle that morning had heard of any crop circles in the area, prompting us to move on to our next port of call—nearby Warminster, once the UFO capital of England.

The short drive took us through the village of Upton Scudamore where, on Saturday, October 9, 1976, I experienced my one and only confirmed UFO (or a should say "ghost light") sighting.[1] At the time, I was a 19-year-old UFO investigator and with fellow researcher Barry King, his two brothers, and one of their friends, we had left London by car late on the Friday evening, arriving in Warminster around two o'clock in the morning. Later that day we would visit Avebury, Silbury Hill, and Stonehenge, among other places, but at that moment all we wanted to do was find a suitably spooky location to spend the night.

Not knowing the town, we found ourselves leaving on the A350 Westbury Road, and after a couple of miles of aimless driving, we chanced upon a secluded farm track, opposite a lane leading down to Upton Scudamore. It looked ideal so, dipping the headlights, we turned off the main road.

It was a dense foggy night, with visibility down to around 100 yards. To our left was a copse of trees and to the right were low trimmed hedges. Unexpectedly, we became aware of an intense white light coming towards us out of the thick fog from across the fields to our right. It was the size, shape, and color of a motorcycle headlamp, and every so often it would gently bob up and down as if navigating the plowed furrows. Our initial thoughts were that it was the farmer coming across to throw us off his land. Yet, as our vehicle bore round to the right and climbed to higher ground, the glowing light moved out of the field below and seemed to cross over the road that we ourselves had just come along. Yet curiously, we did not pursue it. It was almost as if a strange sense of "normality" had overtaken us, for, aside from the occasional comment or passing glance, we merely continued our search to find a suitable place to park up the car.

After waking up later that morning, we checked the plowed field for any sign of muddy tracks. Not only were there none to be seen, but the low hedgerow along the side of the trackway bore no accessible spot where a motorcycle might have left the field.

No more was thought about the matter until January the following year when I purchased a book entitled The Flying Saucerers (1976) by Warminster journalist Arthur Shuttlewood. Page 39 contained an account of just such a mysterious "ghost light" being seen in 1967 on Cradle Hill, which is only about a mile south of where we experienced

5. Sketch of the strange light, like an intense car headlamp, witnessed by the author at Upton Scudamore, Wiltshire, on October 9, 1976.

our sighting. It was described as a Will–o'–the–Wisp with the appearance of a "circular lantern" or "cycle headlight." However, in this case, Shuttlewood and his two colleagues ran towards the luminous ball, prompting it to change from a sphere to an ovoid and jerk up and down like a yo–yo. It had then shot upwards and weaved from side to side with the three observers in hot pursuit. After chasing the poor light through copses, gates, and hedgerows, it was finally lost from view in the direction of the army range at Imber, close to where we saw our own light. Its apparently intelligent actions and shape–shifting capabilities had led Shuttlewood to conclude that it was "surely no earth contrivance" and undoubtedly not of "human construction."

Curiously, the fields around Warminster, and Upton Scudamore in particular, had played host to the crop circle phenomenon in more recent years.[2] As early as 1983, a quintuplet set of circles had appeared at the foot of Cley Hill, a tumuli–capped hill fort two miles west of Warminster, where in the late 1960s and early 1970s UFO sky–watchers had flocked in their hundreds for nightly vigils.

Stop–starting at the traffic lights, I pointed out the tree–lined Cradle Hill at the very edge of Warminster's built–up area. At one time it had been even more popular for sky–watchers than Cley Hill. Dozens of people would climb it each weekend throughout the 1960s and 1970s to wait patiently for something mysterious to happen. Books such as *The Flying Saucerers* and Arthur Shuttlewood's first book *The Warminster Mystery* (1967) had inspired a generation with their graphic accounts of strange UFO events occurring in and around the town.

As I remembered those long hours spent at Cradle Hill, I realized then that they were the precursors to the modern crop watches at places such as Alton Barnes and Cheesefoot Head in Hampshire. They had that same feel about them, those solemn vigils gazing out on to a darkened landscape, patiently hoping that some sign would be given—be it a ball of light, a luminous column, or a return of the trilling noise. In the coming years crop circles were going to be the source of spiritual hope for an awful lot of people, regardless of their true origin and purpose.

So, was there a real link between the thousands of UFO sightings that had haunted Warminster from Christmas Day 1964 onwards for some 15 years and the quite obvious concentration of crop circles in the self–same region in the 1980s and 1990s? The answer was quite obviously yes, but why exactly was going to be the subject of heated debate for some time to come.

7

No Sleep Till Cheesefoot Head

Leaving Warminster, the car passed through Salisbury and Andover and headed out towards Winchester in neighboring Hampshire—the second main center for the crop circle phenomenon. I had been intrigued to see that a map in issue two of *The Cerealogist* showed that most of Hampshire's handful of formations in 1990 had occurred in the vicinity of Cheesefoot Head. So why was there such a clustering in this one area alone? Was there something special about the fields around here? Was it the terrain, the crops, the people, or the media coverage?

To me the only immediate clue was that many of the circles had appeared beneath the dark shadow of St. Catherine's Hill, the ancient, tree-capped hill fort, upon the summit of which is the Mizmaze, one of Britain's last surviving medieval turf mazes. There was also an assortment of earthworks and tumuli in the area, including two upon Telegraph Hill, where circles had appeared in recent years. Also worth noting was that one of Britain's most extraordinary UFO encounters had taken place just two miles from Cheesefoot Head, in the village of Chilcomb, where circles had been appearing since the early 1980s and possibly even before that. I refer here to the case of Joyce Bowles and her friend

31

Edwin "Ted" Pratt, who were driving along a narrow country lane during the evening of November 14, 1976, when they had encountered a
glowing orange, oval-shaped object complete with occupant, just as
their Mini Clubman had lost control and mounted a grass verge. Joyce
herself was a powerful psychic healer, and the investigators who compiled a comprehensive report of the incident were adamant that the
encounter had occurred at the junction of prominent local ley lines.[1]

Perhaps all this was pure coincidence; I could not be sure.

Eventually, I chanced upon the route that took us past St. Catherine's
Hill and on to Cheesefoot Head. Rounding a hill covered in near-rip-
ened wheat, named on the OS map as Chilcomb Down, I espied a clearly
identifiable formation on its southeast-facing slope. It consisted of a
large ring bisected by an axis line, with a smaller flattened circle at
either end. Attached to its northerly extreme was a long spur, and pro-
truding from the other end was an off-center D-shape, its vertical line
bisected into ladder-like sections.

Parking the car on a precarious bend a few hundred yards further
on, our party walked back and stared out at this agricultural work of
art. The one point that immediately struck me was that the width of the
ring and lines was noticeably thinner than their counterparts in
Wiltshire. Indeed, the whole design looked decidedly, well, *weak* is the
word. Still, we were in a different county now.

The field was unofficially entered on the quiet, and, having found
the correct tramline that would take us into the pictogram, we began
the long walk, throwing glances at the passing cars able to witness our
trek from the nearby road. Upon reaching the formation, we realized
that a considerable amount of its flattened crop had righted itself and
was merrily growing back, making its overall image that much more
difficult to discern.

Other people were now leaving their vehicles by the side of the road
and plowing across the crop towards our position. A black dog, off its
lead, bounded wildly through the field, and I cringed at this blatant
breach of the Code of Practice set down for crop circle watchers by the
council of the CCCS. Sorry, next time we really would ask for permission to enter the field; promise!

Our party felt nothing at this site. Shrugging my shoulders, I took in
the different features and spent a little time chatting to the different

groups of circle seekers, who now seemed to be arriving by the minute. Among them was a pleasant girl who entered the field just as we were about to leave. She directed us and another young lad who had tagged along to a further formation in a field marked on the map as Longwood Warren, just south of Cheesefoot Head. It lay out of sight of the road in a wheat field a few hundred yards away.

Following the course of a bridleway, we found and entered the new formation. It was almost a miniature of the Chilcomb Down pictogram, consisting of a ring bisected by a centerline, beyond which was a smaller flattened circle at either end.

Here we stayed for some 20 minutes, chatting and trying to record any anomalous sounds on a pocket cassette. This was the smallest formation I had entered, for it was no more than 40 feet in length, and, as with the others inspected that weekend, I attempted to deduce its method of manufacture. The first flattened circle lay only a couple of feet in front of a major tramline. Straight out from this was a narrow line acting as its central corridor. The wheat had been pushed down in a northerly direction from the top edge of the first circle, right through to the center of the second circle, which could only have been constructed after the corridor was complete. The ring was the last component added, since its swathed stalks rode over the top of flattened crop within the long central line.

Our group felt nothing at all in this one, and it was certainly not for me to cast aspersions on crop circles, but of all the 14 formations we had been witness to in the past 36 hours, this was the most obvious hoax, along with the one at Chilcomb Down, which also did not "feel" right. And that was it. Having run out of further circle locations, it was time for us to venture back to the more predictable reality of our own home territory of Essex.

My introduction to the crop circle phenomenon was complete, and yet, for those who had frequently asked me what my views were on the subject, I could still only shrug my shoulders and say: "Not sure, really." Yet as soon as my body clock and brain were in one piece again, I would sit down and write up the whole circles excursion to see what made sense.

PART TWO
Exotic Energy

8

The Scientific Shaman

In the days that followed our party's return from the crop circle world of Wiltshire and Hampshire, I worked constantly, recording every last detail of that mentally exhausting weekend. Despite my newfound enthusiasm for the crop circle mystery, I was afterwards forced to shelve any active pursuit of new formations due to other, more pressing commitments, which took up my time.

What I was able to do, however, was read Trevor James Constable's *Sky Creatures*, which became my bible for unlocking the secrets of the crop circles and their apparent connection with the UFO phenomenon. Yet to even start to understand how this came about, we must begin with the story of Wilhelm Reich, a scientific shaman if ever there was one, and his discovery of orgone energy.

As early as 1927, Reich—a distinguished Freudian analyst born in Austria in 1897—published a book that provided a full account of his discovery of orgone energy. Entitled *The Function of the Orgasm*, it attempted, among many other things, to express the author's belief that a specific dynamic force lay behind the life energy of the sexual orgasm, the human process of animating matter. Reich wanted to demonstrate the energetic reality of the life energy that Sigmund Freud, the eminent

6. Wilhelm Reich (1897-1957), who might just have discovered the energy that exerts all natural forces in the
universe.

Austrian psychoanalyst, called the "libido." Although its existence was
not disputed, scientists looked upon it as the creation of food processes
alone; something that Reich felt was insufficient to describe its potential.

Reich submerged himself in his own brand of biophysics for several
years, but in 1933 he was forced to leave Germany due to the rising
threat posed to democracy, and his own life, by Hitler and the Nazi
regime. He settled first in Oslo and then moved on to the United States
in 1939.

Using a sophisticated microscope, Reich had noticed that, under extremely high magnifications, luminous blue-green globules would be
released by decaying food. He identified them as pulsating energy
vesicles, or waveforms, which he believed were a form of biological
ether. These he looked upon as the so-called "bions" discovered by H.
Charlton Bastian, a contemporary of Louis Pasteur, the eminent nine-

teenth-century French chemist and scientist. In a book entitled *The Beginnings of Life* (1872), Bastian published details of his discovery of the bion associating them with germs and disease conditions. Unfortunately, Bastian's work was largely ignored—lost in the revelations on bacteriology being advanced at that same time by Pasteur.

Excited by his apparent rediscovery of bions, but cautious as to their nature, Reich set about studying their motion and soon established that they were released by decaying matter. They also seemed to possess quite real properties and appeared to attack bacteria. Bions also discharged into metallic objects and were present even in inanimate substances such as coal and sand.

Reich continued his study of bions until he left for the United States in 1939, realizing that something quite disturbing was taking place. His microscopic study of these energy vesicles was beginning to burn his eyes and produce a form of conjunctivitis. In addition to these unanticipated effects, he found that the skin on his face was becoming noticeably tanned.

What then had he discovered? Were bions a form of previously unknown radiation? If so, then, by isolating this energy, was he exposing himself to a form of radioactivity? His mind recalled the painstaking and often dangerous experiments conducted by Marie and Pierre Curie following their discovery of radium back in 1898.

Sensibly, Reich built a simple metal-lined box to contain and isolate his bions, but this only *intensified* the influence and produced strange side effects. Immediately above its lid he found that the temperature would rise constantly. His inquisitiveness led him to experiment further, and in 1940 Reich constructed his first orgone energy accumulator. It was a six-sided box insulated with alternate layers of organic and inorganic substances (usually glass wool, steel wool, upson board, and galvanized sheet iron). These layers acted as an effective form of caging, deflecting and intensifying this life energy. The more layers that were added, the more efficient it became. It was like a greenhouse to the sun's rays, trapping and concentrating the bion vesicles. He also discovered that this particle release was merely highlighting an actual unknown energy or radiation, which the bion vesicles appeared to emit at a constant rate, and it was this emission that had produced the conjunctivitis and tanning effect. He saw it as an organic radiation present in all living matter. It existed, he established, in *everything*, even in a single drop of blood or in cultivated food, and this previously unrecognized organic radiation he called orgone, or orgone energy.

Reich later came to believe that orgone was universally present in different degrees and concentrations on the ground, in the air, and out in space. It collected in the so-called "orgone envelope," a layer of orgone existing in the upper atmosphere. It also acted as a medium to bring into focus other dynamic forces, for, in orgone, light moves, while electromagnetic and gravitational fields exert force. It is also the blueness of the sky, the heat waves that shimmer above wooded areas and mountains, and the root cause of such meteorological occurrences as clouds, wind, and hurricanes; even the Aurora Borealis or Northern Lights were visible manifestations of orgone's presence. Reich later developed his theories to demonstrate that orgone in the atmosphere is a primordial, mass-free energy produced from sunlight and absorbed into the body through the lungs.

Among the characteristics and properties of orgone was its apparent contradiction of the law of entropy. For instead of flowing from higher to lower potentials, as in electricity or heat, orgone flows from lower to higher concentrations. The earth itself is covered in orgone, and upon its surface some of the greatest concentrations are to be found within water sources, which Reich found acted as natural accumulators. It was also said that reservoirs of orgone, whether in the body or in the landscape, acquired further energy from their environment.

To detect this unclassified energy, Reich constructed an "orgonoscope" to see orgone in the atmosphere and an "orgone field meter" to measure the detailed energy fields that surround living organisms. He was thus able to demonstrate, to his satisfaction, orgone's objective reality visually, thermically, electroscopically, as well as through the process of lumination in vacuums. Reich is even alleged to have produced a motor engine that successfully ran off orgone energy alone.

Knowing that orgone counteracted bacteria in the body, Reich built much larger accumulators using the same principles and shape. In these accumulators, a person could sit in total darkness for short controlled durations. In such experiments the participants would generally speak of feeling body warmth and a tingling sensation on the skin. Often a mild form of reddening or tanning would occur, as would noticeable healing results in everything from mental disorders to cancer. More curious, however, were the reports of luminous particles seen with the naked eye to spin out from the walls and then disappear.

Reich took his great discovery to another German exile, Albert Einstein, whom he met for the first time on January 13, 1941. During the five-hour conversation, Reich explained the process behind the orgonoscope and showed the mathematician the temperature differential existing above the orgone accumulator. Despite all this, the two great men's monumental meeting came to nothing. Einstein was clearly preoccupied with other, more pressing matters, so he decided against any involvement with Reich's work.

In 1951 Reich took a leaf out of Einstein's book and began exploring the relationship between orgone and electromagnetism, using the medium of atomic radiation—his so-called Oranur Experiment. On January 5, Reich placed just one milligram of radium, sheathed in a lead container, inside a specially prepared 20-layer accumulator at Orgonon, the Reich Institute he established at Rangeley, Maine, in 1948. It was left in place for five hours and the experiment was repeated for a whole week, ending with just half an hour on the final day. The extraordinary and rather disturbing results of this exercise were published in Reich's *Oranur Experiment: First Report, 1947-51.*

Problems at Orgonon began when the Geiger counter placed inside the accumulator recorded a steady increase in radiation, before finally jamming completely. Mice used in body cell healing experiments with orgone suddenly keeled over and died, and a peculiar, acrid odor started to permeate the air above the Institute. In the days that followed, thick, oppressive clouds gathered ominously, and both the buildings and surrounding environment began to "glow" at night. Worse still, the effects did not let up when the radium was taken away—they merely intensified. Reich fell ill immediately and was said to have hovered between life and death for days on end.

In the weeks that followed, menacing clouds continued to gather above Rangeley, and the landscape was said to have felt oppressive and somber, as if a sense of impending doom had descended upon Orgonon. Lab workers and visitors became sick; objects began to disappear and then mysteriously reappear; everything seemed tinged with a purplish or purplish-mauve aura, and a constant dryness permeated the air inside the Institute. White birch trees bent over like rubber hoses as if laden with snow. Trees and shrubs blackened and withered as the face of death overshadowed the Reich Institute.

It was even claimed that the "desolation" of the area around the Institute, in the wake of the Oranur Experiment, had begun after "big yellow and reddish pulsing stars" started appearing over Orgonon. Confirmation of this claim soon followed with reports of strange aerial lights seen hanging in the sky above the Institute by Reich's assistants. At first, Reich did not see them himself but whole-heartedly believed in the possibility of their existence, having read with interest the accounts of "flying saucers" seen in different parts of the world since the summer of 1947.

Through the Oranur Experiment Reich realized that he had disturbed the fundamental equilibrium of orgone present in both the environment and atmosphere above Rangeley. As some people put it: "There was something wrong in the air." He eventually decided he had produced a mutated form of orgone—a dense, concentrated, and malignant variant he named DOR (Deadly Orgone Radiation). Whereas OR (Orgone Radiation) was a life-giving process, DOR was its reverse—a death-inducting power source of unknown capability, an anti-life component. Worse still, the chain reaction, started by the Oranur Experiment, was now drawing off its own energy to continually feed the DOR around it. In an attempt to escape from this vicious cycle, Reich, unable to sleep at night, would take a vehicle and drive out to various places, trying to get some rest.

It was during this same period that Reich first developed the cloudbuster in an attempt to dissipate the dirty black DOR clouds. When the strange lights above Orgonon intensified during 1953 and even Reich began to see them, the cloudbuster became a "space gun." For during this bleak period of fragile stability, Reich saw these mysterious lights as interplanetary spacecraft spying on him. They had been drawn to Rangeley, he said, by the radiation sent into space by the Oranur Experiment.

On May 12, 1954, Reich directed the cloudbuster at an unidentified nocturnal light, and it blinked out of view. On subsequent attempts with other lights, the same thing happened. This occurrence led Reich to believe that he was causing the "flying saucers" to withdraw rapidly so that the cloudbuster's rays could not drain away their presupposed power source. These results genuinely shocked Reich to such a degree that he decided against further action, fearing he might initiate an interplanetary war! It was said that Reich also witnessed UFOs in the remote woods around Rangeley, indicating that not all the luminosities witnessed were of atmospheric origin.

Despite his "nuts and bolts" approach to unidentified aerial lights,

7. Wilhelm Reich using a cloudbuster at Orgonon in Rangeley, Maine.

Reich could not have been entirely convinced of their alien origin, for, in a privately published book entitled *Contact with Space* (1957), published the year he died, Reich refers to them by the term *Ea*. The "E" stood for energy and the "a" for primordial, showing that he envisaged these strange lights as products of orgone, the "mass-free primordial energy" he saw as permeating the universe.

Finally, the cloudbusters succeeded in dispersing the DOR that Reich saw as hanging heavy in the air above Orgonon. By updating the devices to include a tiny amount of a radioactive substance referred to as ORUR, the DOR could be made safe before it was discharged into an underground water source, using earthing cables attached to hollow tubes.

During this same period, Reich and his colleagues visited the scrub desert of Tucson, Arizona, intent on conducting further weather-control experiments. Here they set up a new establishment called Little Orgonon. Reich believed that, by coming here, they could leave behind the irradiated fall-out zone created at Rangeley, Maine. Unfortunately, this was not to be, for the events caused by the DOR at Orgonon largely repeated themselves in Tucson. Cloudbusters were used once more, and it was while manning Cloudbuster # 2 on December 6, 1954, that an assistant named Bob McCullough was struck with paralysis, a disorder that resulted in him leaving Little Orgonon (see Chapter 11).

In spite of such tragic drawbacks, Reich's use of the cloudbuster finally resulted in defeat for the DOR. The summer of 1955 was Tucson's wettest in 20 years, with 12 inches of rainfall being recorded. Greenery flourished in this less-than-fertile desert region, and Reich quite rightly believed that his desert-and-drought weather engineering operations were responsible.

Yet, by 1954, Reich was experiencing other, more mundane problems in his life. On March 19 that year, he was issued with a court order by the US Food and Drug Administration directing him to cease research into orgone and discontinue the publication of his Institute papers. This was the culmination of seven years of harassment by the FDA who seemed hell-bent on destroying Willhelm Reich's work and reputation. After much deliberation, the FDA had concluded that the sale, rent, or hire of orgone accumulators across state lines contravened interstate shipping laws. Since there was no such thing as orgone, the devices were, therefore, mislabeled or "misbranded."

In a pitiful scenario that smacks of suppression and conspiracy, the FDA deemed that shipments of orgone accumulators be halted and, those existing, be dismantled. Not content in leaving it there, the FDA decided to ban Reich's ten major books and burn his soft-cover book stocks and unbound scientific documentation. Henceforth, the scientist was prevented from disseminating his work on orgone in any way, shape, or form.

The inevitable legal drama that resulted from the FDA's ruling led to Reich being charged with contempt of court and sent to a federal penitentiary, where he died on November 3, 1957. It was a tragic end for a man who, in 1939, may have stumbled upon the very force that animates matter and causes life.

One additional aspect of Reich's experiments, which caught my eye and seemed particularly relevant to the crop circle debate, occurred during the spring of 1952. It was then that Reich and his colleagues had begun noticing a thick black substance gathering upon rock surfaces close to the Institute in the wake of the Oranur Experiment. It was given the name Melanor, although other distinguishable variations were also discovered, and these variations he named Brownite and Orite. The stuff was even filmed forming on rocks.

Melanor was found to attach to and then destroy rocks. It could crystallize into either rock particles, looking like coal clinker (something that has been found in crop circles), or a dark sticky substance. In this more tar-like form, it simply dried up and evaporated under normal atmospheric conditions. Unfortunately, however, its presence created a detrimental excitation of orgone in the bodies of workers at Orgonon, resulting in cyanosis (a blueness of the skin), nausea, intense thirst, and miscellaneous pains. Trying to collect samples seemed only to make matters worse. Quite naturally, the presence of the substance was put down to high levels of DOR that almost constantly surrounded Orgonon during this period. The sheer existence of a substance like Melanor is disconcerting enough, for it denotes the presence of DOR. More worrying, however, was that something similar had been found in British crop circles.

In 1985 crop circles expert and photographer Busty Taylor and his colleague Alan Twigg found a "white, jelly-like substance" inside one of the circles of a quintuplet set at Goodworth Clatford, Hampshire. It rested in a rectangular clod, roughly the length of an ear of wheat, upon and in the direction of the fallen stalks. Having studied the jelly at close range for some minutes, both men quickly developed a series of side effects that included "stinging sinuses, runny eyes and a sore throat" that lingered for some while afterwards.[1] Earlier, Busty had been startled by a distinct burst of blue light, like a camera flash that had come from the circle itself.

A primary analysis of the substance by a Mr. Moss of the University of Sussex found it to contain a high incidence of starch grains as well as crystals of calcium carbonate and a large amount of bacteria. Despite the analyst noting a slight smell of honey, no sugar crystals were found, and the so-called Fehling's test, to establish whether glucose syrup might be present, proved negative. Commercial sweets and honey are said to give positive reactions to this test.[2]

The University concluded the jelly to be "some kind of confectionary which had gone off," while another separate analysis at the National Testing Laboratory at Wisley also failed to observe any "unusual or distinctive features" in the sample tested. Despite these results, Busty remains convinced that they were wrong, pointing out that only preliminary tests were conducted, as their limited personal funds ran out, and further testing would have involved money they simply did not possess. Certainly, having viewed a clear color slide photograph of the sample *in situ* before its removal from the fallen stalks, I can only say that this is *not* a melted candy bar, as some authors have flippantly suggested.[3]

So, did Busty and his colleague discover a new variation of the Melanor, Brownite, or Orite discovered at Orgonon in the wake of the Oranur Experiment? Certainly, the resultant side effects are similar to both Melanor and the jelly sample. Blue flashes are also indicative of residual orgone and have been reported at circle sites on a number of occasions.

The Goodworth Clatford case is not the only example where a jellylike substance has been found at a circle site either. In the third week of June 1988, a ringed circle surrounded by three smaller satellites was identified from the air in a field of wheat at Oadby, Leicestershire. BUFORA investigators Clive Potter and Ernie Still were on the scene within 24 hours, accompanied by psychic Rita Goold. She rang me that same night to say that, when they had first entered the central circle, a small clod of opaque, jelly-like substance, described as "pink blancmange," was discovered *beneath* the fallen stalks close to the circle's center. It was said to have been "sticky," and samples were taken away for analysis (the results are not known). Rita added that Clive Potter sustained a "thundering" headache in the central circle, prompting them to leave and return later. At the time, he made no connection between his headache and their visit to the crop formation, but, then, having heard of similar incidents dogging other circles researchers, he began to think otherwise. So, had Rita and her friends discovered some form of Melanor at the circle in Oadby, or was there a much simpler explanation that now eludes us?

On the night of the formation's appearance, a lay preacher from nearby Fleckney had seen a glowing ball of light above the field where the circles were later found. Indeed, as far back as 1983, I was with Rita when she received a psychic message suggesting that we watch this particular field for paranormal occurrences. Our enquiries at the time had indicated that the field in question was well known for sightings of mysterious lights. It was with this information in mind that she had contacted me so promptly, wondering whether I could shed any further information on the significance of the location.

The starch basis of the jelly-like substance found at Goodworth Clatford could prove to be significant, for, on the night of November 13, 1833, the skies above the United States had been aglow with strange "meteors."[4] They deposited gelatinous substances on the ground in various locations, and these substances appear to have had marked similarities to the jelly found at Goodworth Clatford. For instance, in Rahway, New Jersey, and in Nelson County, Virginia, a "fiery rain" deposited "lumps of jelly," while in Newark, New Jersey, a similar substance described as "soft soap" was found that same night, and at West Point, New York, a loud "splosh" was heard by a lady who turned to find "a round flattened (and transparent) mass . . . *looking like a boiled starch.*" It quickly evaporated. It might also be suggested that there are correlations here with so-called Angel Hair, the wispy white substance often found on the ground after nocturnal or early morning UFO sightings.

Unfortunately, the preliminary analysis of the Melanor, Brownite, and Orite, conducted in 1953 by Reich and his associates and published two years later in *CORE (Cosmic Orgone Engineering)* by the Orgone Institute Press, is currently unavailable for scrutiny. However, it is known that these substances were linked finally *with the presence of the UFOs above Orgonon in the aftermath of the Oranur Experiment.*

I was beginning to suspect a relationship between the manufacture of crop circles, the strange effects surrounding them, and the orgone energy of Wilhelm Reich. In the knowledge that he saw an intimate connection between orgone, Melanor, and the mysterious lights seen above Rangeley following the Oranur Experiment, I felt that we were on the verge of a major discovery here. It came, finally, after reading what Trevor James Constable had to say about the nature of UFOs and their relationship to the so-called "saucer nests," the precursor of the modern-day crop circle.

9
Return of the Ether Ships

Trevor James Constable studied UFOs for many years before Reich's daughter, Eva, in the mid–1950s, finally introduced him to orgone energy. Previously, he had listened to the prophetic ramblings of UFO contactees, who believed that they had ridden in the "flying saucers" and still retained telepathic communication with their inter-planetary friends. Even though the pronouncements of such people were often of a high moralistic or philosophical content, those who could read between the lines realized that these people might hold the key to unlocking the real mystery of UFOs, which had begun plaguing the world's air space in June 1947.

According to *Sky Creatures*, Constable visited eccentrics such as George Van Tassel, a contactee who gathered his followers together in a hewn–out chamber beneath Giant Rock in the South Californian desert for communion with the Space Brothers. During these séance–like sessions, which often attracted very large crowds indeed, some 60 to 70 people would enter the chamber and join in singing, chanting, and saying prayers, hoping to make their call heard above the background din of the astral planes. Each person would gradually become part of the "biological energies of his gathering" and, in doing so, act as a receiver for alien contact to take place.

The lively calls were usually answered, for out of the darkness a deep, booming voice would issue forth from Van Tassel's entranced body, unlike anything Constable had ever heard before. It was strong and assertive and believable. Using the contactee's vocal chords, the intelligences would speak of their planet, their propulsion systems, and their mission to earth. On one occasion the Space Brothers said they would even appear at a specified time in the nearby desert. Sure enough, at the appointed hour mysterious lights came into view and remained visible until a military aircraft was scrambled to intercept them.[1]

Constable was profoundly affected by Van Tassel and particularly by his alien friends' assertion that the atmosphere was full of invisible life forms that were *not* spaceships. Space, Constable was told, was filled with primary energy of a variety our scientists had no knowledge of whatsoever, and infrared film exposed between dawn and sunrise in hot, dry locations would capture and record these invisible forms, which existed just beyond the visible spectrum.

Even at this stage of the game, Constable was beginning to realize that there was more to the UFO phenomenon than simply men from space visiting us in "flying saucers." He believed there was a direct association between, say, the dynamic force that was able to power him across a room and the energy source behind the UFOs, which seemed to cross the sky as metallic or milky-white disks by day and as mysterious lights by night. Somehow he knew that out there waiting to be discovered was a whole new source of power—not one created by alien mechanics, but one from within ourselves, a "bioplasmic energy," like that discerned and photographed around living matter by the Russians named Kirlian and seen by psychics as colorful auric fields.

Constable accepted that Van Tassel was an honest enough man, but to search for the real answers he began engrossing himself in the study of the occult sciences, particularly the works of Rudolf Steiner, the Austrian philosopher, scientist and founder of the Anthroposophical Society.

Constable's own personal mentor, a man named Franklin Thomas, presented him with a book that was to have a profound effect on his life. Entitled *Man or Matter* (1958), it was written by a Steiner pupil named Ernest Lehrs, Ph.D. The book drew together such seemingly diverse subjects as biology, botany, geology, mechanics, and meteorology, and it showed the correlations between them all. It also dealt with optics, light, and color as well as the so-called visual ray or "eye beam" seen by the Steiner school as a ray of biological energy that could be directed into space through the eye socket.

A new beginning dawned for Constable, and armed with various practices for occult meditations, a camera, and some infrared film, he set about proving the existence of these "sky creatures," as he called them.

During the summer of 1957, the same year as Reich's tragic death, Constable teamed up with a colleague named Jim Woods and chose a suitable location in the Californian desert between Yucca Valley and Old Woman Springs for some photographic experimentation. The agreed plan was for Constable to stand upon a slight eminence and act as a "bio-energetic beacon" by conducting simple "occult" exercises and attempting to call down the "critters." At the same time Woods would stand back and photograph the empty sky against background features using infrared film and filters. The experiments would take place between dawn and sunrise, the time period originally suggested by Van Tassel many years before.

By mid-1958 the results of the two men's early morning photographic sessions were clear for all to see. In just one year they had captured on film over 100 anomalous objects which Constable took to be amoeba-like "bioforms" invisible at the moment the frame was exposed. Some showed dark objects; others, extraordinary ellipses looking like living cells, while still others were of more obvious UFO shapes. All appeared to be of considerable size and were framed by physical features such as hills, desert landscape, and people.

The potency of what Constable and Woods had achieved may be summed up by the remarkable series of images taken with an infrared motion film in the Mojave Desert on an unspecified date. The sequence, shot at 24 frames per second and reproduced in *Sky Creatures*, shows five consecutive pictures in which Constable stands some way away with his hands raised in the air. Descending down towards him is an object that, in a mere quarter of a second of exposure, divides in two, joins back together, before finally ascending towards the top of the last frame.

Whatever the true nature of these photographic anomalies was, Constable came to believe that they were living "critters" composed of orgone radiation similar to the mysterious lights that Reich had encountered above the Orgonon ranch in Rangeley, Maine, between 1952 and 1954. This he deduced through various factors. Firstly, he found that Reich had seen the luminosity of the Aurora Borealis, the Northern Lights, as a product of atmospheric orgone and not simply the result of electrical discharges as conventional science maintains. This highly ionized phenomenon is generally accompanied by electrical storms, which Reich saw as severely disrupting the level of atmospheric orgone in the same manner as a cloudbuster. Constable considered this observation as an indisputable link between orgone, weather control, and aerial luminosities. He also realized that UFOs were often observed descending from, or disappearing into, clouds. Somehow it all added up to the clear fact that his "critters" were integrally involved with the orgone process, and, as Reich had already discovered, they could be forced either to manifest or dematerialize simply by exciting or disrupting the orgone potential of the atmosphere.

In the years that followed, Constable built a cloudbuster and used it to make his "sky creatures" descend into the infrared or visible ranges of the electromagnetic spectrum. Almost instantly he had further photographic successes, with some pictures even showing a strange aerial mass against a backdrop of Jim Woods operating the cloudbuster.

Of the greatest importance to the crop circle debate were the many shots taken by Constable and others of silhouette–like blobs seemingly in motion across the sky. They appeared this way, he said, because Reich had discovered that objects of a high orgone charge reproduce on photographs in reverse polarity, in other words, as absorptive bodies, their charge nullifying the film emulsion instead of reacting with it.[2]

This hypothesis could, perhaps, explain the two "black darts" that appeared in a color picture of a circle at Chilcomb Head in Hampshire, taken by Busty Taylor in 1987 and featured on page 50 of *The Crop Circle Enigma*. One is rising vertically from ground level inside the flattened crop, while the other appears to be on the surface of the standing wheat. Nothing was visible when the picture was taken. In addition to this, other types of photographic anomalies have become associated with crop circle research. One picture, taken by George Wingfield of the 1991 "middle" formation at Alton Barnes, shows a dark ovoid mass hanging in the air. He, apparently, possesses "a file full" of similar such photographs sent to him by circles enthusiasts.

More satisfying to me was the remarkable resemblance between the

8. Strange black darts caught on camera by Busty Taylor in a crop circle at Chilcomb Head, Hampshire, in 1987.

silhouette images caught on film by Constable, Busty Taylor, and George Wingfield and a dark image I captured on two separate 35mm frames while investigating a UFO sighting in Prestatyn, North Wales, during October 1979. A colleague named Martin Keatman and I had visited the home of a young girl who had witnessed an alleged UFO above the rooftops of houses opposite her home. I had taken black and white photographs of the view from the front door step, only to find that a significant silhouetted aerial form had appeared above an outline of chimney stacks in two frames showing the selfsame area of sky. At the time a young psychic and contactee named Gaynor Sunderland—who had accompanied Martin, me, and her mother, Marion, on the investi-

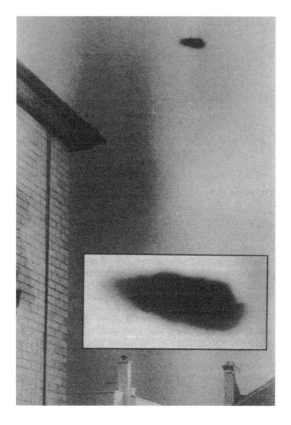

9. The first of two pictures taken by the author at Prestatyn, North Wales, during a UFO investigation in October 1979.

gation—quite independently felt the "presence" of a UFO "watching" us from this very area of the sky.[3]

No other similar marks appeared elsewhere on the reel of film, and no logical reason has ever been given to suitably explain these images. If not simply an emulsion fault, was it possible that the camera had caught on film an invisible object, arguably one of Constable's "critters," whose presence was somehow becoming known to young Gaynor?

To Constable his "bioforms" were hidden from scientific detection for the simple reason that, for most of the time, they inhabit the higher regions of the electromagnetic spectrum and, only occasionally, shift

10. The second of the two images taken at Prestatyn, North Wales, in October 1979.

down in frequency to its infrared or ultrasonic ranges. Yet, when this shift occurred, they could be tracked on radar, caught on camera, and, just occasionally, seen by the naked eye. Constable believed they changed density, shape, and size, and proposed that some might even be up to a mile long and appear like lenticular clouds. Of course, Constable knew that his theories could not explain the appearances of *all* UFOs, especially the well-attested sightings of "nuts and bolts" spacecraft and alien entities, but he was sure that these also utilized biological energies in their propulsion systems. Van Tassel had taught him this, and Constable's solid belief in interplanetary communication made sure he continued to accept such a hypothesis.

Constable, however, needed confirmation of his beliefs and so searched the annals of "flying saucer" lore for signs of others before him who had reached similar conclusions. There were many. For instance, the physicist Carl F. Krafft wrote prodigiously on the power of ether in a book entitled *The Ether and its Vortices* (1955). Essays on the same subject by Krafft were included in the appendix to W. Gordon Allen's 1959 work *Spacecraft from Beyond Three Dimensions*. He proposed that the atmosphere was not empty but filled with primary energy currents, or ethers, eddying like vortices beyond the detection of scientific instrumentation.[4]

Yet, as early as 1946, one year before the advent of the "flying saucer" craze spread across the United States, the concept of etheric aero-forms in the atmosphere was advanced by Meade Layne, MA, the founder of the Borderland Sciences Research Foundation in San Diego, California. In a later book, *The Ether Ship Mystery and Its Solution* (1950), he argued that unidentified aero-forms were "thought constructs"—intelligent entities that form bodies from etheric substances. The profusion in shapes and sizes of "flying saucers" led Layne to conclude that these "etherian entities" were atmospheric "mutants" that could permeate land, air, or sea.[5]

Apparently, when Meade Layne was shown an assortment of photographs of "critters" taken by Constable, he became ecstatic, pronouncing them "the death knell of the old order." But, unfortunately, the world was not ready for any kind of ether-related physics.

In 1955 the Countess Zoe Wassilko-Serecki, an Austrian noblewoman, wrote an article in the occult publication *Inconnue* suggesting that UFOs were life forms that dwelt in space and fed on pure energy, creating "bladder-like bodies for themselves out of colloidal silicones." The Viennese publication *Neue Illustrierte Wochenschau* allowed the Countess to follow up her theory in two articles published in May 1959 under the title "Creatures from the Stratosphere."[6]

The early 1960s saw further suggestions that UFOs were not as "nuts and bolts" as the public so wanted to believe. American scientist and inventor John M. Cage saw them as "sentient life forms of a highly tenuous composition, charged with and feeding upon energy in the form of negative electricity." For him they could better be described as "life fields" rather than spaceships from another world.[7]

Cage's own brand of etherian physics was, like all the others, totally ignored, not just by the scientific community, but also by the supporters of the UFO phenomenon. No one wanted to see their emotionally based belief in the "nuts and bolts" world of interplanetary craft called into question. Yet, even Kenneth Arnold, the pilot who ignited the whole "flying saucer" craze after spotting nine aerial forms skimming gracefully through the skies above the Cascade Mountains of Washington

11. Kenneth Arnold (1915-1984), the founder of the modern flying saucer craze.

State on June 24, 1947, was unconvinced of the phenomenon's extraterrestrial origin. Writing in ufologist Ray Palmer's *Flying Saucers* magazine in 1962, Arnold admitted:

> After some 14 years of extensive research, it is my conclusion that the so-called unidentified flying objects that have been seen in our atmosphere are not space ships from another planet at all, but are groups and masses of living organisms that are as much a part of our atmosphere and space as the life we find in the oceans. The only major difference in the space and atmospheric organisms is that they have the natural ability to change their densities at will.[8]

As Constable himself put it so boldly in *Sky Creatures*: "By the year

2000—if there is one for our species—hosts of young investigators in exobiology will be in full pursuit of the critters of our atmosphere. They will undoubtedly marvel at our stupidity in not tumbling to such presences far earlier."[9] However, he also warned that ." . . nobody on this earth will understand UFOs in a technical sense unless they first master Reich's discovery of the orgone energy."[10]

It seems that Constable's prophecy failed to come to fruition, although, hopefully, within the foreseeable future the idea that many genuine UFO sightings are intelligent plasma constructs is something that will be taken more seriously by the scientific community.

Having come to some decisions on the nature of UFOs, Constable next turned his attentions to the subject of their landing traces, seeing only further evidence for his theories. He noticed in the May–June 1969 issue of the respected British journal *Flying Saucer Review* reports coming out of Queensland, Australia, of so-called "saucer nests," which were being discovered in remote regions following the appearance of unidentified aerial phenomena.

The main case in question is well known to UFO lore and occurred on January 19, 1966. It concerns a banana grower named George Pedley, who, around nine o'clock on the morning in question, was driving his tractor through a cane farm at Euramo, some seven miles out of Tully, a famous sugar town in Queensland, Australia. According to his story, Pedley had reached within 25 yards of a swamp known as Horse-Shoe Lagoon when he heard above the tractor engine a loud hissing sound, compared to air rapidly escaping from a tire. It was then that he saw a "vapor–like saucer" about 30 feet above the reeds. Open–mouthed, he watched it rise to a new height some 60 feet off the ground, before it spun wildly, made a shallow dive, and vanished in a south–westerly direction. It possessed no portholes or aerials and displayed no signs of life. He did, however, report a smell likened to "sulfur" that had seemed to hang in the air after the event. He also said that the tractor engine had started missing before finally stopping during the "saucer" sighting (a classic consequence of coming too close to a powerful electromagnetic field).

On moving into the reeds, Pedley was astonished to find a 30–foot circular area of flattened plants in an otherwise dense reed growth. As in the Wessex crop circles, the swirled stems were radially distributed in a noticeable clockwise rotation.[11]

12. Swirled circle found in a reed swamp at Tully, Queensland, Australia, on January 19, 1966.

George Pedley became so excited by the incident that he reported it to Albert Pennisi, a local cane grower as well as the owner of the land on which the incident had taken place. He claimed that around 5:30 a.m. that very morning, his dog—like the one belonging to John Hussey's son on the night the Hackpen Hill formation appeared in July 1991— had gone uncontrollably "mad," before bounding off in the direction of the lagoon (had it been disturbed by infrasound or ultrasound?).

The two men decided to return to the location of the reed circle, and, upon their arrival, Pennisi promptly stripped off and waded out to the nest (a brave act since the lagoon was infested by crocodiles). It consisted of a nine-inch layer of reeds torn away from the lagoon's muddy bed with untouched green reeds up to 30 inches tall all around it. Color photographs taken at five o'clock that afternoon showed that the upper surfaces of the floating reeds had already turned brown, whereas the plant surfaces still underwater remained green. What this meant, the two men were unsure.

In the weeks that followed, six additional "nests" were discovered in

the thick swamp grass of Horse-Shoe Lagoon, and, since 1966, Tully
UFO researcher Claire Noble has recorded details of no less than 84
circular or elliptical ground indentations found in the area, including
five further examples discovered on the Euramo property on February
20, 1987.[12] Many have appeared during spates of unusual light phenomena, while local aboriginal legends speak of "moving lights" seen in the
Tully region long before the arrival of white settlers during the 1920s.

Constable's observations on the nature of these nests are revealing,
for, on page 199 of *Sky Creatures*, he describes them as the result of a
descending "bioform" with "high orgonotic potential," its "whirling
plasma" browning the "upper edge of the flattened reeds." In conclusion, he was in little doubt that:

> The UFO nests thus appear as examples of orgonotic ef-
> fects, and mechanical crushing of the reeds by a weighty
> object descending from above is insufficient to account for
> the observed effects.

To support this hypothesis regarding the mechanism behind the
"saucer nests," Constable cited a French UFO case involving a baker
named Germain Tichit who encountered a landed UFO and occupants
in 1959.[13] He was said to have experienced a "veritable tornado blowing" out from the object, described as "warm and pungent."

Constable noted, too, that "plasmas" in the order of 200°–400° Fahr-
enheit might be created in the atmosphere by intense etheric fields of
orgone, resulting in microwave-like effects within anything that comes
into contact with them. In other words, an intense amount of heat is
produced almost instantaneously upon contact with living matter as in
the case of the reeds at Tully. He also believed that the "landed disk" was
absorbing water to sustain its orgone potential and referred to another
nest case where the flattened plants involved were found to have been
drained of all moisture.[14] He went on to describe the affinity that
bioforms appear to hold for bodies of water as "cold, contractive, water-
hungry energy." Water hungry the Circlemakers certainly are, for the
paddy fields playing host to the circles phenomenon in Japan are sometimes found to have lost literally thousands of gallons of water on the
morning after their nocturnal arrival. Why exactly, no one can rightly
say.

To round off the subject, Constable observed:

> The (bioform's) affinity for water may account for part of
> the drying and scorching observed in these nest cases. Such
> withdrawal of water from plant substance may be taking
> place simultaneously with the generation of the whirling
> plasmas around the discs already mentioned.

Constable went on to state that, according to Reich's law of reversed or "orgonotic" potential, a body of higher charge attracts a body of lower charge. If so, then a person coming into contact with a "bioform" held in a plasmatic state would have his own orgone potential sucked away, causing a number of bodily effects such as numbness, blindness, conjunctivitis, burning, instant tanning, and unconsciousness. Remember, it was while observing the tiny blue–green bion vesicles beneath a microscope that Reich suffered very similar effects.

UFO files across the world abound with cases where the witnesses involved have come close enough to the phenomenon to suffer a variety of side effects, some of which are particularly unsavory in nature. These include everything from tingling sensations to headaches, hair standing on end, hair loss, nausea, tanning, burns, welts, and even death. All these physical disorders have either been linked with overdoses of orgone energy inside accumulators or with the DOR that appeared in the wake of the Oranur Experiment at Orgonon in 1951.[15] This experiment, it should be recalled, was originally designed to study the relationship between orgone and electromagnetic energy using atomic radiation.

It would be pointless quoting case after case where such physical effects have resulted from close encounters "of the second kind," as the late J. Allen Hynek referred to them, although we will return to these at the end of the next chapter. For the moment it is better we steer closer to the crop circle debate and take a nostalgic trip back through the annals of UFO literature to sample a few further cases of UFO landing traces in the hope of seeing how they might relate to Constable's orgone solution to "saucer nests."

10

Nesting Habits

Never in my wildest dreams had I expected to return to my hoards of pulp paperbacks and hardbacks on the UFO phenomenon, originally digested at a quick pace between 1975 and 1979. At the time I was a young, naive UFO investigator who took in their every word. To me, we really *were* being visited by extraterrestrial spacecraft from other planets, and there *were* those who experienced close encounters with their occupants.

Glancing through these same books now, I just could not believe the amount of dross propagated in each and every one of them. An interplanetary invasion was a forgone conclusion before the text had even begun. Not one author—save for the unique, inspired works of individuals such as F.W. Holiday, John Keel, John Michell, Jacques Vallee, and Carl Jung—kept an open mind on the hidden nature of the phenomenon and its relationship to ourselves.

Still, they made amusing reading this time around and kept me occupied for some days. Accounts of alleged UFO nests were scattered between chapters on ancient astronaut theories and why exactly the Space People were not making open contact with us just yet. Despite this sea of outdated trivia, a little searching did produce some dynamite cases from Britain and abroad that not only reflected the modern-day circles phenomenon but also greatly supported the idea that orgone energy might be a key component in both the UFO phenomenon and the sudden appearance of genuine crop circles. Here are some of the examples I discovered.

Isle of Wight, 1967

Beginning in Great Britain, Robert Chapman's classic *UFO—Flying Saucers over Britain* (1968) devoted space to the severe crop damage discovered in adjoining barley fields on the Isle of Wight during the summer of 1967, a time coinciding with the largest UFO "flap" or "wave" the country had ever seen. "Strange whirligig patterns" of flattened crop were discovered along a strip of land some three quarters of a mile long and up to six yards wide. In the main it consisted of flattened and depressed stalks, forming circular patterns. Just as with modern crop circles, the flattened areas were swirled in either a clockwise or anticlockwise direction. Some areas had centers with the tufts removed, while others merely formed the dead center of the swirl pattern. Aerial photography later revealed damage over three separate fields, running roughly parallel with a road side hedge some yards away.

There was also clear evidence that the circular damage had made right-angled turns along its course of devastation, even swerving to avoid a dilapidated hut on one occasion.

Children from a nearby primary school had watched a "milky-white disk" in a cloudless sky on two occasions during the morning of July 10. It was seen to drop like a falling leaf in the vicinity of the barley fields in question, before accelerating out of sight. The boys later saw the strange crop marks from a bus on their way home from school.

Leonard Cramp, an aeronautical technician called in to inspect the scene, certainly considered the marks to have been the result of a UFO, adding that the damage was "very mechanical in appearance . . . (but looked like) a vortex pattern."

The matter was never resolved, as local authorities involved in the case could draw no conclusion.

Warminster, c. 1970

Warminster features both in UFO lore as the "mecca" for the phenomenon in the 1960s and 1970s, and as the point of commencement of the current crop circle furor in the early 1980s, with examples found beneath the shadows cast by Cley Hill and the Westbury white horse.

Warminster journalist Arthur Shuttlewood, who dedicated his life to understanding the nature of "The Thing," as one regular strange light was known to locals, often wrote of "landing sites" discovered in the vicinity of Cradle Hill the morning after nocturnal sightings. These generally took the form of swirled grass or field crop, flattened into circular depressions. However, in the frontispiece plates to his 1971 book *UFOs— Key to the New Age* he cited two examples of unaccountable crop damage of a particularly unusual nature.

Plate # 1 showed two 50-foot furrows lying parallel to each other, found one morning in a cornfield close to Cradle Hill.

Plates # 2, 3, and 4 showed a precise triangular shaped area of flattened corn, some 50 feet in length and 30 feet across its base. The depression was noticed after a bright light had been seen to descend into the same field the previous night. The fallen crop involved with both the furrows and the triangle possessed a "whirligig" pattern, the same term used to describe the swirling lay of the crop in the Isle of Wight case from 1967.

Triangles, as features of the circles phenomenon, did not reappear in the fields of Wessex until the very end of the 1990 summer season. Therefore, if genuine, this Warminster triangle predated the evolution in crop circles by some 20 years.

Van Horne, Iowa, USA, 1969

J. Allen Hynek (1910–86), who, when alive, was probably one of the world's foremost authorities on the UFO phenomenon, devised the categorization of UFO reports that we know and use today. These classifications followed his extensive involvement in the US Government's Project Blue Book during the 1950s. One of these categories, Close Encounters of the Third Kind, went on to become the Spielberg blockbuster of the same name.

Close Encounters of the *Second* Kind are those where physical traces of a UFO are reported in association with close proximity sightings. It is in this category, Hynek wrote in his 1970s classic *The UFO Experience: A Scientific Inquiry* (1972), that he had documented over 300 cases of "landing marks" found at sites following a UFO's departure. Of these marks, many were "scorched, denuded circles," some involving dehydrated soil and plants as well as blighted treetops and burnt areas upon the ground.

13. Forty-foot diameter circle of crop damage found at Van Horne, Iowa, on July 12/13, 1969.

Probably the most well attested of these so–called "landing" trace cases occurred on July 13, 1969, following an inexplicable incident over-night in Van Horne, Iowa. Two girls became anxious when, upon lean-ing out of a farmhouse window, they were shocked to see a "traditional lighted craft" gliding away from a nearby field of soybean, accompanied by a sound likened to a jet engine roar.

The following morning the farmer entered the field in question and came upon a 40–foot circle of devastated crop—the leaves of each plant hanging wilted on their stalks as if forced downwards from above. Yet, despite this extraordinary damage, no plants had been broken, and no marks could be found upon the soil itself. Hynek, who later visited the site, was totally baffled, suggesting that the plants had been subjected to an intense heat, as if the "destroying agent" was applied from above and at close range, yet without direct contact.

The object seen rising from the field by the two girls was said to have been a "dull gray–black metallic color with a circular reddish–orange band of light" around its horizontal rim. It vanished into the night, leaving behind a glowing orange residue in the sky.

My immediate thought on reading this case was to recall the damage to the trees around the Reich Institute at Rangeley, Maine, following the Oranur Experiment: "The white birch trees were bending over like rubber hoses, as if laden with invisible snow," while trees and shrubs in the same vicinity blackened and withered.[1] If these effects were caused through the presence of DOR, deadly orgone radiation, was it also to blame for the plant damage at Van Horne in 1969, and, if so, was the "craft" seen by the girls really some kind of orgone construct of the type described by Constable and encountered also by Reich over Rangeley, Maine, in the wake of his Oranur Experiment? Were the lights seen on the object really ionized gas, plasma, held in place within some kind of powerful electromagnetic field? All of these answers were distinct possibilities.

North Island, New Zealand, 1969

Now you might think that a book, badly entitled *Laser Beams from Star Cities?* (1975) by Robin Collyns, would contribute little to our greater understanding of the UFO phenomenon. Certainly this was my sentiment when I first picked it up to read. Yet how wrong could I have been, for among its series of all–too–familiar "Was God an astronaut?" plates were three beautiful images of UFO nests filmed on agricultural land south–west of Taupo, on New Zealand's North Island, during April 1971. In a chapter entitled "Spaceship Nests," it describes the appearance of a large number of circles amid a spate of mysterious light sightings over North Island between August and October 1969.

The first circle was found on September 4 by a farmer named B.G. O'Neill in a field of tea–tree, or manuka, just over 2 miles south of Ngatea, on the Hauraki Plains (the same case is mentioned briefly in *Sky Creatures*). In appearance the small bushes were described initially as "bleached," and in the dead center of the damage were three curious V-shaped grooves, 90 centimeters long, 50 to 75 centimeters in depth, and evenly spaced. Some 27 meters away, a number of treetops were found to have been "burnt" and "bleached."

Extensive tests on "bleached" manuka by a horticultural expert named John Stuart-Menzies resulted in these extraordinary findings:

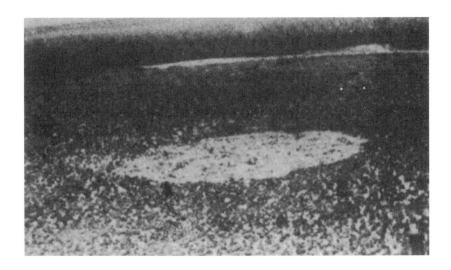

14. First of two pictures showing one of the many circular traces found on North Island, New Zealand, in 1969.

15. Second picture of the circular marks found on North Island, New Zealand, in 1969.

> Every ounce of moisture in the plant had been instantly va-
> porized, and it was bone dry and brittle. This is most un-
> usual in manuka, which normally takes a long time to dry
> out ... Some kind of high-frequency radiation had cooked
> the material from the inside out ...The effects appear to be
> instantaneous ...The energy received (by the manuka) has
> reduced the pith to black carbon, without the outside show-
> ing any signs of burning ...The cells in the medullary rays
> were burst by the sudden vaporization of the cell sap.

Stuart-Menzies likened the "cooked" effect upon the manuka to "the infrared" (i.e. microwave) cooking of food, but in this case on an "enormous scale." A separate test indicated the presence within the crop samples of extraneous substances, such as measurable radioactive isotopes of Strontium-90 and Uranium-235 as well as traces of silver and titanium.

Members of New Zealand's DSIR (Department of Scientific and Industrial Research), a leading scientific body, eventually visited the crop circle. They sowed seeds in soil taken from the nest and found that they withered and died, while seeds from the same packet planted in control samples extracted from elsewhere in the field, sprouted and continued to grow normally.

It was later found that a resident of nearby Paeroa witnessed a "pulsating light" traveling on a direct path towards the position where the nest was afterwards discovered.

Further UFO nests began appearing with frequency upon North Island and continued into October. These included a circle of "bleached" grass located on a farm at Whitford. This also possessed V-shaped marks carved into the ground and in its center was a bisected cavity. The farmer in question had heard a "low-pitched droning noise" in the same vicinity some days earlier.

Three more circles of burned grass were noticed on the Rotorua Farm belonging to a C.T. Johnson, who was first alerted to their presence after a horse became "spooky" and refused to go near them. The farmer said he had never seen anything like them in the 18 years he had owned the land.

Mid-October saw the discovery of a nine-meter circle of dead grass and plants at Takapuna and three days after that, a "burnt-out" circle of blackened vegetation of four and a half meters located on a "floating

island" situated on farm property belonging to Charles Blackmore of
Puketutu, just over 14 kilometers south of Te Kuiti. Apparently, the affected vegetation was some 60 centimeters lower than the rest of the
plants on the island, and in all, no less than five species of plants had
died within the circle. All were pressed down in the now familiar radiating spiral pattern which, as the author pointed out, was a feature of
the Australian nests (presumably those at Tully, Queensland, in 1966).

Collyns also detailed the apparent strange effects upon the indigenous fauna of the island around the time of the circle's appearance.
Overnight four resident ducks and the entire frog population simply
vanished. Cows and ducks that had previously visited the island's ponds
to drink would not go near them any more.

Blackmore is said to have suffered a lingering headache after finding
the circle, and this pain persisted without letup for some weeks. Collyns
suggested this was due to the short-lived radiation he assumed to have
been present when the nest was found.

Other circles continued to appear elsewhere on North Island during
mid–October, such as the four found at Mahuta, a coastal farming settle-
ment near Dargaville. The very same period saw the alleged appearance
of mysterious lights in the night sky, some even being tracked on radar.
They were variously described as "fluorescent," "intensely bright," "glowing," and "pulsating" with colors ranging from blue to yellow and white.

These sample cases clearly show that some hitherto unknown agent
is not only responsible for some circles but also leaves noticeable traces
compatible with the idea of an intense, unknown energy making contact with the ground. This agent is comparable, in some instances, to the
more disturbing effects of orgone energy's more deadly counterpart,
DOR. Hynek described the "destroying agent" involved with the soybean damage in the Van Horne case as an "intense heat" coming "directly from above," which left no signs of actual contact with either the
plants or the ground.

Stuart-Menzies spoke of the damaged manuka from the circle at
Ngatea, North Island, as appearing to have been cooked from the inside
out using microwave radiation. He also said the moisture inside the
circle had been vaporized, drying out the plants to the point of death,
as in the Van Horne case. The pith inside the shoots had been turned to
carbon, and its living cells had been "burst by the sudden vaporization
of the cell sap." Exposure to intense amounts of orgone was found by

Reich to result in similar physical effects. Large dosages "irradiated" living matter, causing an excitement comparable with infrared heating processes. Constable graphically described orgone as "water-hungry energy," due to its apparent ability to vaporize water upon impact, and Reich warned against the possibility of exploding blood vessels should the human body be subjected to megadoses of orgone inside multilayered orgone accumulators.

With the added presence of extraneous substances such as radioactive isotopes in plant samples taken from the same circle, Stuart–Menzies had himself been left to conclude that the energy force involved was a "high frequency radiation."

Other telltale symptoms of orgone in the North Island cases point dramatically to this conclusion. The accompanying light shows, the "low–pitched droning noise," the irregular animal reactions (the "spooky" horse, the changes in grazing habits of the ducks and cows as well as the vanishing tame ducks and frog population), and the seeds dying were all either side effects of orgone radiation or have been reported in association with modern–day crop circles.

The gouged–out holes found in the flattened and burned circles on North Island are difficult to understand in terms of orgone. Despite this difficulty, it is still a plus point for the British crop circles as similar holes have been found in these as well. The obvious case is the ringed circle with a spur found in a field of wheat at Childrey, Oxfordshire, in 1986. When the indentation was first entered, a bowl–shaped hole— some 0.35 meters in diameter and 0.23 meters deep—was discovered at the arrow–headed end of the spur. It looked like it had been gouged out with a tool, yet no displaced soil could be found, baffling the police who investigated the formation with circles experts Colin Andrews and Pat Delgado. Soil samples taken from the base of the hole resulted, apparently, in a spate of inexplicable poltergeist activity in Colin Andrews's home.[2]

One final comparison between the North Island cases and modern-day crop circles is the negative results obtained by New Zealand's DSIR when they tried to grow seeds in soil taken from the Ngatea nest. During the summer of 1990, a 45–foot diameter crop circle was discovered on farmland owned by Brian Lawrence of Great Holland near Clacton in Essex. It was harvested at the end of the season, and the field was plowed out in readiness to grow oilseed rape in 1991. However, the following year Mr. Lawrence had been amazed to find that the rape seeds in the precise area defined by the 1990 crop circle refused to sprout until a full two weeks after the rest of the field had begun to grow. Consequently, when the rest of the rapeseed was in flower, the circular area of stunted crop remained green. When it did finally bloom, the rest of the rapeseed had lost its distinctive flower, leaving a precise yellow patch of noticeably shorter plants to define the area where the circle had appeared.[3]

The clear indication, in both this case and the Ngatea nest site, is that changes occur in the soil that can either prevent or stunt plant growth once a circle has occurred. Thankfully, this disconcerting phenomenon is very rare in British crop circle cases.

Australia (1966–1989)

To end the review of UFO nests worldwide, we return to Australia where, ever since the Tully reeds case of 1966, flattened circles of crop have continued to appear. UFO researcher Keith Basterfield has made a detailed study of all reported incidents in his paper *Circles Down Under*.[4] He cites 13 prime examples of Australian crop circles appearing in everything from grass to berries, oats, strawberries, thistles, and swamp grass. Keith's list begins at Tully, Queensland, and ends with an account of the much-publicized story of Max and Nancee Jolly of Speed, Victoria. The couple ran a farm at Turriff with their son Stuart in the Mallee wheat belt of western Victoria.

On December 6, 1989, a contractor took a combine harvester on to the Jolly's property to strip wheat from a 600-hectare field. Unexpectedly, he came across five flattened circles, so steered around them and reported their presence to the owners.[5] Two were found to be approximately three meters in diameter, while the other three were just one meter across. All were swirled in an anticlockwise direction. No stalks had been broken or crushed, and each one bore a striking resemblance to their British counterparts. Eight further examples were eventually located elsewhere in the same field.[6]

The discovery of the circles was dramatic enough, but to the Jollys, it merely climaxed a series of strange occurrences involving their 9,000-hectare property. The most remarkable of these events took place around nine o'clock one evening in May 1989 when Stuart decided to investigate the terrible commotion coming from a distant sheep pen filled with 700 ewes and lambs. He could see them dashing about in a wild panic and, upon looking up, saw the source of their distress—

stationary above the paddock was a huge yellow light, pulsating rhythmically. He jumped into a farm vehicle, but, by the time he reached the spot, the light form was nowhere to be seen. However, Stuart could hear a loud, high-pitched noise coming from the empty sky above the paddock likened to the slow rotation of a helicopter blade without the sound of an engine.

When Max and Nancee arrived home from a twenty-first birthday party an hour later, the sheep had still not calmed down, and what's more, they quickly learned that animals on a neighboring farm had gone wild at exactly the same time. In the paddock itself they were amazed to find a wedge-tailed eagle stumbling and flapping its wings, as if unable to fly. It appeared to be totally disorientated and in some kind of shock. Never before had they seen an eagle act in this manner. The Jolly family concluded that the presence of the yellow light had destroyed its sense of balance. Happily, the effect could only have been temporary, for it had gone by the morning.

This was not the only strange incident of its type to occur on the Jolly's farm, either. In November 1987, following the appearance of an unidentified aerial light in the area, Nancee Jolly went out one morning and found that a 4,000-liter water tank had completely emptied overnight. No explanation was ever found. Then, one night in December 1988, Stuart Jolly was shocked out of bed by an ear-shattering noise that came from the clear sky. Upon investigation he found no trace of its origin.

Other mysterious lights were reported in the vicinity as well, and the family was in no doubt that the flattened circles were linked in some way. This assumption was strengthened when aerial photographs of their property showed that as many as 400 circles, some like the tiny "grapeshot" holes found in Britain (see Chapter 15), had appeared over a five-mile radius in the past ten years, but not one of these holes had been observed at the time. Subsequent investigations by local UFO researchers revealed that the magnetic variation inside the wheat circles was considerably higher than the background level on other parts of the farm, giving us our first clue as to why the Jolly's property should have been repeatedly graced by strange phenomena of this kind.

During my potted survey of the battered UFO books in my personal library, I also came across two cases originally used as evidence in favor of the extraterrestrial debate but, in the light of any proposed orgone hypothesis to crop circles, now seem to take on a new (and in the second case, somewhat disturbing) significance.

The first example has been extracted from *Flying Saucers come from Another World*, written by a Frenchman named Jimmy Guieu and published in 1956. In a year-to-year account of developing events in the "flying saucer" debate, he detailed a remarkable case that took place at Charleroi in Belgium on May 16 or 17, 1953. It concerned a man named Hermann Chermanne, of the town of Bouffioulx, who was able to capture on film two remarkable shots of an unusual aerial phenomenon he witnessed in the sky.

16. First of two pictures of a remarkable aerial object witnessed and photographed in Charleroi, Belgium, in May 1953.

17. Second of two pictures showing the remarkable aerial object witnessed at Charleroi, Belgium, in May 1953.

According to the *Le Peuple* newspaper of May 18, Chermanne was on his way home from work at around 8:15 p.m., when he was drawn to look skywards by a peculiar sound likened to "the prolonged vibrations of a sheet of iron," accompanied by "a dry rattle like that of a machine-gun."

Turning around, he saw a mysterious object rising upwards with a long funnel of spiraling mist or smoke that trailed up from behind a tree–capped ridge a short distance away. What he saw can only be described as an intense ball of light, surrounded by a fluctuating, white halo of plasma. From its edges came tiny "satellites" that darted off in all directions. Chermanne took hold of his camera and clicked one shot before the mysterious light turned sideways to reveal more of its brilliant central sphere.

A second photograph was taken just as the object moved rapidly into the sky and vanished, leaving only the long white vapor trail that soon evaporated under the force of the wind.

Several people from nearby Bouffioulx and its environs independently reported the clear sound of "a loud rumbling explosion" at a time coincident to Chermanne's extraordinary sighting.

The two photographs came out uncannily well, and, when I first set eyes on them, I could not help but wonder why they had never reappeared in any other books on UFOs. I present them in this book for the sheer mesmerism they induce.

The second case is lifted from the book *Laser Beams from Star Cities?* by Robin Collyns. It is not a good idea to take at face value the majority of the book's claims of transdimensional contact, but aside from the North Island circles, it does quote one incredible example of a "meteorological occurrence" from Venezuela that occurred in 1886, the details having originally been published in the scholarly journal *Scientific American*. It takes the form of a letter to the editor dated November 7, 1886, and is signed "Warner Cowgill, US Consulate, Maracaibo, Venezuela," and reads:

> During the night of October 24 last, which was rainy and tempestuous, a family of nine persons, sleeping in a hut but a few leagues from Maracaibo, were awakened by a loud humming noise and a vivid, dazzling light, which brilliantly illuminated the interior of the house.
>
> The occupants, completely terror stricken, and believing, as they relate, that the end of the world had come, threw themselves down on their knees and commenced to pray, but their devotions were almost immediately interrupted by violent vomiting, and extensive swellings commenced to appear on the upper part of their bodies, this being particularly noticeable about the face and lips.
>
> It is to be noted that the brilliant light was not accompanied by the sensation of heat, although there was a smoky appearance and a peculiar smell.

The next morning the swellings had subsided, leaving upon the face and body large black areas. No special pain was felt until the ninth day, when the skin peeled off, and these blotches were transformed into virulent raw sores.

The hair of the head fell off the side, which happened to be underneath when the phenomenon occurred. In all nine cases, the same side of the body was the more seriously injured.

The remarkable part of this occurrence is that the house was uninjured, all doors and windows being closed at the time.

No trace of lightning could afterwards be observed in any part of the building, and all the sufferers unite in saying that there was no detonation, but only the loud humming already mentioned.

Another curious attendant circumstance is that the trees around the house showed no sign of injury until the ninth day, when they suddenly withered, almost simultaneously with the development of the sores on the bodies of the occupants of the house.

This is perhaps a mere coincidence, but it is remarkable that the same susceptibility to electrical effects, with the same lapse of time, should be observed in both animal and vegetable organisms.

I have visited the sufferers, who are now in one of the hospitals of this city; and although their appearance is truly horrible, yet is hoped that in no case will the injuries prove fatal.

Let us hope the family made a full recovery! No other information on this remarkable incident has been made available to me. However, it was soberly reported and readily categorized as a "meteorological occurrence," due to the lack of alternative explanations available in 1886. And in some strange way this conclusion may not be so far removed from the truth, as it might have seemed during the height of the UFO craze in the 1970s.

Yet how much of this perplexing and often disturbing material relating to alleged "saucer nests," UFOs, and their accompanying side effects on flora, fauna, and human life, relate to the modern crop circle phenomenon? Certainly, we can say that a number of strange effects have been noted in connection with visitors to crop circles. Yet, as we shall see in the coming chapters, many of the other occurrences associated with "saucer nests" have reflections not only in modern lore associated with crop circles but also in folklore beliefs regarding the existence of a very similar phenomenon going back hundreds of years.

11
Orgone Aftermath

Unusual effects inside crop circles were noted as early as August 1989, when high tech video equipment used during the filming of Colin Andrews and Pat Delgado at a large circle at Beckhampton, near Avebury, for a *Daytime Live* program, continually malfunctioned. Each time the camera approached the main circle (as well as other smaller examples nearby), bars of interference crossed the viewing screen and red lights flashed, warning of functioning problems. This interference was then followed by a loud noise that cut across everything being recorded.

Professional photographer Richard Ansett told me of another good example of cameras malfunctioning at crop circles. He was commissioned by *The Mail on Sunday's You* magazine to take some human interest shots at the 1991 Barbury Castle formation for an upcoming feature. From the offset his professional equipment was dogged with unique problems he had never before experienced. The radio–linked flash gun held by his assistant failed to respond to the camera's trigger mechanism and had to be operated manually. Even then it would flash only intermittently, prompting him to bring out a reserve flashgun. But this too failed to work, and, to add final insult to injury, the camera shutter decided to jam.

Richard is very skeptical about the paranormal, and yet these bizarre effects on his usually efficient photographic equipment, led him, somewhat reluctantly, to conclude that the crop formation was jinxed in some manner. Crop circle photographer and researcher Busty Taylor has experienced similar problems on many occasions as have a number of other visitors to circle sites across the country.

Other forms of electrical anomalies have also been reported. At the end of August 1991, for instance, a quadruplet set of wheat circles was found on farmland belonging to Roy Tetzlaf at Warner, just outside Lethbridge in Alberta, Canada. Their arrival signaled a spate of microwave oven malfunctions in the immediate area, including one owned by Mr. Tetzlaf, which supposedly switched itself on! In addition to this incident, a radiotelephone on the farmer's harvester repeatedly failed to operate when he first entered the circles on the day of their discovery. Interestingly enough, the normally placid Malamute dogs belonging to Roy Tetzlaf had become agitated, noisy, and continually howled the day before the circles were discovered.[1]

Spinning compasses and electrical malfunctions are familiar problems to earth mysteries researchers, for they also occur at ancient sites, such as stone circles, barrows, and dolmens. Here they are put down to the varying susceptibilities of rocks and minerals to the earth's magnetic field. Such places of magnetic variation were perhaps marked as sacred by ancient cultures, which recognized their special properties and usually associated them with inducing altered states of consciousness.

Is it possible that the capture and accumulation of orgone at places of power stimulates localized geomagnetic fields to produce fluctuating electromagnetic effects at ground level, thus intensifying the existing properties of a site? This answer might help explain the spinning compasses reported by Colin Andrews and others at circle sites as well as the accounts of interference with electrical apparatus, including photographic equipment and video cameras.

Is it possible that, once a crop formation has been created, a strong residue of energetic orgone may exist? The deadly form of orgone, known as DOR, was thought by Reich to be very volatile with the ability to either draw away or overdose the orgone potential of living matter, along with several other quite worrying side effects.

On many occasions a cloudbuster was used to draw down DOR accumulating above the Reich Institute of Orgonon in Rangeley, Maine. This accumulation generally occurred only on dull or "flat" days, but, when it did, the resultant effects could be dangerous. For instance, on December 6, 1954, Reich's assistant Bob McCullough, in charge of a cloudbuster, directed the device into the air at the Reich Institute known as Little Orgonon, in Tucson, Arizona. He said later that the DOR in the air was leaving a bad taste in his mouth likened to offal—strong and sour. Then suddenly he felt a crippling sensation in his right leg and found he had been paralyzed down the whole of his right side. It eased enough for him to be back on the cloudbuster the following day, when he found the same affliction occurring for a second time. He was forced to leave Little Orgonon and was not fit to work again until January the following year. McCullough still dragged his right foot when Constable came to write *The Cosmic Pulse of Life* in 1976.

18. Cloudbuster under the controls of orgone expert Tony Beddow.

Constable spoke of a similar incident that took place in December 1971 when he was using his own homemade cloudbuster for weather control operations in Southern California. A visitor to the site became excited when he realized that a disk of light had appeared in the general area of the sky where the device was directed. In that same instant there was a sharp crack as a bluish bolt of light hit the tube on which the man rested his hand. His whole right side was jolted by the shock, leaving him temporarily paralyzed for some minutes. The pain brought tears to his eyes and made him feel as though every nerve in his body had been "irradiated" by the bolt.[2] Blue flashes of this nature have been reported by many visitors to crop circles.[3]

Reich himself found that discharging particles of orgone often resulted in a blue–green luminosity, so blue became the color most often associated with orgone radiation (azure, or blue, is one of the two primary colors of ch'i, the life energy equivalent to orgone in the Chinese tradition of feng-shui–see Chapter 14). In fact, Reich even believed that the blueness of the sky was the result of orgone in the atmosphere and so decided that, when deflecting harmful orgone with a cloudbuster, the Institute's technicians should wear blue protective clothing.

The foul taste reported by Bob McCullough when using the cloudbuster to draw down DOR is important, for similar bad tastes have been reported by visitors to crop circles. Circles researcher and crop artist Rob Irving is aware of two cases where a lingering and somewhat unpleasant metallic taste was reported by visitors to circles, while members of our own party experienced a sour and bitter taste inside some of the circles visited in July 1991. Such bad tastes are perhaps a side effect resulting from exposure to high levels of orgone radiation.

The nature and intensity of the orgonic residue left at such sites might well define its physical and psychic effect upon humans and animals. If it is present in healthy, stable quantities, it will provide visitors with a feeling of well-being upon entering the circle. Should, however, the crop circle be left with unhealthy pockets of DOR, then direct contact might lead to anything from bad tastes to dizziness, fuzziness, headaches, sore throats, disorientation, sudden temperature changes, nausea, skin or eye problems, swollen glands, muscular problems, flu symptoms, or worse. All of these physical effects have been reported in connection with crop circles and were recorded by Wilhelm Reich in connection with his Oranur Experiment at Rangeley, Maine.

In nearly every instance of formations appearing in Alberta, Canada, in 1991, there were reports of headaches, dizziness, nausea, and general uneasiness experienced by visitors to the circle sites.

Animals are much more sensitive than humans, and, aside from seemingly being able to hear sounds inaudible to the human ear (most probably caused by infrasound or ultrasound), it seems they might overdose on excessive amounts of orgone present at circle sites. There are two well-documented cases of dogs becoming violently ill after entering circles. One incident occurred at the flattened ring of crop in a field at Kimpton in Hampshire on June 29, 1987, when Colin Andrews took his parents and family dog to visit the formation. The animal was "pulling keenly" on its lead as they advanced along the tramline towards the hidden ring, where a mysterious "orange glowing object" and "odd noises" had already been reported since the ring's arrival on Saturday, June 13. However, drawing parallel with its flattened perimeter track, the dog would go no further. Colin Andrews' father coaxed the animal into the center, but within minutes it was violently sick and remained quite ill for some 20 minutes afterwards.

Puzzled by the number of strange events happening in association with the Kimpton ring, including a black flash he himself had witnessed there, Colin Andrews returned to the field that evening. It was then that, upon entering the formation, he experienced "a static electrical cracking noise" that started up some three yards away and grew with intensity until suddenly, after some six seconds, it abruptly ceased. The experience severely unnerved Colin, although it seemed that "warbling, humming-like noises" were also heard in the same field during the second week of June by a Mr. and Mrs. Hitchcock who were out walking their Alsatian dog early one morning.[4]

Most animals would probably choose to avoid entering crop circles if they had the choice. However, sometimes circles seem to draw animals to them, and at other times they will simply repel them. Aerial photographs of the huge "key" formation that appeared in July 1991 upon Preshute Down, near Marlborough, Wiltshire, show a peculiar anomaly. Narrow animal tracks are seen to pepper the immediate area around the circles, many of them coming to an abrupt halt. There is no real explanation for these tracks although it seems likely they record the frenzied reactions of rabbits, which abound in English crop fields. Rabbits are known to halt suddenly and either change direction or return back along their own tracks when in a state of blind panic. Could these crop marks provide some indication of animal reactions to the crop circles?

Another very important clue concerning animal reactions to already formed circles comes from a farm in Canada belonging to Fred Watmough of Lethbridge, Alberta. A series of circles in a unique configuration appeared there in late August 1991 and an in-depth study was undertaken by Canadian cerealogist Chad Deetken. One of the first things he discovered was that the farmer's dog had gone crazy on the night they formed. Yet this episode was nothing when compared to the reaction of the local geese to the presence of the circles.

Chad noticed a large flock of some 100 or more geese feeding in a field about one kilometer from the formation. Once in a while they would take flight and head in its general direction. However, every time they approached the circles, the whole flock would veer to one side or the other before regrouping to continue their journey. Never once did they pass directly over the formation. On each occasion this activity took place, Chad would crouch down to become as unobtrusive as possible, and, once away from the circles, the birds would fly directly over both people and vehicles, showing it was not his presence that had prompted the birds to react this way.[5]

Similar responses from animals and birds are constantly noted in association with ancient sites where magnetic variation, radiation, and ultrasound anomalies have been recorded. In fact, it was the observation of birds spiraling above a stone and earthen henge monument named Arbor Low in Derbyshire during the Dragon Project (see Chapter 14) that reignited the debate over whether ultrasound was a component of so-called earth energies associated with places of ancient power. Horses, too, have been observed clearly making detours around monuments such as stone circles when the easiest route would have been to pass directly through them.

The unusual effects associated with crop formations, whatever their origin, was, I sensed, down to undefined energy discharges, perhaps connected with Wilhelm Reich's orgone radiation. Yet, if so, then reading his suggestions about the practical use of orgone energy accumulators was perhaps a good idea,[6] for he advised spending only short durations inside man-sized accumulators and strongly recommended that people not sleep in them. Failing to follow his recommendations could result in some very unpleasant side effects. So, for orgone accumulator, *read crop circle*. But then this type of inherent danger from entering strange circles, associated with mysterious lights and chanced upon in the countryside, was something clearly understood by rural communities long before the advent of the "saucer nest" or modern crop circle, as we shall see now from a cursory examination of English folklore.

12

Lights of the Damned

The modern–day interest in crop circles began on Friday, August 15, 1980, when the *Wiltshire Times* ran a brief report on the appearance of three plain circles of flattened crop found in a field lying below the gaze of the Westbury white horse. After this time, the circles phenomenon gained a steady pace in evolution and popular interest. This was until 1983 when a sudden explosion in circles progression catapulted the subject to national media attention. From then on the crop configurations accelerated rapidly in style and design until the first landscape pictograms began to appear in 1990. These attained majestic perfection with the dramatic appearance of the first Alton Barnes formation in July the same year. Designs like the one at Barbury Castle in 1991 indicated that the remarkable evolution of the phenomenon was still on the increase.

It was quite clear, however, that the first crop circles of 1980 were nothing new and that single circles had been appearing in the Westbury area for some years. They had also been reported since the 1960s in association with UFO sightings, under the guise of "landing traces" or the ill–named "saucer nests." Indeed, Barry King and I had investigated two swirled circles of barley found in a field at Wooburn Green in

Buckinghamshire in the summer of 1977, even though they had failed to impress us at the time (see Introduction).

Yet, this activity was not the beginning of the enigma, for there is ample evidence that crop circles have been occurring for hundreds of years. For example, they are known to have appeared with frequency in the Cotswolds region of central–western England between 1939 and 1946. A woman of integrity, an Essex councillor named Gwen Horrigan of Southend–on–Sea provided this information to me in 1991, and her story is truly fascinating and of extreme importance to the crop circle debate. During the Second World War, she was evacuated from London to Kingham, Oxfordshire, which is close to the county border with Gloucestershire. Here, between the ages of six and twelve, she quickly found herself leading a new lifestyle among a rural farming community which adhered to ancient customs and superstitious practices unknown to children living in London.

Gwen said that throughout this period the fields were constantly planted with cereal crops to cater for wartime needs, and on several occasions she and her young friends came across huge flattened circles of varying sizes while out "gleaning," i.e. collecting, fallen wheat. Like modern–day examples, each circle had sharp cut off edges and radial swirl patterns, always clockwise she remembers. Some were up to 50 feet across, while others were much smaller. They appeared most frequently on sloping land belonging to Slade Farm, to the south of an east–west track running between Kingham Hill School and Daylesford Hill Farm (SP260262), close to the woods of Whitequarry Hill. Local farmers always considered them a genuine mystery, and villagers referred to them as "fairy rings," despite the use of the *same* term to describe ring-like discolorations of grass caused by *Basidiomycota*, a type of fungi. A certain amount of superstition was attached to their presence—children would never step into them, just glean crops from their edges before moving on.

The association with the fairy folk is important here, as mysterious balls of luminosity, know locally as "fairy lights," were often seen in and around the woods at Whitequarry Hill. Under alternative names such as *Ignis Fatuus*, meaning "foolish flame," Will-o'-the-Wisp, corpse candles, or even ghost lights, rational scholars of the past viewed these mysterious light sources as the result of the spontaneous combustion of decomposing matter, an interpretation that does little to explain their prolonged manifestation, incredible intensity, and maneuverability. To the more superstitious, these "dancing lights" were usually seen as the lanterns of elves and fairies ready to lead lone travelers astray should they decide to follow one. Such lights were often said to possess the ability to transform themselves into the likeness of a beautiful girl or a crock of gold in order to lure their victims. Regionally, the lights bore a variety of curious names including Jack o' Lantern, Jumping Jack, Jenny Burtail or Greenteeth, Joan o' the Wad, Spunkie, Pinket, and Peggie with th' Lantern.

Gwen said it was also common knowledge that these same woods were used at night by a local witch coven that saw this location as in some way special. She told, too, how the Cotswold villagers would speak of an ancient power the land held, especially at local prehistoric sites. These sites would have included the Rollright Stones—the megalithic stone circle three miles to the northeast of Kingham Hill—various barrows and tumuli, along with a circular Iron Age earthwork named Chastleton Barrow Camp. This can be seen on the top of a ridge, a mile and a half north of where both the crop circles and mysterious lights would appear. Interestingly, a straight track still runs down through the fields from the earthen fort for a distance of just over a mile, before curving to the right beyond Whitequarry Hill.

Skeptics might doubt the research value of an account over 50 years old, remembered by a woman from her childhood. However, I scanned the records for any possible confirmation of her words and discovered that one of the only documented cases of a circular indentation appearing in Britain prior to 1980 came from the village of Evenlode, Gloucestershire, *not three miles* from Whitequarry Hill, and just two miles west of Chastleton Barrow Camp. *The Evesham Journal* carried a news story in its issue of June 8, 1960, concerning two perfectly formed concentric rings of flattened crop, one 23 feet across, the other 16 feet, which appeared one inside the other. The farmer, Bill Edwards of Poplars Farm, who was out tending sheep, found them during the early morning of June 3 in a meadow halfway between Evenlode and Chastleton. He had never seen anything like them before. They were so perfectly round, he said, it was as if a giant stamp had come down and left a deep imprint. The long grass had been pressed so flat that it looked like a heavy wagon had made precise six-inch wide bands without marking anywhere else, and yet their remoteness ruled out the possibility of a simple explanation. A local reporter also witnessed the rings first hand and later said it was as if they had been drawn with a giant pair of compasses.[1]

I was subsequently able to interview Bill Edwards on what he recalled of the incident. I spoke also to an elderly lady named Ethel Wood of Evenlode, who worked on a local farm at the time and clearly remembers visiting the double ring formation. She said they became quite a local attraction, much like the crop circles of today, which have returned in recent years to the Chipping Norton area, just four miles east of Whitequarry Hill.

The area of the Cotswolds that incorporates the Rollright Stones complex of megalithic sites is known to be an intense region of paranormal activity. This is shown by the findings of Paul Devereux's Dragon Project (see Chapter 14), which focused much of its efforts in this region. In his book *Earth Lights Revelation* Devereux cites the tradition of a light phenomenon, often blood red in color, seen in the area between Chipping Norton and Burford since at least the turn of the century and known locally simply as "The Light." It would appear to have haunted a road on a ridge above Shipton-under-Wychwood, some five miles south of Whitequarry Hill.[2]

Aside from the examples from my own files, Terence Meaden has recorded many cases of crop circles appearing prior to 1980, including one from Aberystwyth in West Wales during 1936 and another from Kent in 1918. Ralph Noyes also received a personal communication from a woman whose husband came across circles while farming in Hampshire some 60 years beforehand (i.e. around the 1940s). She claimed that when they did appear, the superstitious country folk would refuse to hand reap the wheat, fearing that they were "uncanny and of devilish origin."[3] This reaction bears out the superstition surrounding the crop circles found on the Oxfordshire–Gloucestershire border during the very same period.

From these early accounts it seems clear that, until comparatively recently, rural farming communities treated the presence of crop circles with the utmost caution and saw their formation not as acts of God, but as the work of infernal spirits. Why exactly, we can only guess, although I suspect this reaction might well have had something to do with the side effects experienced by visitors to "fairy rings."

This brings me to the extraordinary account of the so-called mowing devil cited in a little-known Hertfordshire pamphlet dated 1678 (and republished by Hertfordshire folklorist W. B. Gerish in 1913), which could be the oldest recorded account of the circles phenomenon. The publication's full title is an adequate description of its contents:

THE MOWING DEVIL: OR, STRANGE NEWS OUT OF HARTFORDSHIRE
Being a True Relation of a Farmer, who Bargaining with a Poor Mower, about the Cutting down Three Half Acres of Oats: upon the Mower's asking too much, the Farmer swore That the Devil should Mow it rather than He. And so it fell out, that very Night, the Crop of Oat shew'd as if it had been all of a Flame: but the next Morning appear'd so neatly mow'd by the Devil or some Infernal Spirit, that no Mortal Man was able to do the like.

Also, How the said Oats ly now in the field, and the Owner has not Power to fetch them away.

Licensed, August 22, 1678

The existence of this pamphlet was brought to the attention of UFO author and crop circle researcher Jenny Randles by Betty Puttick, the editor of a 1970 edition of *Hertfordshire Folk Lore*, put together from material originally compiled by Gerish, c. 1905–1915.

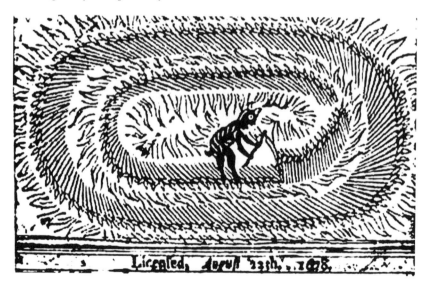

19. Woodcut of the Mowing Devil creating a crop circle in Hertfordshire in 1678.

The text elaborates in a prosaic manner the statements of the front cover. It tells of a farmer who refuses to pay the price asked by a neighbor to reap his crop, and so that night a strange fire is seen to illuminate a field of oats. Upon approaching the area in question, the farmer discovers circular areas of the crop perfectly flattened in a manner we can only presume fits the general description of circles today.

The woodcut accompanying the pamphlet shows a small impish figure using a scythe to mow flat concentric bands of oats in order to create a circle. Beyond the fallen crop are tongues of flame representing the infernal fire seen in the field while the mowing devil was at work.

Certain conclusions can be drawn from the existence of this single pamphlet. Firstly, if such an incident did take place, and I see no reason to doubt its authenticity, then it implies that more than one circle appeared in a Hertfordshire field one night in August 1678. The farmer was drawn to their presence by mysterious luminosities, seen in terms of flames, above the crop, leading him to accredit their formation to an evil spirit known as the "mowing devil." He considered the presence of the circles a misfortune brought about by his failure to pay the neighbor, and the title's last statement about the oats lying in the field untouched, while the farmer "has not Power to fetch them away," may also be important. It seems highly probable that, afterwards, the farmer was struck down by some kind of illness resulting from the presence of the circles.

A name like "mowing devil" would indicate that a mischievous spirit of this title existed in folklore beforehand and was an accepted phenomenon known to cause grief to farmers by visiting their fields at night and striking down crops. Until comparatively recently the trolls of Norway were likewise made scapegoats for all manner of mischief occurring in remote farming districts. All this points to the fact that crop circles were frequent occurrences in Hertfordshire before 1678 and that, like those in Hampshire during the 1940s, they were considered bad omens.

I can go further on this topic. For the apparent tendency to blame the mysterious appearance and side effects of crop circles on infernal spirits, such as the mowing devil or the fairy folk, opens up new doorways to archive material not previously explored in this debate.

Gwen Horrigan is quite certain that the crop circles she saw in the fields around Kingham Hill in the Cotswolds were known locally as "fairy rings," and that the dancing luminosities seen in the same vicinity were explained as "fairy lights." If so, then in the light of the mowing

20. Seventeenth-century woodcut showing fairies dancing in a ring.

devil account of 1678, just how many stories in English folklore mask bastardized versions of mysterious light displays associated in some instances with crop circle formation? Let me give you three good examples of fairy encounters from Wiltshire, the center of modern–day crop circle activity. They are drawn from the writings of John Aubrey (1626–1697), the well-known English historian and antiquarian, who was the first person to bring the mysteries of Avebury and Silbury Hill to the attention of the world.

The first two accounts concern Hackpen Hill, where a crop formation appeared under quite dramatic circumstances in 1991. Both come from a local character described as "old Ambrose Brown" in 1645. One relates how "a hinde [that] goeing upon Hack-pin with corne" was led a merry dance by the fairies to the village, for it was firmly believed that these infernal spirits inhabited the location. The second account tells of "a shepherd of Winterbourne Basset," a small village four miles north of Avebury, who seems to have encountered an opening into a "fairy hill," most likely one of the Bronze Age mounds that grace the locality. Unex-

21. Mysterious light hovering over a marsh.

pectedly, the "Ground opened and he was brought into strange places underground," with fairies "that used musicall instruments, viz. viols and lutes (such as were then played on)." Aubrey stated that nothing good came of such visits to the fairy realm, for "never any afterwards enjoy themselves."[4]

What on earth was going on at Hackpen Hill for local people in the seventeenth century to conclude that this place was the domain of fairies? Were strange lights dancing about at night? Were there fairy rings in the form of crop circles? And what of the experience of the "hinde" and the poor shepherd—what did they stumble upon? We have no way of knowing, but the main importance in citing these accounts is to show that for many centuries Hackpen Hill has been considered a place of supernatural manifestations accredited to the fairy folk.

Similar sentiments were obviously widespread in Wiltshire at the time, for Aubrey records a third fairy encounter that featured his curate from Latin school, a Mr. Hart, who lived around 17 miles west of Avebury

22. The fairy ring, showing fairies and imps dancing to music.

in the village of Yatton Keynell, near Chippenham. In the year 1633 or 1634, when out walking on "the downes" thereabouts, he too had been "annoy'd one night by these elves or fayries." Apparently, in the "neere darke," Mr. Hart had chanced upon "one of the fairy dances, as the common people call them in these parts, viz., the greene circles made by those sprites on the grasse." What happened next I shall leave Aubrey to describe:

. . . he all at once sawe an innumerable quantitie of pigmies or very small people, dancing rounde and rounde, and singing, and making all maner of small odd noyses. He, being very greatly amaz'd, and yet not being able, as he sayes, to run away from them, being, as he supposes, kept there in a kind of enchantment, they no sooner perceave him but they surround him on all sides, and what betwixt feare and amazement, he fell down scarcely knowing what he did; and thereupon these little creatures pinch'd him all over, and made a sorte of quick humming noyse all the time; but at lenght they left him, and when the sun rose, he found himself exactly in the midst of one of these faiery dances.[5]

Aubrey learned of what had happened to the poor curate just "a few days after he was so tormented," and so enthused had he been by the man's sincerity that with his "bedfellow Stump" he went "at night time to the dances on the downes," but they "saw none of the elves or fairies." This, Aubrey admitted, was because it is "saide they seldom appeare to any persons who go to seeke for them."

Despite Aubrey and Stump's disappointment, it is clear that Mr. Hart encountered something very unusual while out on the downs beyond Yatton Keynell. The trigger for this event was his entry into a "fairy dance," which was clearly not a crop circle but a ring or circle of dark coloration in grass. Somehow it caused a bizarre sequence of events, which included unearthly singing and "small odd noyses" as well as an otherworldly feeling of absolute enchantment accompanied by the sensation that the "pigmies" or "very small people" had "pinch'd him all over." Such strange effects eerily echo those often reported in connection with UFO close encounters, and, in the knowledge that Gwen Horrigan is firm about the crop circles she saw in the Cotswolds being classed as "fairy rings," then their connection with unidentified aerial phenomena in the guise of "fairy lights" is most revealing indeed. Similar pinching sensations have been reported also by patients using full-sized orgone accumulators, presumably as a result of the device's energy potential affecting the individual's central nervous system. Thus, whatever it was that Mr. Hart encountered, it would appear to have had highly energetic properties comparable to those of orgone energy.

So, did the curate at the Latin school where John Aubrey learned grammar chance upon an exotic light form, perhaps one of Constable's orgone bioforms, in the process of discharging into the ground? Could it have caused the hallucinations and sensations Mr. Hart was said to have experienced that night out on the downs? These are intriguing possibilities, but how all of this might have been triggered simply by stepping into a ring of discoloration caused by fungi is a complete mystery. If it had been a crop circle, then the whole story would have made much more sense.

There is good evidence to suggest that crop circles have been around in one form or another for a long time indeed, but for just how long? And why has there been the sudden evolution during the 1980s and 1990s? These were the questions that I knew I had to address in order to understand what was truly going on in the crop fields of southern England.

13

How Did It All Begin?

Was prehistoric man aware of the crop circle phenomenon, including the accompanying light manifestations and physical effects? Up until the demise of the Mesolithic culture of Europe between 5000 and 4500 BC, our ancestors had been hunter–gatherers, following the migrating cycles of animal herds, setting up temporary settlements for limited periods before moving on again. After this time Britain was introduced to a new lifestyle involving permanent settlements and shaping the land for agricultural and ceremonial purposes. These people began constructing monuments such as huge stone circles, standing stones, chambered barrows and dolmens, many of which were aligned towards prominent solar and lunar events in the calendar year. A great many were also positioned in relation to each other, a conclusion some archaeologists are beginning to accept. These sites formed an overall arrangement on either a local or regional basis.

It is clear that the Neolithic and Bronze Age races, like many primitive cultures today, were very much in tune with the seasonal cycles and natural qualities of the environment in which they lived, a knowledge they had to possess in order to survive.

Was it possible that our Neolithic ancestors became aware of natural nodal points upon the earth's surface not just through divinatory practices but also through the appearance of both crop circles and light manifestations? Such blatant intrusions into their natural order would not have been ignored in a primitive society where omens and portents governed the actions and movements of everyday life. Recognizing the potential power of such locations through circle–related events might have meant it being "roped off" from open inspection and preserved through the construction of a monument of some sort. This is likely to have been a circular earthen henge, a mound, or circle of stones. It would then have acted as a symbol to outsiders that this place was sacred and, thus, out of bounds to the curious.

There are many good examples of megalithic stones bearing beautiful carvings. Most depict concentric rings linked with lines, some with hollowed out "cups" or indentations in their center. Among this ancient art are clear representations of what we might refer to as crop circle designs with circles, spurs, and halos.

Most carved megalithic stones belong to a particularly early date, approximately between 4500 and 2200 BC, and have been found only in certain areas of the British Isles. They include the Orkneys, the Scottish Western Isles, the Boyne Valley of Ireland, West Wales, and the north of England. They are very rare in other parts of the country, although this fact does not mean they did not exist in these areas. Artistic and symbolic imagery of this kind was probably painted on wood, in caves, or upon the standing stones themselves.

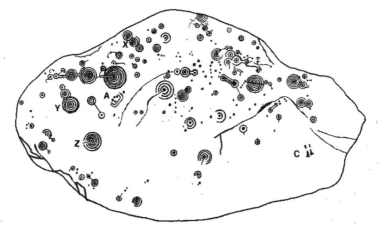

23. Prehistoric rock carvings from a now buried stone at Cochno, near Bearsden, in Scotland.

The subsequent Bronze Age culture, c. 2200–500 BC, left behind very few petroglyphs in stone. Instead, their artistic abilities were channeled into the design of metal objects such as swords, breastplates, and personal items of adornment. Their art styles show little similarity to the crop circle formations, and yet it was this culture that built the final phase of Stonehenge and left as a legacy the hundreds of round barrows scattered across the Wessex landscape. Many of these cemetery groups, as they are known, cluster around Stonehenge and consist of several separate types of mound, including bell barrows, bow barrows, disk barrows, pond barrows, and round barrows. Most of them were constructed between 1600 BC and 1350 BC—this later date being calculated through the discovery in the barrows of Egyptian-style faience beads similar to those made during the reign of the Pharaoh Akhenaten, the so-called Amarna period of ancient Egyptian history.

Crop circle researchers have often noted the great similarity between the shapes and sizes of circular mounds and crop circles. The late F.W. Holiday in his enigmatic book *The Dragon and the Disc* (1973) pointed out the obvious correlations and similarities between the Bronze Age circular monuments, the UFO phenomenon, and age-old legends of fiery dragons seen in the sky. I know it could never be proved one way or another, but it is possible that the Bronze Age peoples of Britain were familiar with both terrestrial and atmospheric light manifestations as well as crop circles and other forms of atmospheric or meteorological discharges within the landscape.

Even accepting these tantalizing views, we must ask ourselves why there has been such a concentration of circles in southern England? Was it linked somehow to the presence of the Neolithic and Bronze Age peoples who built the prehistoric monuments? One has only to look at an Ordnance Survey map to see evidence of early field systems: dykes, ditches, and indistinguishable earthworks that show the intensity of human habitation in the very areas where crop circles appear today. For instance, the final few miles of the Ridgeway weave their way through a region of intense crop circle distribution, which includes sites such as Barbury Castle, Hackpen Hill, Avebury Down, East Kennet, Lurkeley Hill, and, finally, East Field, Alton Barnes. Can it be coincidence that this ancient trackway comes to a halt in probably the most important location for crop circle formations in Britain?

Other major formations have appeared close to the Wansdyke, a curious defensive ditch that slices through the Wiltshire countryside and passes along its course such familiar circle sites as Bishop's Canning, Morgan's Hill, and Lockeridge Dene. With its mass of prehistoric sites, ancient trackways, "Celtic" field systems, undulating downs, and steep escarpments, Wiltshire seems perfect crop circle country.

Just how much all these diverse threads hold together is impossible to say. What we can say, however, is that there appears to be some relationship between the effects of orgone energy and places of ancient power. Moreover, what happens to visitors to these sites parallels exactly what happens inside crop circles.

14

Places of Power

The characteristics and qualities of places of natural power are best understood by looking at comparative cultures that have accepted and utilized natural energies and geo–magnetic forces of the earth for thousands of years. For example, the so–called geomancers or earth diviners of the ancient Chinese practice of *feng-shui* (pronounced *fen-shway* and meaning "wind and water") appear to have recognized Wilhelm Reich's orgone radiation as a universal life–force known as *ch'i* (or *ki* in Japan), meaning "two breaths" and orgone's negative or de–structive form, DOR ("deadly orgone radiation"), known to them as *sha*.

This term *ch'i* expresses this energy's dualistic nature, its so–called Yin and Yang components—one female and the other male, one negative and the other positive. In *feng-shui* these two aspects are symbolized by the white tiger and azure (or blue) dragon, their misty breath weaving together to become one harmonious life essence that exists in all living matter. For many centuries *ch'i* has been used in eastern healing prac–tices, such as acupuncture, and in martial arts, where it is utilized to focus, heighten, and project the physical potential of the body.

To the *feng-shui* geomancers, *ch'i* exists in different concentrations upon the earth's surface and flows (or discharges) from place to place

along winding paths known as *lung-mei* or "dragon veins." Through ritualistic attunement and the use of magnetic instrumentation, these highly
skilled men can predict the nature of the *ch'i* present at a location and
believe that there are different conditions involved with its accumulation, direction, and flow. These conditions include the shape and design
of the surrounding landscape—factors borne in mind when deciding
upon the location of new buildings and monuments. Great care is taken
to construct new towns in strict accordance with *feng-shui* principles in
the belief that, by regulating the *ch'i*, it will enhance the quality of life of
those who live there. Landscaped settings are created with the specific
purpose of accumulating, enhancing, and channeling *ch'i* energy, and
today we refer to the study of this age–old earth divination as geomancy.

The black or negative form of *ch'i*, known to the *feng-shui* geomancers
as *sha*, meaning "noxious vapor," or *feng sha*, "noxious wind," can result
from many things. These causes might include the configuration of a
land form, channels of cold and blustery wind, opposing influences,
interrupted lines of energy, or even bad soil. All of these situations can
disrupt the harmony of any person or building. In the case of people,
this disruption can result in serious illness and personal catastrophe.
Dowsers, too, would seem to have identified a very similar dark and
unhealthy form of earth energy, which they refer to as a "black stream."
Quite simply, both the *sha*, or *feng sha*, of the *feng-shui* geomaners, and
the "black streams" of the dowsers, bear uncanny similarities to Wilhelm
Reich's DOR—deadly orgone radiation, which he saw as having the ability to either draw away or overdose the orgone potential of living matter along with several other quite disturbing side effects.

Is it possible that the geomancers of the Neolithic and Bronze Age
cultures, which thrived in Britain between 4500 and 500 BC, recognized
natural reservoirs of *ch'i* or orgone energy? If correct, then this knowledge might well have decided the placement of their key stone and
earthen monuments. We speak here of stone circles, standing stones,
dolmens, chambered barrows, earthen mounds, hill forts, and henge
monuments—sites seen by the archaeological community as originally
having possessed ceremonial, sepulchral, or celestial functions only.
Such conclusions for anyone who studies ancient sites with an open
mind have always seemed a little short of the truth.

For those of an intuitive or psychically aware nature, these prehistoric monuments are storehouses of natural energy, "earth energy" as it

is known, regulated and connected by their alignment and configuration. Such energies have on many occasions been identified with the *ch'i* of the Chinese geomancers or the *prana* of Hindu yogic mystics. To researchers of the earth mysteries, these places of power were constructed upon earth acupuncture points, and function as organic batteries: channeling and enhancing the richness of life and fulfilling the agricultural cycles, both in the past and, to a lesser degree, in the present day.

It is a fact that the *ch'i* of the *feng-shui* geomancers is considered to travel along "secret arrows," the name given to straight courses such as those formed by avenues or rows of trees, ditches, paths, stone walls, trackways, water courses, even lines of posts, and railway lines; in fact, anything straight or in lines. All of these lines can, it is believed, become powerful conductors of the life force existing within nature.

Such linear courses of least resistance between man–enhanced and natural nodal points may also provide the answer to the age–old association between unidentified aerial phenomena and ley lines—alignments of ancient and sacred sites thought to be ancient trackways, spirit paths, or death roads, first marked out by our Neolithic ancestors. It was an idea first popularized in the 1920s by the Herefordshire antiquarian and photographer Alfred Watkins (1855–1935), with books such as *Early British Trackways* (1922) and *The Old Straight Track* (1925). Although his theories were largely ignored by mainstream archaeology, a modern breed of archaeologist is gradually coming to grips with the idea that straight lines might have been an important feature in religious ideas connected with shamanic practices and altered states of consciousness.

Early earth mysteries pioneers, such as Tony Wedd, founder of the Star Fellowship, saw ley lines as associated with the flight paths of UFOs. Moreover, it was believed that, where ley lines crossed, there existed nodal points in the earth's terrestrial matrix where mysterious lights were more likely to be seen. Wedd saw this connection purely in terms of interplanetary visitors using the ley system for navigational purposes. However, if the orgone hypothesis to mysterious lights and crop circles is applied, then this material can be reviewed with a new perspective.

Wedd first made the link between flying saucers and ley lines after noting a statement in a book by 1950s UFO contactee Buck Nelson. He wrote that: "The Space People tell me that the places where magnetic currents cross is comparable to a crossroads sign."[1] This simple sentence made Wedd recall the findings of Aimé Michel, who had investigated a very famous French wave of UFO sightings during 1954. He had discovered that a great many of the sightings occurred on well–defined straight courses. Moreover, at certain "sighting points," where two or more "air lanes" converged, the object or objects involved would drop "like a falling leaf." These geographical alignments Michel referred to as "orthotenies," while the study of the apparent relationship between UFOs and terrestrial lines of force he termed "orthoteny."[2]

Wedd came to believe that the places where orthotenies converge were one and the same as the magnetic "crossroads" spoken of by Buck Nelson's "Space People" and as the nodal points on the landscape where ley lines crossed. At such locations a prominent earthwork would invariably be found, strongly indicating that both ancient sites and ley lines were places of natural "magnetic" energy, utilized by the UFOs in their downward descent.[3]

Despite his clichéd view of UFOs, Tony Wedd, who was himself a contactee, is accredited with having inspired a generation into studying everything from ley lines to earth energies as well as Glastonbury to New Age consciousness *before* the advent of the 1960s hippy movement. Indeed, he is seen by some as the founder of the earth mysteries subject. Philip Heselton's books *Tony Wedd: New Age Pioneer* (1986) and *The Elements of Earth Mysteries* (1991) are essential reading in this respect.

The believed association between UFOs and ritual landscapes was a subject discussed in detail in an important earth mysteries work entitled *Quicksilver Heritage—The Mystic Leys: Their Legacy of Ancient Wisdom* written by Paul Screeton and published in 1974.[4] The book details the early work of Tony Wedd and Aimé Michel before presenting the case for the relationship between leys, orthotenies, and UFOs. Inevitably, Paul Screeton was forced to conclude that, unless we fully understood the nature of the UFO phenomenon, no definite answers would be forthcoming.

Paul Screeton assimilated all available information and put forward various suggestions as to why UFOs seemed to be attracted to leys, quoting the sentiments of writers who had each made their own observations on the matter. One, the mystic Frank Lockwood, who wrote many inspired articles in the late 1960s and early 1970s under the pseudonym "Circumlibra," had this to say in a 1969 article on ancient sites as "etheric centers" of force:

> Unidentified objects appear to use these connecting lines
> (leys) and also seem to appear at certain times. I know there
> are extraterrestrial beings who have a far wider knowledge
> of the forces surrounding the earth than any man on earth,
> but don't jump to the conclusion that all that passes be-
> tween the (etheric) centers has a "man from space" within
> for a sudden outpouring of energy flowing above the level
> of the earth would show shape and color on occasions. This
> phenomena could give rise to the dragons of old.[5]

It seems clear now that Lockwood's inspiration may just turn out to have some basis in fact and that his ideas were very much ahead of his time. UFOs exist—of that there should be little doubt—but 35 years as a ufologist have convinced me that their appearances are in no way hard evidence of extraterrestrial visitations. They do, however, represent strange and highly significant events that desperately need to be stud- ied and understood in scientific terms. However, I have felt it prudent to cite here the pioneering work of people such as Tony Wedd, Aimé Michel, Philip Heselton, Paul Screeton, and Frank Lockwood, as I feel they were touching at the roots of a mystery that we are now only beginning to comprehend properly for the first time.

The idea of a relationship between unknown terrestrial energies and ancient sites was first noted in the 1930s by the occultist Dion Fortune as well as the artist and sculptor Katherine Maltwood, who discovered Glastonbury's so-called terrestrial zodiac. Both were Glastonbury resi- dents for a while, and both recognized the energy potential at sacred places, whether they be natural or manmade. Previously, very few oc- cultists and mystics had taken enough interest in magical sites such as stone circles, barrows ,and other stone and earthen monuments for their hidden potential to be investigated. For most people prior to this time, they were simply rude monuments where the druids of old had made their sacrifices.

It was not until the birth of the earth mysteries movement, coinci- dent to the pioneering work of people like Tony Wedd in the early 1960s, that people started to realize that prehistoric sites deserved closer attention, which is something that earth mysteries writers such as Philip

Heselton, John Michell, Anthony Roberts, Janet and Colin Bord and Paul Screeton began to do when they saw their associated folklore as the key to understanding their original functions during the Neolithic Age. Fueled by the work on ley lines by Alfred Watkins and the theories on earth energies by dowsers such as Tom Lethbridge and Guy Underwood, they explored the view that the earth's surface was covered in subtle energies unknown to science. Moreover, it was their opinion that major megalithic sites, such as Stonehenge, Avebury, and other similar such complexes, were key meridian points in a national ley system, built on the nodal points of an unseen telluric power.

Scientific evidence for the existence of anomalous terrestrial energies in the landscape had, however, been around since the 1930s, as is shown by the remarkable work of Dr. E. Mathias, a physician of Toulouse. He conducted a detailed study of geomagnetic field differentials in different parts of France and concluded that the surface of the earth is "streaked" with "telluric currents" passing from west to east. He found also that sudden irregularities in geomagnetic readings on the surface or subsurface were usually caused by caverns, deep gorges, underground rivers, and valleys, which disturb and deflect the flow of these natural energy fields.[6]

Clearly, all of these wild ideas became the mainstay of the earth mysteries subject, and when it tried to become more respectable, the whole subject was, of course, shunned entirely by academia. Mad hippies talking about the power of the stones and how they were centers of the ley system, just did not go down very well with mainstream archaeologists. By the late 1970s, the debate over the existence of earth energies and their relevance to ancient and sacred sites became such a contentious issue between different factions of the earth mysteries community, that Paul Devereux, then editor of *The Ley Hunter* magazine, initiated the so-called Dragon Project. Its purpose was to ascertain the scientific reality of hitherto unknown terrestrial energies at prehistoric sites.

Experiments of both a psychic and scientific nature were conducted over a several-year period at ancient sites throughout mainland Britain. Early results strongly indicated that megalithic sites, such as stone circles and dolmens, were indeed hotbeds of detectable anomalies but only of known energies already recorded by science. These energies were principally infrasound, ultrasound, magnetic variation, and natural radiation—all of which have been associated also with crop circles.

The findings of the Dragon Project were published in Devereux's important work *Places of Power, Secret Energies at Ancient Sites* (1990), in which he concludes that prehistoric man was fully aware of natural energy sources and enhanced them by using stone and earthen structures. That was as far as he could go. No *new* scientifically detectable energy had been discovered during the Dragon Project. The reality of "earth energies," the *ch'i* of the *feng-shui* geomancers, remained elusive, and it would have to be accepted that, in scientific terms at least, it simply did not exist.

Yet, to any open–minded earth mysteries researcher, dowser, or psychic who has come into contact with places of ancient power, such terrestrial "energies" are an unquestionable reality. So what *are* these people experiencing on a subtle, psychic level? Has it been Wilhelm Reich's orgone radiation all along? And how does it relate to crop circles and the side effects that people seem to experience within them?

As early as 1978, I began working with psychics who spoke extensively about the inherent energies at ancient sites and monuments. These energies they experienced either as visible bands of colored light or audible sounds, such as a buzzing, humming, or clicking noise. They spoke of such energies "accumulating" at ancient sites and could even predict where and when they would overload and "discharge." I wrote extensively on this subject in my journal *Earthquest News.*[7]

One person, known to me, named John Day (see Chapter 22), was involved with the Dragon Project during its early stages, visiting the Rollright Stones in Oxfordshire and working alongside key earth mysteries figures such as John Glover and Paul Devereux. He spoke of being able to see clairvoyantly a ring of light build up inside the circle of stones at Rollright over a period of several days. At the end of the apparent cycle, the stored earth energy would reach a tension point and then discharge as a laserlike beam of light into the local landscape from a gap between two specific stones.

On one occasion John and a party of friends visited the Rollright Stones late one evening. Upon entering the ring of megaliths (a word meaning "great stones"), he looked around and noticed a subtle band of burnt orange light encircling them. From its color John realized that the site was about to discharge its built–up energy and so suggested that they leave immediately, as to be present when this happened would, he believed, result in adverse physical effects, such as nausea, dizziness, and muscular weakness.

Similar experiences were reported at an ancient site by someone else known to me, someone whom we shall refer to only as "Bernard," his first name. In 1981 he, too, was engaged in work for the Dragon Project—in his case scientifically monitoring the Kit's Coty House dolmen in Kent. Although Bernard was able to take an extraordinary infrared photograph of foglike energies above the dolmen, he experienced no adverse psychic effects there. It was a different story, however, when, in the company of fellow investigator Bill Eden, he visited a tree-covered tumulus named Wormwood Hill, close to Wandlebury Camp, on Cambridgeshire's Gog Magog Hills.

The date was February 15, 1981, and, upon approaching the earthen mound, Bernard clearly saw it engulfed by swirling bands of light, unseen by his colleague. Ignoring this sight, he stepped on to the mound amid the vibrant colored light and instantly sustained a powerful headache, as well as an intense pressure on his chest and head, a bitter metallic taste, acute nausea, and dizziness. With these physical effects came the rising sound of a deep tonal note that resonated from the ground and rose in pitch the higher he climbed. Even more curious was the disconcerting sensation that he was about to experience astral projection–the detachment of some part of his consciousness from the physical body. He also saw, clairvoyantly at least, priestly figures in saffron-colored robes, approaching the site in a ceremonial fashion.

The moment he was helped away from the mound by Bill Eden, the physical and quite bizarre psychic effects suddenly ceased. Yet, on tempting fate and approaching the site again with Bill Eden on April 5th that same year, the whole process restarted, beginning with the swirling lights, and then moving on to the physical problems, the rising tonal sound, the out-of-body experience, and culminating with the vision of the saffron-clad priests in procession. It all ended as abruptly as it had begun when he was again ushered away from the ancient monument. The pair left convinced that some sort of inherent power source contained within the tumuli had caused Bernard's ill effects, due to his psychically sensitive nature. The experience made him very wary of visiting ancient sites in case any similar incidents occurred.

Was it possible that unidentified aerial forms, Constable's "critters," sought out or were attracted to primary meridian points on the earth's surface, just as Aimé Michel had suspected back in the 1950s? If so, was this why mysterious lights appeared to "follow" ley lines, i.e. alignments of prehistoric stone and earthen monuments? Might this also explain why crop circles can appear in ritual landscapes, filled with ancient stone and earthen monuments? Remember, hundreds of years before the advent of the crop circle, the downs around Avebury were the haunt of fairy folk, who could manifest as both light and audible phenomena. There is something very special about this area in particular—something that does set it aside from most other places in England.

Such sentiments should have seemed obvious all along, especially as archaeologists have often found that tumuli and barrows are constructed of alternating levels of organic and inorganic material, just like Wilhelm Reich's orgone accumulators. For instance, earthen mounds have been found to contain layers of chalk, charcoal, straw, stone, flint, and crushed quartz, all compacted together and covered with turf. The obvious example of such a monument is Silbury Hill, Europe's largest man-made mound, located close to Avebury at the very heart of crop circle country.

Once again I could recall visiting Silbury Hill with psychic colleagues as early as 1978 and hearing them speak of this powerful ancient monu-

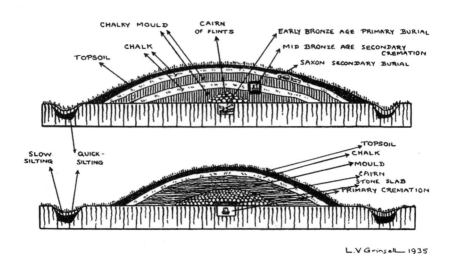

24. Cross section of a British round barrow, giving an example of how they are constructed of alternative layers of materials.

ment as a storehouse of natural energy. Bernard even referred to the Wormwood Hill mound by Wandlebury Camp, where he experienced his own altered states of consciousness, as a powerhouse of "accumulated" natural energy.

Of possible significance to the orgone debate were the findings of "earth energy" dowsers, whose fieldwork suggested that water courses in the form of blind springs or underground streams were almost always found beneath prehistoric stone and earthen structures. Many dowsers even consider these water sources to be the "fountain of energy" they detect at such places.

Underground water acts as a natural conductor, and, according to Reich and Constable, such water sources become attractive to atmospheric orgone, like oak trees attracting lightning. Blind springs might, therefore, be seen as earthing mechanisms—natural variations of the long cables that were attached to the base of the hollow tubes connected to Reich's cloudbuster. The atmospheric orgone was earthed into the ground through an underground water source, enabling Reich to disperse excess orgone drawn downwards by the device during cloudbusting and rainmaking experiments. Blind springs at ancient places of power could well perform similar functions. If true, it means that, whether by accident or design, they might attract atmospheric orgone, which would then arguably be contained and stored by the monument. Since we know that various barrows and tumuli possess alternating layers of organic and inorganic substances, then this explanation becomes a very neat idea indeed.

What percentage of prehistoric sites might have been planned for energy accumulation is impossible to say, and how many function in this manner today is equally difficult to answer. Many monuments were probably constructed in a copycat style by other tribes and so may never have had any hidden functions. Certainly earthen mounds continued to be used as both beacon hills and sepulchral monuments well into Saxon times, c. AD 650, although by this time it is extremely unlikely that they were planned with energy accumulation in mind.

Continuity is a term used to describe the reuse of a site by different cultures, and it is known that a great many Neolithic stone and earthen sites were reused by the Bronze Age and Iron Age cultures as well as by the Romano-Britons. Many heathen temples were later taken over by Saxon and Norman communities who built chapels, churches, and

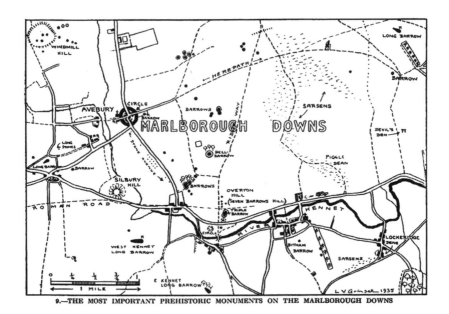

9.—THE MOST IMPORTANT PREHISTORIC MONUMENTS ON THE MARLBOROUGH DOWNS

25. Map of the Marlborough Downs, showing principal prehistoric sites.

standing crosses at such places. These buildings might continue to act as storehouses of natural energy due to their geophysical setting and the site's continued religious worship (dowsers are often able to locate blind springs beneath church floors, particularly under altars). Therefore, early Christian buildings and structures can perhaps also serve as efficient orgone accumulators.

Having dealt with man–made structures built upon natural nodal points upon the earth's surface, mention must be made of purely natural sites that were equally revered as places of ancient power, for these, too, have been seen as sites of orgone accumulation. Moreover, such places are viewed by *feng-shui* geomancers as collecting points of *ch'i* energy. This list includes waterfalls, springs, wells, and lakes, as well as caves, rock features, and holy hills. Due to the presence at such places of varying geological factors, hilltop sites are revered as locations of supernatural potency—most often associated with legends of light discharges and mysterious tongues of fire.[8]

The *feng-shui* geomancers believe that water is a perfect conductor of *ch'i* and can be utilized in its accumulation. Best for this purpose are fountains, lakes, and ponds, which can all be installed in geomantically landscaped environments. Fast rushing watercourses such as streams would, on the other hand, tend to disperse *ch'i*. This seems an important point, for as early as 1984 Pat Delgado and Colin Andrews noted the close proximity of dew ponds, reservoirs, and underground water tanks to crop circle locations.[9] It might also explain why some dowsers suggest that crop circles are often sited upon underground springs and streams.

It is highly possible that what Constable saw as descending masses of condensed orgone, his so-called bioforms, are drawn towards the earth's primary places of power, whether they be natural or enhanced by human hands. When this movement does happen, unidentified aerial phenomena of this nature might well produce sound emissions audible as high-pitch whistles, hums or low frequency rumbles and roars, like those reported the night the Barbury Castle formation appeared. In addition to this, inaudible sounds—most obviously infrasound and ultrasound—might also be a byproduct of such energy discharges. These inaudible sounds could well explain the reactions of both the guinea fowl and the dog belonging to John Hussey's son on the night the Hackpen Hill formation appeared in July 1991 as well as other similar accounts of adverse animal reactions associated with "saucer nest" appearances around the world.

Since sound can create geometrical and symmetrical *shapes* upon anything able to hold a mark of force, we might speculate that the infrasound or ultrasound, associated with both exotic light forms and Constable's orgone bioforms, can produce tensional pressure waves that are contained and manipulated in some manner, potentially creating additional features, such as rings and spurs, around forming crop circles. Like some cosmic graffiti artist, these discharging energy constructs might well sing out their signatures as they impact with the earth's surface.

The idea that plasma-based vortices might be responsible for crop circle appearances was first proposed by Dr. Terence Meaden during the 1980s, and, although it is a theory that has failed to gain much favor among crop circle enthusiasts, there is every possibility that he came closer to the truth than any of his contemporaries. What is more,

Meaden's body of work, as we shall see next, highlights the strange relationship that has always existed both in folklore and in real-life experiences between prehistoric sites and control of the weather.

15

Wild is the Wind

Sitting next to a lake one day, Wilhelm Reich picked up a hollow tube and stared through it at the rippling waters before him. After a few seconds he was intrigued to see the wind ripples upon the surface–changing course. He removed the tube from his eye, and the ripples returned to their original motion. He returned it to his eye and, upon looking again, saw them change direction once more.

After careful deliberation Reich deduced that linear vessels, such as tubes, can act as focuses to allow a direct particle link with sources of orgone, such as that which supposedly gathers upon the surface of a lake. Reich, thus, came to believe that he could suck in or push out orgone at his command using this rather unique process.

Reich got to work. He gathered together different hollow tubes of varying sizes, then bound and mounted them upon a pivoting turntable so that the resulting contraption looked like a rocket launcher. That was all it was—there were no fancy scientific dials and no instrumentation.

When the device, known as a "cloudbuster," was unveiled at Orgonon in 1952, Reich announced to his bewildered staff that it was to be used to attract and draw off excess orgone from the atmosphere. However, it would have to be earthed, so he attached thick cables to the ends of the tubes and inserted them into a water source at the bottom of a well.

I am not entirely sure what Reich expected when he first focused the cloudbuster upon the open sky, but, whatever it was, the actual results were somewhat spectacular. Not only did it appear to draw orgone down from the sky, but it also made the atmosphere levels fluctuate, dissipate, or change potential, severely affecting local climatic conditions. In short, he found he could affect the weather.

Cloudbusting came easy to Reich. To disperse a cloud, all he needed to do was aim at its center, and the tubes would reduce its orgone potential, hence its ability to hold water in vaporized form. By aiming the cloudbuster to one side of a cloud, Reich found the orgone level was disturbed, and the cloud would immediately enlarge to fill the new space. This activity increased its orgone potential and thus its ability to carry water vapor. Repeat the process again and again, and the cloud would be unable to hold the volume of water any longer, so it rained.

Time after time Reich was able to repeat his experiments, busting clouds and making rain. Ultimately, the cloudbuster acted in the same capacity as an oak tree does to lightning and certain environments do to discharging light forms. Yet, as Constable worked out in the late 1950s, pointing hollow tubes in the air was not the only means of cloud dissipation. You could just stare up in the air and bust clouds by thought alone; this meant, he speculated, that there was a clear and direct relationship between the human mind and the orgone potential governing the continuation of cloud formations. He concluded that the eye socket acted as a focus for pulling orgone downwards. This conclusion I would contest, believing that we are dealing here with a subtle form of mind over matter. For, although the tubes allow a drawing off process to take place, it is helped dramatically by the activation of orgone produced in our own bodies.

Reich demonstrated that we ourselves could affect the weather, simply by interfering with the orgone potential of the atmosphere and artificially drawing it towards a point of discharge on the ground. Was there some kind of relationship between orgone energy, crop circles, ancient sites, and weather control?

There is an old saying among archaeologists, which states that when a new excavation is started, it will always rain. Even older tales recorded in folk tradition speak of retribution in the form of thunder, lightning,

26. Old woodcut showing witches conjuring up the wild wind.

hail, and rain on those who try to dig up or damage ancient sites, such as barrows and tumuli.[1] Legends speak also of witches and wizards being able to conjure "fierce storms, . . . hail and wind, or violent thunder and lightning" at places of ancient power such as stone circles or standing stones. Indeed, the whole image of the supernatural is stereotyped by the clichéd presence of lightning and thunder on a cold dark night.

If we accept prehistoric monuments as places of orgone accumulation, then it seems reasonable to suggest that the presence of people at a site can unbalance its orgone potential. This imbalance might result in an immediate ionization of the air, leading to a thunderstorm, rain shower, or wind squall. How exactly such a process works, I cannot say, although if we can accept such ideas, then it goes without saying that the priest–magicians of the Neolithic and Bronze Age cultures would have been aware of this process.

Dowser and earth mysteries researcher Tom Graves, in his classic work *Needles of Stone* (1978), speaks much about weather control and its connection with both orgone energy and places of ancient power.[2] He convincingly argues that the regions in Britain with the highest concentration of stone circles suffer least from thunderstorms, suggesting, therefore, that prehistoric monuments were actually constructed with weather control in mind. He describes standing stones as earth acu-puncture needles drawing down or pushing out positive and negatively charged ions, while accompanying barrows or henges act as organic energy accumulators, collecting and then disgorging their potential in association with natural cycles.

Man's interaction with ancient sites appears to affect their fine bal-ance of orgone potential, and, when this occurs, some form of localized weather change takes place. It is a natural progression, therefore, to suggest that through controlled ritualistic activity Neolithic and Bronze Age communities almost certainly used such places to affect the weather.

In 1982 I became so intrigued by the possibility of ritualistic weather control at ancient sites that I took a group of Earthquest members to a secluded stone circle called the Nine Ladies, situated in woods near Birchover in Derbyshire. The idea was to conduct a seasonal observance inside the ring of stones at dawn on Sunday, November 1. This date corresponds with the old Celtic cross–quarter day of Samhain (pro-nounced *sow-wain*), a time when dowsers and psychics believe that great changes occur in the energies present at ancient sites. The real purpose of the event was to try and make the stone circle discharge its energetic potential through mental interaction at the exact moment of sunrise.

The day came, and before dawn seven weary figures left the rented house and made their way in thick fog across the bleak terrain of Stanton Moor, eventually finding the stone circle in the half–light of the early morning.

The air was perfectly still, but, by the time we had made a circle inside the ring of stones and had begun the ritual meditation, the fog had retreated slightly. In the 20 minutes that followed, creative visual-ization was used to activate the site's assumed energies. This activation was seen in the mind's eye as swirling light spiraling around and around, gradually forming itself into a cone of radiant blue–white en-ergy that stretched high into the air. Simply by visualizing the supposed energies present at a site, occultists, witches, and mystics believe it can trigger these natural forces into responding in a similar manner through the intervention of what can only be described as quantum entangle-ment or nonlocality (see Chapter 22).

As the visualization came to a crescendo, a ferocious wind squall suddenly whipped up, totally engulfing the circle and surrounding tree line. It quickly grew with intensity until I had to shout to make myself heard. My words of power acted as a further impetus as the wind increased in force until it became difficult to stand up without swaying about. At that moment I reached the final stage of the preplanned observance, where I told those taking part to see the ground tremble through the discharge of energies, and it almost did!

But, then, as quickly as it came, the freak wind ceased abruptly, and once more the site became calm and silent. The whole experience lasted for around 45 seconds, and most curious of all, the squall had appeared to be *only in the vicinity of the circle.*

With the visualization over, those present exchanged their views on the matter. Not one considered the freak wind to have been merely coincidence. There had been no wind before and none afterwards, just a mild breeze that arose some 15 minutes after sunrise. Since the purpose of the ritual act was to cause an energy discharge in the hope of producing physical and/or psychical effects, it was concluded that the freak wind had been a product of our mental and physical actions at the site.

Only later was I to recall a reference to this precise type of energy discharge in Tom Graves' *Needles of Stone,* and it is worth quoting his actual words on the subject:

> A side effect of this (energy discharge and weather control) is that since high charge moves off a point as an "electric wind"—a vertical "wind" in this case—a conductor "spraying" a high charge into the sky would send up a charged airstream as well. This air stream will carry up with it a fair amount of dust, grit, bits of leaves and so on, all of them becoming charged by the "wind" in the process.[3]

Could such an "electric wind" cause a violent upward air current of the sort experienced by the Earthquest group at the Nine Ladies stone circle in 1982? I summed up my views on the matter in an article for *Earthquest News:*

> If our conclusion is correct then it means that the interaction of the human consciousness with a stone circle in the form of rigid preparation and meditation will, under the correct conditions, produce an apparent energy discharge—an effect brought about by the release of kinetic energy stored,

captured and generated by the configuration of the stones.[4]

That "kinetic energy" now appears to have been orgone related—an energy almost certainly present at crop circles as well. Evidence of very similar electrically-charged wind squalls have been reported in cases of eyewitness accounts of crop circles being made. For instance, in late July or early August 1983, a Wiltshire man named Melvyn Bell from Keevil, near Devizes, was out horseback riding at dusk along a valley on Littleton Down, Little Cheverell, on the northern edge of Salisbury Plain, some seven miles east of Westbury. His interest was suddenly drawn to frenzied activity going on in a wheat field some 60 yards in front of him. He then saw, quite plainly, a 30-foot circle being flattened before his very eyes. No noise was heard, but what seems most revealing is that the incident was accompanied by "dust, dirt, and light debris spiraling into the air."[5]

Mr. Bell later described the cause of the circle as a "stationary whirl-wind," so did he witness an "electric wind," which under different circumstances might have been plasma charged and, thus luminous, like some kind of illuminated energy construct? Was it the same sort of phenomenon we induced at the Nine Ladies stone circle in 1982?

Interestingly, it would seem that in the past such electrically charged dust whirls, as they were known in meteorological terms, also bore the name "fairy dances," seemingly because they were likened to the sight of the fairy folk in the midst of their circular revelry. If some crop circles have been created by wind vortices, then it is understandable why they might have gained the appellation "fairy rings."[6] This said, such mundane actions on the part of wind squalls hardly square up with the description of the circles being made in the Hertfordshire mowing devil story or the mysterious objects usually associated with the appearance of "saucer nests." Thus it is likely that the association between the fairy folk and crop circles has a more disturbing origin—one more likely connected with the appearance of mysterious lights and the side effects that might be expected from entering the circle after its appearance.

Another eyewitness account that could be relevant to this debate is the case of Roy Lucas, a farm worker from Avebury Trusloe, one mile west of the Avebury megalithic complex.[7] Around 7:15 a.m. on June 16, 1988, he was busying himself cutting the verges near the village when his eyes were drawn to what appeared to be a "puff of smoke" some yards in diameter rising upwards from a field of wheat. Upon reaching a height of 15 feet, it billowed about and spun rapidly, its center appearing as a dense gray mass. Then, without any further notice, the vortex of thick "bonfire smoke" merely dissipated on the spot. A few minutes later another very similar phenomenon occurred elsewhere in the same field. Curious now, Mr. Lucas went to investigate but found no evidence of fires or any other explanation. Five minutes later the same thing happened again, this time on the other side of the field boundary.

The air at the time was relatively humid, and the sky overcast. Despite the term "bonfire smoke" used to describe the dense column, it was said to have been more like a vertical cloud of water vapor or mist than anything else. Although these strange occurrences may not at first seem connected with the circles debate, their importance lies in the fact that just two hours later two single circles were found in barley some 300 yards west of the field where the thick columns of "bonfire smoke" were seen by Mr. Lucas.

More significantly, in 1989 the Circlemakers visited the actual field where Roy Lucas had witnessed his columns of rising "smoke" the previous summer. From the middle of May onwards, up to 28 circles of different sizes and configurations were found here, including two quintuplet sets and a large number of smaller examples of "grapeshot"—tiny circles of perfectly–flattened crop often only two to three feet in diameter.[8] There has to be a possibility that what Roy Lucas witnessed were wind vortices, which under different circumstances would have laid flat the crop to create circles of the sort that turned up at the same location the following season.

This type of unusual wind squall has marked similarities to the meteorological solution to crop circles proposed by Dr. Terrence Meaden, who is an academic physicist by profession. Dr. Meaden's exhaustive twelve–year search for an answer led him to conclude that circle formation "involves the descent of an energetic vortex from the atmosphere, a vortex of air which is ionized to the point at which it is better regarded as a species of low–density cool plasma producing a high–energy electromagnetic field."[9]

According to him, when a stationary whirlwind is formed upon a steep escarpment, it will gain terrific momentum as it slides down a slope and comes to a halt in the basin or lee of a hill. This momentum, caused through its descent, will, on occasions, produce a complex interaction between the upward flow and its horizontally spinning component. The resulting effect is an unstable, down-flowing vortex containing a bulge inside the funnel of fast spinning air. It also causes an electrification of the air described by Dr. Meaden as a "plasma"—a quasi-solid mass of ionized gas with a defined shell held together by strong electromagnetic fields.[10]

If this globular mass reaches a field where standing crops are to be found, Dr. Meaden proposed that it would leave a swirled circle with a sharp cutoff edge. The electromagnetic field that accompanies it also accounts for the various anomalies reported in association with not just crop circle appearances but also UFO sightings. These anomalies will include audible sounds, magnetic variations at circle sites, radio interference, ghost images on radar, and even vehicle interference.

In March 1991 Terence Meaden's often neglected work was given a major boost when it was announced that a Japanese Professor of Physics, Dr. Yoshi-Hiko Ohtsuki of the Waseda University, Tokyo, had made a dramatic breakthrough in establishing the plasma vortex hypothesis as the mechanics behind crop circle production. For a number of years, Dr. Ohtsuki had been studying the curious light spheres known as ball lightning, a plasma-based phenomenon often associated with UFOs, which usually, although not exclusively, appears during electrical storms. Dr. Ohtsuki was the first physicist to actually create spinning balls and vortices of ball lightning under laboratory conditions by pumping microwaves into specially built apparatus. However, during more recent experiments he had found that, if a tray of aluminum powder is placed in the apparatus, circular marks will be left in the dust after the production of ball lightning—so, for dust circles, read crop circles. Of course, the research was only in its primary stages, but early results looked promising.

Of all the eyewitness cases of crop circle formation, that of Ray Barnes, a farmer from Westbury, is potentially the most important for the series of strange effects attached to the case. The date of the occurrence has been fixed as Saturday, July 3, 1982, although this is uncertain. The time was around six o'clock in the evening. A little earlier there had been a thunderstorm, indeed it was still drizzling slightly. While in a field, Ray Barnes' attention had been drawn to a "wave" moving through the heads of the crop in a straight line while keeping a constant speed of around 50 mph. Although nothing could be seen, this dynamic force acted like a solid object. There was no deviation in speed, course, or strength in

27. Old illustration of ball lightning appearing in a household.

the vortex, and after crossing the field in a shallow arc, it dropped down into the crop and radially inscribed a classic circle in around four seconds flat. The force involved then simply dissipated on the spot. In an interview given to Terence Meaden, Ray Barnes had spoken of hearing a "hiss and a rustle" as the crop was being flattened. The rustling could be put down to the stalks being laid flat, and the hissing could be linked with the agency involved with the circle's manufacture.

In the weeks, months, and, then, years that followed, Ray Barnes kept a careful watch on the field in question, during which time several odd incidents occurred. These events included a "time warp," the witnessing of distorted shadows, and various localized meteorological anomalies—all indications that what he had witnessed was more than simply a discharging wind swirl. Clearly, it was a multifaceted phenomenon, and one which, in my opinion, can be explained only in terms of the location's proximity to Warminster, an area plagued by strange events since the 1960s, including the appearance of some spectacular "saucer nests" in the form of swirled circles of grass and crop. The crop circle that Ray Barnes saw form, along with the other strange incidents he reported in connection with the same field, just seem to confirm the anomalous nature of the locality.

Orgone is integrally linked with both geology and meteorology, so if the crop circle researcher dismisses the basic principles of Dr. Meaden's prosaic theories on crop circle creation, then he or she will be throwing the baby out with the bath water. For, every time I look at the evidence to support the plasma vortex theory, I see only further evidence to support the orgone hypothesis. The two are intrinsically linked, as I have tried to show with the accounts of creating a vertical wind vortex at ancient sites. That intrinsic link, I feel, concerns our apparent ability to utilize orgone for purposes of weather control, just as Reich himself realized at Orgonon back in the early 1950s, and, as we shall now see, the indigenous peoples of North America and ancient Palestine realized a long time before that.

16

The Rainmakers

Before sunrise upon a sunbaked place of the ancestors, revered and sacred since the beginning of time, a Native American shaman approaches a medicine wheel of power—an earthen circle of sanctity with radial lines and concentric rings marked out with small stones and entered along an arrowlike pathway. It also contains rings carefully traced by other materials, some organic, others inorganic, like the compact layers of the ancient monuments of Britain.

Amid the pathways the painted man commences a low chant that gradually rises in pitch and intensity, matched only by the constant stomp his bare feet make upon the dusty ground.

The orange solar orb slowly appears, but still the archaic ritual continues. In the hour that follows the scattered clouds trailing across the blue sky steadily grow in number and spiral within themselves. They meet and join, making the sky progressively darker as time goes by.

Finally, the shaman ceases his dance and walks away from the medicine wheel, his task fulfilled.

Within a short time the welcome patter of rain is greeted by the confident tribe with much enthusiasm—its fall bringing new life and regeneration.

This is a vision of the rainmaker, one of the most revered and power-ful shamanic figures in Native American tradition. Bizarrely, the early settlers saw him as a madman and magician who bewitched the weather and invoked demons. Superstitious colonials were in no position to question the reality of his rainmaking techniques, so his existence be-came shrouded in mystery within misinformed folklore. The idea of Native Americans bringing forth rain was ridiculed by more "civilized" European cultures, and thus our knowledge of this important relation-ship between man and weather will never properly be understood.

28. The Big Horn medicine wheel in Wyoming, dating from AD 1200.

Despite this lacuna, the study of contemporary American Indian tra-ditions has shown that many tribes still believe in the abilities of the rainmaker. Although the recipe for a successful rain dance is largely lost, these shamanic practices were almost certainly conducted at sa-cred places, like the great medicine wheels of the Plains. Examples have been found measuring up to 92 feet in diameter, and they are almost always located upon high places. Some wheels are represented by sa-cred designs and patterns depicted in petroglyph form upon cavern walls and rock faces. All such images have shamanic and highly sym-bolic roots, and one has only to view them to see their extraordinary similarity to the more obvious crop circle formations appearing in North America and Britain today. The circle, the so-called "Hoop of the Na-tion," was sacred to many Indian tribes who saw it as the symbol of the earth, sun, moon, seasons, and universe as a whole.

Medicine wheel is the traditional name for a sacred place usually constructed upon far older sites already revered in Indian tradition. Usually they consist of carefully chosen rocks, placed end to end in radial lines, but many incorporated rings of other materials such as crystal, sodden turf, wooden posts, branches, and even bones. In many ways they are the Native American version of British ancient sites, even to the point of being orientated towards prominent solar and lunar events of the year. Some wheels are said also to align with other ritualistic sites, and, as in British tradition, dowsers frequently detect underground water sources beneath them such as springs and streams.

Although the precise ceremonial uses of medicine wheels have largely been lost and rainmaking processes are today conducted anywhere, some idea of their original construction and purpose can be gained from a study of Native American sand paintings, used either for divinatory or healing purposes. These circular, mandala-like images were constructed upon the ground and were often up to 20 feet in diameter. Many different designs and configurations were used, and one appropriate for the occasion would be chosen by the local medicine man. He would begin the painting with a layer of sand scattered upon the earth, and on this layer various organic and inorganic materials, such as ground rock pigments, charcoal, root bark, crushed flowers, and pollen, would be laid to form colorful rings and representational pictures. If healing was involved, the person would be placed upon the sand painting and left there for a set period of time, decided by psychic communication with the ancestor spirits. Afterwards, all traces of the design would be removed and kept by the family as effective charms to ward off evil spirits.

It seems almost as if the sand paintings acted as flat plan orgone accumulators, like miniatures of the circular henge and fort monuments of Britain. Reich found that bion activity was prolific within inanimate substances such as coal and sand, showing their potential to contain and concentrate orgone. This explanation would also make sense of the carefully raked rings of sand, often tens of feet in diameter, that were laid around natural features in landscaped gardens constructed in ancient Chinese and Japanese towns. The purpose of these sand gardens was to regulate and enhance the ch'i (or ki in Japan) of the environment and raise the spirit of the soul through sheer ascetic beauty, a practice forming part of the Japanese zen (Chinese ch'an) tradition. Modern-day

29. Navaho sand painting created for a healing ceremony.

examples of *zen* gardens may be seen in the old Japanese capital of Kyoto, which was originally constructed according to ancient geomantic principles.

It is no quantum jump, therefore, to suggest that the layering effect in the medicine wheels formed efficient orgone accumulators. Seeing this ground force only in terms of "the Great Spirit," the American rain-making shamans would stimulate this energy both within the circle and inside themselves, using intense ritual actions such as chants and circle dancing. This would create the same climate as a cloudbuster by allowing the rainmaker to act as a means of drawing down atmospheric orgone. As with the cloudbuster, this drawing away leaves an orgone vacuum that is rapidly filled by ionized clouds. The Indian shaman instinctively knew how to draw down orgone from the atmosphere by first containing its terrestrial form upon the surface of the earth.

One of the best anecdotes concerning the message of the crop circles was told to me a while back. A Westerner visited the Hopi Indians of Arizona and showed a wise old man a picture of an Alton Barnes–style crop pictogram. For a long moment the old man remained silent, transfixed by the majestic design in this wheat field far away. Then a tear formed in his eye, which gently trickled down his cheek, for he recognized the pictogram as a symbol sacred to his tribe's unwritten faith.

Whether true or not, it is a brilliant story and expresses the very real link that may exist between the ancient symbolism of the Amerindian tribes and the crop circle enigma.

The association between rainmaking and shamanism is a universal one and is found particularly in Judaic Talmudic tradition. From an early stage in the history of Israel, there have existed wandering *zadoks* or "righteous" holy men who were not part of the orthodox priesthoods. These figures were keepers of an arcane knowledge known as *zohar*, a doctrine much later made popular under the name *Qabalah*, meaning "to pass on orally." They were also shamans and ascetics, often spending long periods in the caves around the Dead Sea before moving on to other parts of the country. What is more, biblical scholars such as Robert Eisenman have clearly shown these holy men to be connected with the Essene communities of Qumran and Engedi, close to where the Dead Sea Scrolls were unearthed in 1947.

Among their magic powers, these "righteous ones" of the Jewish faith possessed the ability to make rain, a virtue bestowed on them by birthright. For it seemed they considered themselves to be descendants of an ancient biblical line that included such enlightened characters as Elijah, Phinehas, the grandson of Aaron, and Noah, who was seen as the original rainmaker through his covenant with God at the time of the Flood.

Among the most important rainmakers in Jewish Talmudic tradition was Onias the Righteous, known as Honi the Circle drawer. His daughter's son, Hanan the Hidden, and another grandson named Abba Hilkiah were both able to repeat their grandfather's rainmaking feats. Eisenman shows that the *zadok* tradition permeated into the early Christian Church and proposes that figures such as John the Baptist, James the Just, even Jesus himself, may have stemmed from this rainmaking line.[1]

For our purposes it is Honi's epitaph—"the Circle drawer" —that is significant here, for it seems clear that the rainmaking ceremony involved the *zadok* constructing rings of sand upon the ground, within which he would perform. There is no indication where this would have taken place or what form the rite might have taken. However, the result would appear to have been the same—the discharging of atmospheric orgone and the creation of rain clouds, like their shamanic counterparts in North America.

Quite obviously there are traditions of rainmaking and weather control among many cultures of the world, from the Buddhist lamas of Tibet to the Huichol Indians of Mexico. So, if archaeologists can accidentally trigger off energetic reactions and create rain during excavations at ancient sites, and witches and earth mysteries enthusiasts can summon a wild wind, then it should be possible to regain the key to unlocking the mechanism to make rain, so to speak. Should this feat be achieved in an environment playing host to the circles phenomenon, then it could lead to noticeable weather alterations and the appearance of aerial light forms.

Tom Graves saw all this as a vision of the future when he wrote *Needles of Stone* in 1978; for, after discussing the correlations between ancient sites, *ch'i*, earth energies, orgone, UFOs, and weather control, he concluded:

> ... if the barrows in that "stone-and-barrow" weather-control system are indeed orgone accumulators, a definite link is beginning to emerge between orgone and UFOs—but a link that only makes sense if we abandon the idea that UFOs are "spacecraft from Outer Space." The way things are going, "craft from *Inner* Space" seems more likely.[2]

The relationship between UFOs and inner space we'll explore in due course. Yet, before we can do this, we need to better understand first the relationship between exotic light forms and the planet's geophysical properties, which might well be responsible for the manifestation of many of the strange lights that appear both at ground level and in the night skies.

17

Earthlights Revelation!

In 1979 I turned my attentions to what was then Britain's most popular mystery—the Loch Ness monster. In the weeks leading up to Christmas that year, I visited Inverness, the closest large town to the loch and, together with UFO investigator Martin Keatman and parapsychologist Graham Phillips, spent a whole week in its main library examining newspapers and sighting reports going back over 100 years. We tracked down and interviewed several key witnesses to the monster and also talked to various individuals who either worked or lived in the vicinity of the loch. This research trip was to have formed part of an intended television documentary on the subject of the monster. Unfortunately, the program was never made, but the wealth of material uncovered at the time proved invaluable to our understanding of this little understood topic of fortean lore.

Extraordinary accounts of monster sightings never before quoted in books were unearthed, including many that simply did not fit the usual description of the monster we know and love. There was one case where a camel-like animal had walked out on to the shore at the western edge of the loch, and others of beasts that were in bright colors, not the usual brown or gray you might expect. More importantly, it was found that the environs around Loch Ness were home not just to an alleged lake serpent, but also to many other types of strange phenomena such as bizarre UFO encounters, big cat sightings, contemporary accounts of Little People, and witches conjuring the wild wind.

Most bizarre of all, we uncovered a folk story regarding a young couple who had gone missing in the eighteenth century while riding in a horse and trap near Loch End on the southern shores of the loch. It was assumed that they had been abducted and killed—their bodies cast into the water. However, no trace of them or the horse and trap were ever found, making the disappearance a complete mystery. Then, in the mid-nineteenth century, over 100 years later, two strangers walked into a local almshouse seeking refuge from a freak storm. According to the priest who took them in, they were dressed in clothes of the previous century and could offer no explanation as to their origin. The pair, a man and a woman, passed the next two days in a highly confused state, after which they simply walked out into the open and were never heard of again. It was only afterwards, when the old folk of the village recalled the mystery of the couple who had gone missing locally, that the connection was made.[1]

To all of us it became apparent that the monster was just one facet of a much stranger picture centered upon Loch Ness, with the lake acting as a "window area" for these inexplicable occurrences. Comparisons with other similar areas of intense paranormal activity around Britain hinted at the possibility that the Great Glen Fault, which runs the entire length of the loch, produced intense geophysical anomalies, resulting in paranormal activity on a dramatic scale. It was also feasible that fault lines in other regions must likewise produce window areas, or "ufocals," as they are called. In addition to these hypotheses, the proximity of ancient sites such as mounds and barrows to Loch Ness was noted, leaving the feeling that they might mark important nodal points locally. These points included a chambered cairn lying below the Loch's water line, which lay precisely on the Great Glen Fault.

What was unknown to me at the time was that two earth mysteries researchers, Paul Devereux and Andrew York, had been studying hundreds of unexplained incidents in the English county of Leicestershire and were coming to similar conclusions regarding the relationship among UFOs, underground faulting, geophysical anomalies, and the location of prehistoric monuments. They acknowledged the French ufologist Ferdinand Lagarde for having first examined the apparent relationship between UFOs and geological faulting, following his own extensive study of the legendary wave of French sightings in 1954. This was the same source material that had inspired Aimé Michel to establish his orthoteny theory of UFOs following linear courses.

Paul Devereux, at the time editor of the *The Ley Hunter* magazine, finally published his findings in two groundbreaking books—*Earth Lights*, co-written with Paul McCartney in 1982, and *Earth Lights Revelation*, written with a team of co-authors in 1989. Both titles adequately demonstrate that the stresses and strains of geophysical features, most obviously fault lines, working in association with an assortment of atmospheric conditions, produce light manifestations Devereux refers to collectively as earthlights. These manifestations may take the form of hill or mountaintop discharges, earthquake lights, ghost lights, spook lights, even Will-o'-the-Wisps. He also believes this theory accounts for those aerial light forms seen today as extraterrestrial spacecraft, in other words UFOs. Devereux was able to show the close correlations between earthlight manifestations and tectonic strains, particularly during earthquakes. He and his colleagues have also been able to photograph tiny globes of light released moments before the controlled crushing of granite core samples, caused most probably by the so-called piezoelectric properties of the quartz they contain.

When put under severe pressure, as the earth is shortly before an earthquake, quartz (and other types of minerals) generate an electrical current, which activates an electromagnetic (EM) field within the rock. Apply even more pressure, and the EM field becomes stronger and more unstable, creating tiny vortices of ionized gas, or plasma, which take on their own independent existence and can escape from the rock moments before fracture. As I have said, these lights, which bear uncanny similarities to the bion vesicles discovered by Wilhelm Reich, have been seen and photographed under laboratory conditions. This is one means of creating plasma balls, but there are many others, including the manner in which Dr. Yoshi-Hiko Ohtsuki, Professor of Physics at the Waseda University in Tokyo, has been able to produce ball lightning, what he calls "plasma fire," using microwaves.

Clearly, the larger the plasma construct becomes, the more existing names are used to describe them. Ball lightning, earthquake lights, earthlights, plasma vortices, and, of course, UFOs might all start their lives through the creation of plasma constructs within powerful elec-

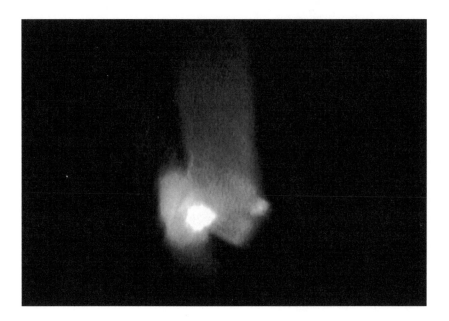

30. The piezoelectric effect of quartz caused through tension in crystals.

tromagnetic fields, produced either within the earth or in the upper atmosphere. Not that this accounts for all UFOs or that the process is that simple, but it does provide some kind of starting framework for understanding the sentient nature of exotic light forms that we call UFOs. Moreover, as we shall see in Chapter 23, the recent discovery of a protoform of life that exists only in a plasma environment, leads us to some stunning conclusions regarding the true face of alien contact.

Other researchers, such as Dr. Michael Persinger, a Canadian psychologist studying brain chemistry, and his partner Gyslaine Lafrenière, have been coming to similar conclusions concerning the nature of UFOs.[2] Their main area of study has been the relationship between paranormal events and electromagnetic fields, especially their effects on the human brain. They have proposed that a spinning column of ionized air, described by them as a "space–time transient," can be produced by tectonic stress below ground level and then released into the air. Through atmospheric ionization it would attain luminescent form, and should observers come into the proximity of this light source, and in particular, the electromagnetic field that surrounds it, they would experience varying degrees of physiological effects. These effects would include many of the symptoms generally associated with the close proximity of witnesses to UFOs, such as tingling sensations, hair standing on end, headaches, nausea, eye problems, skin tanning, and, if close enough, visionary experiences (see also Chapter 22 for more on this subject).

The revolutionary work of researchers such as Devereux, Persinger, and Lafrenière have brought us closer to understanding the manufacture and physiological effects of strange light phenomena on a worldwide level. It did not, however, explain *all* UFO sightings, as no theory ever can, but their discoveries are of paramount importance to the crop circle enigma for a number of reasons. Firstly, a realization of the relationship between underground faulting and paranormal activity allows the prediction of past, present, and future UFO hotspots, and perhaps even areas where genuine "saucer nests" and crop circles might appear. For instance, Paul Devereux conducted an extensive survey of the Warminster light phenomenon and discovered that the only two surface faults in the area both pass close to the base of Cley Hill. Their presence, therefore, supports the large number of paranormal and UFO-related events reported in the area.[3]

As we have seen, there has been a high incidence of strange light phenomena reported either at the time of a circle's formation or later by those visiting the site concerned. In addition to these phenomena, small, white or metallic-looking balls have been captured by camcorders at Wessex circle sites on several occasions. One such film sequence, shot by two German students on August 18, 1991, at a formation near Marlborough nicknamed the "Manton Ant," is featured on the video *Crop Circle Communiqué*, released in 1991. The viewer sees a tiny milky-white ball pass over a circle before continuing its course across the heads of the sunlit wheat until, after some 20 seconds, it is finally lost from view. It then reappears and is eventually seen five times in all. Interestingly enough, the small globe looks more like a globule of liquid mercury than a ball of light, an effect that gives the whole video a distinctly eerie quality.

Such cases are good evidence of the relationship between strange light phenomena and crop circles. They are not, however, evidence that the circles themselves are actually producing these lights—far from it. It seems much more likely that the qualities of prospective circle locations as potential orgone accumulators can allow dense concentrations of orgone to manifest as fully formed earthlights, or "space–time transients," of the sort envisaged by Devereux, Persinger, Lafrenière, et al. Such manifestations are almost certainly also reliant on the geophysical qualities of the landscape thereabouts. In other words, if the area is already known as a hot spot for strange light phenomena due to its geophysical anomalies, then the appearance of crop circles in the same vicinity, whatever their cause, will only enhance the light–making process.

That such a potential exists in the areas of Wiltshire which have become a mecca for crop circle events over the last 30 years is evidenced by the fact that mysterious globes or spheres of light were appearing in the vicinity of the megalithic complex at Avebury and the nearby mound of Silbury Hill years *before* the area became a hotbed for the circles phenomenon. One such sighting occurred in November 1978 and was related to me by the observer, a life–long resident of Avebury named Heather Peak–Garland. She said that around ten o'clock one evening she left her house on the High Street for a quiet stroll with her dog. As Heather entered the southwest quadrant of the henge monument at the edge of the village, she observed what she first took to be the full moon. Upon looking closer she realized that this "moon" was, in fact, a soft, yellow–white orb of light, gently drifting towards her position from the direction of Beckhampton in the southwest. The luminous globe moved in silence over the earthen ditch and bank, before finally settling down just inside the ring of stones. It then blinked out like a light bulb being switched off.

As a countrywoman, Heather is familiar with the area at night and is not likely to have made a mistake about what she saw that evening in 1978, ten years before the first quintuplet set of circles appeared within sight of nearby Silbury Hill on July 15, 1988. Within eight weeks of this date no less than 51 crop circles of various configurations peppered the fields around this great earthen mound.

The Warminster story is another prime example of light phenomena preceding the modern–day resurrection of the circles phenomenon (even though a few reported cases did come out of the area during the 1960s and 1970s), and I might cite other examples as well. UFO encounters such as the one experienced by Joyce Bowles and Ted Pratt in November 1976 as well as further sightings during the same period, exemplify the susceptibility of the Cheesefoot Head and Chilcomb areas of Hampshire to this type of phenomenon. The field at Oadby in Leicestershire where a crop formation appeared in 1988, had long been associated with strange light manifestations, as Rita Goold and I discovered in 1983. The location on the Oxfordshire/Gloucestershire border, where Gwen Horrigan chanced upon crop circles during the war years, was also quite separately associated with the appearance of mysterious spheres of light. A relationship between UFOs, crop circles, prehistoric sites, and the natural forces of the earth seems certain. All are inextricably linked, whether it be through orgone energy or human intervention.

Late August, 1991. My review of the crop circle enigma since our party's return from the fields of Wiltshire and Hampshire in July, was, I felt, complete as I had written down everything I could remember or thought relevant to the whole debate. I now had other publishing commitments to take care of, and so, in the meantime, I bought tickets for the first ever "Cornference," an event being organized by *The Cerealogist* magazine for the weekend of September 7th and 8th. It would give me the chance to socialize with others who shared my interest in crop circles and, at the same time, enable me to gauge whether anyone else had linked the orgone energy of Wilhelm Reich with crop circle creation. It would also be a final summer break before plunging myself into writing a book on the subject of crop circles and its relationship to UFOs, prehistoric sites, and the human mind, which I would call *The Circlemakers*.

PART THREE
The Furor

1. Barbury Castle hill fort, which, since 1991, has played host to a number of major crop formations, including a sequel to the original design in 2008.

2. Hackpen Hill white horse, just north of Avebury, Wiltshire. In recent years it has played host to various crop formations, but in the seventeenth century "Hack-pin" was the haunt of the fairy folk.

3. Silbury Hill, the largest manmade mound in Europe, where on the night of July 13, 1988, a huge amber-colored light emitting a tube of light portended the arrival of a quintuplet set of crop circles, the first of many in the locality.

4. Avebury henge monument, built 2600-2000 BC. Long before the modern crop circle era, it was the setting for the appearance of mysterious lights.

5. The Rollright Stones in Oxfordshire. The area around this mysterious ancient monument has long been renowned as a place where strange lights and crop circles, identified as "fairy rings," were reported.

6. Stonehenge, Britain's most famous prehistoric monument at the time of the winter solstice. It is surrounded by hundreds of Bronze Age round barrows, next to which some classic crop formations have appeared.

7. Formation found in East Field, Alton Barnes, Wiltshire, on June 30, 1996. It was 648 feet long and consisted of 89 circles in all. Some saw in this the DNA double helix pattern.

8. The "snowflake" formation discovered at Oliver's Castle, near Devizes, Wiltshire, on August 11, 1996. A video was taken here allegedly showing it being formed in seconds as balls of light spun wildly overhead. However, the video is a hoax.

9. This formation, based on the Julia set fractal, appeared near Stonehenge (pictured) on July 7, 1996. It became the center of a controversy when claims were made that the formation was created in broad daylight during a window of less than 45 minutes.

10. To find a Julia set in the fields of Wiltshire was extraordinary, but this was topped on July 29, 1996, with the discovery of a triple Julia set beneath Windmill Hill, the site of a Neolithic camp, a few miles away from Avebury.

11. This grid design found at Etchilhampton, Wiltshire, on August 1, 1997, was made up of 780 squares in rows of 30 and 26. It was interpreted as the number of days (30 x 26-week periods) between the creation of the formation and the date in 2012 marking the end of the Mayan Long Count calendar.

12. This magnificent formation found at Avebury Trusloe on July 22, 2000, gave the impression that it possessed three-dimensional "magnetic fields," the name by which it became known.

13. Five years after the single and triple Julia sets, a six-armed Julia set was found on August 12, 2001, at Milk Hill, northwest of Alton Barnes. It spanned across ten tramlines, meaning it was over 800 feet in diameter.

14. Crop circle evolution continued in 2001 with the appearance on August 14 of a strange cerealogical face within a rectangular frame, which appeared next to the Chilbolton radio telescope in Hampshire.

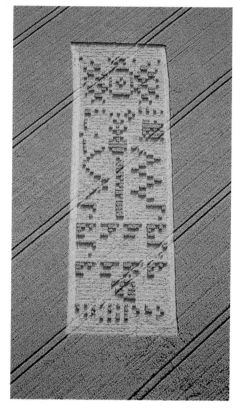

15. On August 19, 2001, five days after the Chilbolton face, another formation appeared in the same field. It was a variation of the famous message sent out into space from Arecibo, Puerto Rico, in 1974, implying it was a reply 27 years later.

16. Crabwood, Hampshire, was the scene on August 15, 2002, of the most auda-
cious formation ever—a three-dimensional alien face. It bore a circle with a binary/
ASCII message reading: "Beware the bearers of FALSE gifts & their BROKEN
PROMISES. Much PAIN but still time. EELRIJUE. There is GOOD out there. We
Oppose DECEPTION ..."

17. On August 27, 2002, Crooked Soley, near Ramsbury, Wiltshire, played host to one of the most perplexing formations ever, showing an unbroken DNA double helix strand. Its dimensions and proportions contained incredible mathematical geometry.

18. View of the North Downs of Wiltshire taken on July 5, 2003, showing a line of round barrows with a majestic crop formation aligned perfectly upon their axis. Round barrows were seen in the past as fairy hills and entrances to the otherworld.

19. On August 2, 2004, this "sun wheel" formation appeared beneath the gaze of Silbury Hill, visible in the background. Its design highlighted important Aztec and Mayan symbolism relating to the all-important 2012 date.

20. This giant formation appeared next to the Avebury henge monument on July 24, 2005, reconfirming the intimate partnership between southern England's temporary temples and those that have existed here since prehistoric times.

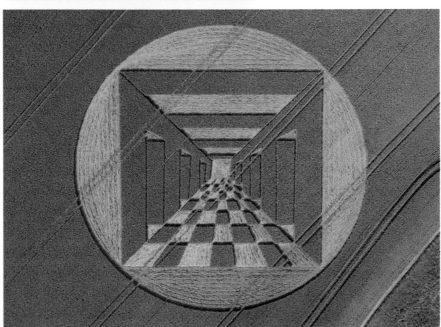

21. On June 28, 2007, this mesmeric formation, dubbed the "Doors of Perception", turned up in the field next to the West Kennet long barrow, near Silbury Hill. Sadly, it was quickly mowed out by the local farmer, depriving people of experiencing this wonderful design.

22. Pole shot of the Doors of Perception formation, showing the grass-covered earthen bank of the West Kennet long barrow in the background.

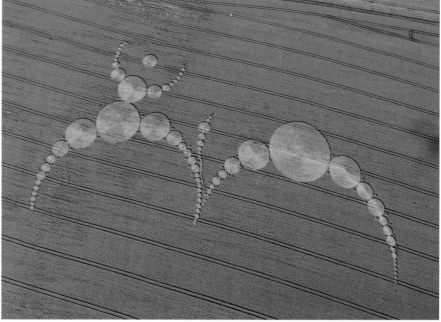

23. The significant 7.7.7 date in 2007 saw the arrival of a gigantic formation in East Field, Alton Barnes, resembling the OM symbol. Although initially hailed as having appeared in a flash around 3 am, video footage revealed that it had been made across the night.

24. On August 1, 2007, a spectacular formation appeared at Sugar Hill, near Aldbourne, Wiltshire, which was seen as a "clear sign" of inter-dimensional communication, coming on an important date in the Mayan calendar.

25. On June 1, 2008, Barbury Castle was the setting for another extraordinary formation consisting mainly of a ratchet spiral, an element of its 1991 predecessor. Some saw its design as encoding data on musical scales and mnemonic harmonies; others, an exact representation of *pi*.

26. Re-writing this book on July 15, 2008, I discovered that a stunning crop formation had been discovered in a wheat field next to Avebury Manor. It shows the solar system complete with the orbit of the planets as they will appear on December 21, 2012, the date marking the end of the Mayan long count calendar.

27. One of the 12,000-year-old circular cult buildings at Göbekli Tepe in southeast Turkey. Were the "watchmen" responsible for the construction of this proto-Neolithic cult center communicating with otherworldly life forms associated with the UFO phenomenon?

28. Ground plan of the circular cult buildings at Göbekli Tepe in southeast Turkey, constructed as early as 12,000 years ago, over 7,000 years before Stonehenge and the Great Pyramid. This site is now known officially as the oldest temple in the world.

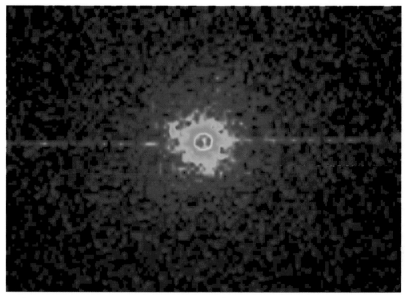

29. The binary star system Cygnus X-3. Although 37,000 light years away, it could well have influenced waves of geophysical and anomalous phenomena, leading to contact with trans-dimensional intelligences and advances in human evolution.

18

The Cornference

Saturday, September 7, 1991. *The Cerealogist's* first annual Cornference in Glastonbury, Britain's New Age center in the southern county of Somerset, was packed to capacity with circles researchers, UFO believers, national journalists, and members of the general public. I arrived at the venue late and had to watch from the rear of the stiflingly hot hall as circles experts Colin Andrews and Pat Delgado enthusiastically reviewed that year's crop of formations and cryptically announced that they were on the verge of revealing even greater marvels. Andrews passionately vowed that, at every lecture in the future, he would pass on a poignant message the Hopi Indians had asked him to give to the world. It says that "mother is crying" and speaks of how we as a "brother" are destroying the planet. The Indian elders were claiming that, if we did not learn how to become caretakers of the planet pretty soon, then it would all be too late. The speaker's words were very emotive and meaningful, and I assumed by this speech that he now believed the crop circles were visible signs of this desperate plea from the earth itself.

It would be stupid to ignore the wise words of such spiritually aware people. Like the Neolithic and Bronze Age cultures of Britain, the Hopi's understanding of man's relationship to Gaia, the name given to the living earth during the 1970s by research scientist James Lovelock, has always been deep and profound.

The next lecture came from George Wingfield, an ex–IBM physicist and full-time circles researcher. In a factual, though humorous, tone he reviewed the evolution of the circles during the 1991 season by showing the audience a series of breathtaking aerial photographs that flashed up on the screen. For the first time I now saw images of those formations that had appeared in the ripened fields of Wessex beyond our visit to the area in the third week of July.

It seemed that the first major development of the season had been the appearance of three–circled dumbbells with features that gave them the distinct appearance of looking like "insectograms," complete with antennae and stamens, an early form of which we had encountered at Chilcomb Down in Hampshire. Although these insectograms were mainly confined to Hampshire, two had been found in the same field, just beyond Stonehenge in Wiltshire. George emphasized that the insectograms were different in feel and style to the rest of the pictograms that had appeared in Wiltshire.

Aside from the Barbury Castle formation in mid–July, the Wiltshire quota of crop indentations had continued in the basic style laid down the previous year, typified by the well-publicized example at Alton Barnes. Dumbbells had been very popular at the beginning of the season, and these included the examples we had encountered at Avebury Trusloe, Alton Barnes, and The Firs farm, Beckhampton. One dumbbell found at Morgan's Hill, near Devizes, was discovered first thing on June 29, despite the field in question being monitored extensively from all sides. In previous years this field had played host to various circle formations, so cerealogists such as Terence Meaden and Mike Carrie had decided to keep a careful watch there in 1991. Not only was there a considerable amount of technical equipment trained on the crop itself, but infrared sensors had been positioned across the tramline entrances on each side of the field. On the night concerned, a thick mist had descended, and, when it lifted shortly after dawn, the dumbbell formation was noticed by the baffled group of crop watchers. No one had been into the field; no sounds had been heard; no movement was seen, and none of the sensors had been activated. When Mike Carrie entered the dew–laden circles, he found no evidence of any human involvement in their construction.

As the season had got into full swing, the insectograms evolved into another variation, amusingly christened the "curlyman" or "curlygram." Their principal features included linear spurs ending in curved turns, either placed at the edges of the formations' flattened circles or jutting out at angles from their main axis line, giving the impression of enormous matchstick men. There were also six–petaled flowers, encircled by a single ring, found at Cheesefoot Head.

It was at this stage that the evolution pattern had started to move in very strange directions indeed. For Tuesday, July 30 had seen the appearance of the first, well, what shall we say, dolphin or whale formation. It was found at Boreham Wood, Lockeridge Dene, in a field quite close to the original formation we had encountered on the way to Alton Barnes in mid–July. This unbelievable design could be described as an enormous, elongated ellipse with a linear spur encircled by a ring at either end. To complete its fishy appearance were two further angled spurs two–thirds of the way down its "back," giving the overall impression of a gigantic bottle–nosed sea mammal, closely resembling the Ganges river dolphin of India and Nepal. It also had undeniable similarities to the aerial image of the serpent mound at Peebles, Ohio, USA, a pen and ink drawing of which could be seen in F.W. Holiday's essential book *The Dragon and the Disc* (1973).[1]

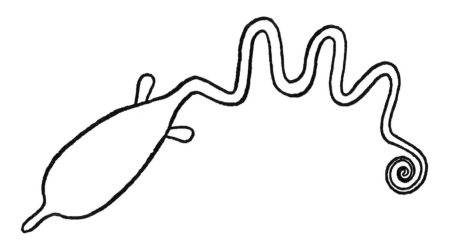

31. Outline of the serpent mound at Peebles, Ohio.

My initial response upon seeing this bizarre image was to consider that, if a formation such as this was for real, then we really have got problems. Yet other ellipses with spurs and rings were to follow, including one at Alton Priors, two at The Firs farm, and two close to the Kennet stone avenue leading into Avebury. Even more obscure was the formation nicknamed "The Brain," found at Chilton Foliat, Hungerford, in mid-August. To me it looked more like the curling tracks left by a snake in the sand than a brain, but to others apparently it resembled a DNA molecule.

32. The "dolphin" formation that appeared at Lockeridge Dene, Wiltshire, on July 30, 1991.

One point that did disturb me slightly during this lecture was the passing references to outlying circles or patterns found in the vicinity of larger formations. In Wiltshire these aptly named "signatures" consisted of either two small circles of different sizes or a scroll composed of two circles joined by a curve. In Hampshire and at Stonehenge the telltale signature had been two "eyebrows" or double-D's discovered edging out of tramlines. These figures were found next to nearly all the insectograms, the curlymen, and the flower designs.

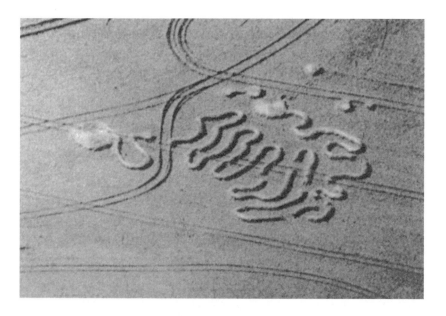

33. The crop formation nicknamed "The Brain" which appeared at Chilton Foliat, near Hungerford, Berkshire, on August 18, 1991.

Did a natural force with a computer-like consciousness need to sign off its works of art with signatures? The answer did not bear thinking about in the euphoria accompanying the lectures here at the first ever Cornference.

George Wingfield left the most sensational pictogram of the season till last. The slide changed, and on to the screen came an extraordinary masterpiece—an enormous formation composed of an inverted heart attached to a large number of smaller circles of varying sizes, and a further satellite circle well beyond the uppermost tip of the formation. It had appeared during the dark early hours of August 12 in an isolated wheat field near the village of Ickleton, ten miles south of Cambridge and close to the Essex border. It was positioned upon a ridge, completely hidden from obvious view, virtually on the course of the prehistoric track known as the Icknield Way, which joins the Ridgeway in Buckinghamshire.

This magnificent formation was first noticed on the morning in question by a Mr. Cherry–Downes of Snailwell, who was making a regular air journey to Hatfield in Hertfordshire. However, it had not been until George Wingfield was shown a drawing of this unique formation, that its full significance was realized. For he recognized that it was a near perfect representation of a Mandelbrot set. In common with almost the whole audience there that day, I had no idea what he was talking about. Yet straining my ears in the hope that it would ensure his words were digested, I listened carefully to what he had to say.

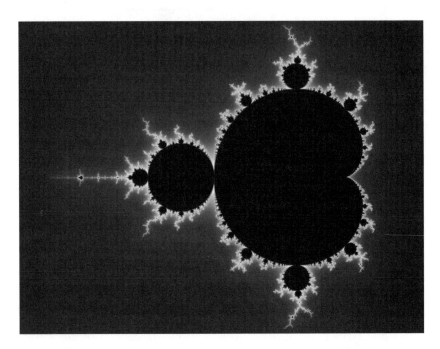

34. The Mandelbrot set computer fractal created in 1979 by Benoit Mandelbrot.

Apparently, the Mandelbrot set is looked upon as among the most complicated of patterns possible in chaos mathematics. In simple terms it is a visual representation of infinite possibilities derived by an endless mathematical equation, like two mirrors turned in on each other. Within a Mandelbrot set are more Mandelbrot sets, and within each of these are further Mandelbrot sets, and so on, so forth—it is a constant process displaying a vision of infinity itself. Technically, the design does not exist in nature and can only be produced artificially using complex computer graphics. It takes its name from Benoit Mandelbrot, the first person to utilize high–powered computer enhancements in the 1970s to demonstrate these so–called geometric "fractals." The actual design was first created by Mandelbrot in 1979 using a highly sophisticated IBM computer.

The study of chaos mathematics, fractal geometry, and their allied subjects of astrophysics and quantum physics were all born at Cambridge University, just a few miles away from the location of the extraordinary crop formation. So, was the cereal Mandelbrot set simply a prank undertaken by students as part of a rag week celebration? Some students initially claimed responsibility but offered no evidence. Despite this claim, a well–promoted campaign by CCCS agronomist Montague Keen to find those responsible through university journals failed to produce one single culprit, even though amnesty had been assured to anyone who came forward and admitted to the hoax.

For the crop circle experts this was merely a cosmetic affair, as those who studied the cerealogical version of the Mandelbrot set were convinced of its authenticity, citing as evidence the fine detail of its outlying circles, some less than two feet in diameter. The larger of the appended circles were separated from the great cardioid by a thin curtain of standing corn that diminished to the width of *just one stalk*, a feat of great artistic achievement, whatever its origin.

It was said that Cambridge quantum physicist Dr. Stephen Hawking, author of the best–selling book *A Brief History of Time*, quickly dismissed the formation as a hoax. *The Sunday Telegraph* of August 25 had reported on the formation, quoting the words of Mandelbrot himself, who was apparently "very pleased to hear of the theory taking root . . . I can't wait to see what the next one will look like."[2]

Whatever the origin of the Mandelbrot set formation, its presence was perhaps an indication that we should look towards chaos mathematics and quantum physics for clues as to the nature of the crop circle enigma.

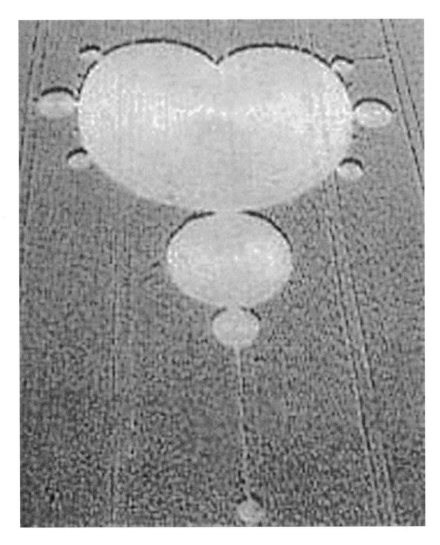

35. The Mandelbrot crop formation, which appeared in a field at Ickleton, Cambridgeshire, on August 12, 1991.

If it was a hoax, then its construction would have necessitated precision drawing of a kind previously unknown in crop circle creation. Even the complex patterns found in the formation at Barbury Castle would have been easier to hoax than the Mandelbrot set.

And it was the Barbury Castle formation that featured in the next lecture by *The Cerealogist*'s editor, John Michell. He explained how the measurements, proportions, and general design of this unique work of art, contained hidden dimensions of great cosmic significance to the study of universal or "canonical" geometry, like that incorporated in the measurements of Stonehenge.³ Certainly, this was another point in favor of its authenticity.

No one even made a passing reference to orgone energy in connection with crop circles until a panel discussion at the end of the first day, when a man standing at the back shouted out: "Do any of the panel have any views on whether Wilhelm Reich's orgone energy is connected with crop circles?"

What kind of response would this question receive? I waited with baited breath. Yet, to my surprise, the panel shook their heads, passed around the question before admitting that they knew of the work of Wilhelm Reich and his orgone energy but did not link it directly with crop circles.

The man who had posed the question turned out to be a Glastonbury resident. I sought him out and asked him what his thoughts were on the subject. He pointed out that many crop circles appear in the proximity of ancient sites, particularly mounds and barrows. These sites often are composed of alternating layers of organic and inorganic materials, making them ideal orgone accumulators. Perhaps there was some link, he suggested, between these storehouses of energy and the supposed ley lines that ran out from the ancient sites into the fields where the crop circles appeared. To him there was an undeniable relationship between orgone and crop circles, and he simply could not understand why no one else had recognized the fact.

Sunday, September 8. The second day of the Cornference began at a leisurely pace with a panel discussion headed by a group of dowsers on crop circles and "energy leys." Among their number was Hamish Miller, co-author with Paul Broadhurst of *The Sun and the Serpent* (1989), a fine book on the St. Michael Line—a corridor of ancient sites stretching from Cornwall to the Norfolk coast. Hamish spoke about dowsing this super ley, which passes through Glastonbury, Avebury, and the White Horse of Uffington.

Later, those people still remaining sauntered over to the majestic abbey ruins where, in the lazy afternoon sun, CCCS chairman Michael

Green and dowser Colin Bloy conducted a simple meditation in recognition of the Circlemakers. Embarrassment very nearly descended upon the proceedings when one hippy sort fell into a trance and momentarily began "channeling" the voice of the Circlemakers. I knew this sort of thing would happen once dolphins started turning up in the crop fields!

Back in the bar of the George and Pilgrim Hotel, two astute circles researchers, Rob Irving and Adrian Dexter, spoke ominously of "something big about to break," and that frantic telephone calls were currently passing between primary researchers in the circles fraternity. No one knew exactly what was happening, only that a major meeting had been planned for the coming Tuesday evening in Winchester, Hampshire.

Something fishy was obviously taking place, and I needed to know what. It didn't feel good, and I could sense that others lingering behind at Glastonbury were agitated by the sketchy news. I had no idea what was going on but was to find out soon enough.

19

The Dream Shattered

Monday, September 9, 1991. It was to be my final day in Glastonbury—a time to mellow out and do very little before the long drive back to Essex. However, Glastonbury resident Geoff Gilbertson, co-author with the late Anthony Roberts of the 1970s cult classic *The Dark Gods*, sought me out and suggested that I purchase a copy of the *Today* newspaper. He said it contained a front cover story that would interest me—something about two men who had come forward to admit that they were responsible for creating the crop circle mystery.

What the hell was this? The appearance of the article the day after the finish of the Cornference was too much of a coincidence. The Sunday newspapers had carried favorable reviews of the event. The frantic telephone calls between circles researchers the previous evening were obviously linked with this breaking news story.

Finding a copy of the newspaper, I saw immediately the source of Geoff's anxiety. Under the headline "The men who conned the world" and "Exposed: Two artists admit they pulled off the greatest corn circles hoax for 13 years" was the story of Doug Bower and Dave Chorley—two sexagenarian jokers who were now putting claim to over 200 crop circles, which they had been making every year since 1978. Their handiwork included many of the pictograms in the Cheesefoot Head area, all the insectograms, the curlygrams, the six-petaled flowers, and many, many more. Indeed, their signature had been those telltale double-Ds found bucking up to the tramlines closest to the formations in question.

Using only a plank of wood tied to a loop of rope, along with an eye sight affixed to the peak of a baseball cap, they had done them all. The whole episode had been a yarn thought up in a pub over a few beers. Doug claimed that, while in Queensland, Australia, during the 1960s, he had come to hear of farmers who had "made a few circles for a joke" (he was probably referring to the Tully reed nests of 1966). So they had decided to go out on Friday nights, have some fun, and see whom they could fool. After their first circle close to Cheesefoot Head near Winchester in 1978, Doug and Dave say they spent three years hoaxing further circles before anyone noticed they were there. I'll take up Dave's account at this point.

> ." .. for three rotten years they never noticed what we were doing and it never got in the papers. We wanted the papers to catch on so we could have a good laugh about it. . . .
>
> "Then all of a sudden we saw an article in the local paper and then articles in the national papers and we knew we had done it.
>
> "We heard this bloke Delgado had reported them—that was the first time we had heard of him.
>
> "When we heard he had worked at NASA in Australia we were even more pleased. He started saying they had been done by a "superior intelligence"—we liked the sound of that. We laughed so much that time we had to stop the car and pull into a lay-by because Doug was in stitches so much he couldn't drive. . .
>
> "Once the papers started saying a UFO had landed we started to go down to Warminster in Wiltshire, where there had been a lot of UFO sightings, and do the circles there to create a bit of a stir."

The *Today* news feature said that, after a weeklong investigation, the newspaper was convinced that Doug and Dave had fooled the world and created the mystery of the crop circles as an elaborate hoax. Pictures of the pair showed them pushing their plank, their "stomper" as they called it, across crop in one of the Hampshire pictograms. Another shot showed them arranging the components of a proposed insectogram with pieces of cardboard.

As a test of their crop circle skills, Doug and Dave had been asked to construct a pictogram in a Kent field. Pat Delgado had then been contacted and, upon seeing it just a few hours later, proclaimed it genuine, saying: "In no way could this be a hoax. This is without doubt the most wonderful day of my life." He was then informed it had been created specifically to fool the supposed experts, like him. The newspaper called these statements the most damning evidence of all.

This was a terrible moment for me. The candid smiles on the faces of the two men showed that they had pulled off a major hoax. I could do little more than admit to it being a bleak day for the crop circle enigma. I was gutted and felt as if I had been kicked squarely in the stomach.

But Doug and Dave had made reference only to those circles and formations in Hampshire that bore their telltale signature of the double-D as well as others they had apparently made around Stonehenge, Warminster, and Westbury. There was no mention of the vast majority of crop formations in Wiltshire, such as the one at Barbury Castle or those at Alton Barnes, despite Doug and Dave's suggestion that other teams of hoaxers were creating the *rest* of the circles. There was also no mention of the Mandelbrot set at Ickleton, but that could be put down to students, surely. It was also said that Doug and Dave had created some 200 circles or formations, and since an estimated 2,000 had been reported to date from locations as widespread as Canada, Hungary, Turkey, even the paddy fields of Japan, it looked as if the hoaxers would have had their work cut out to have achieved this lot!

The funny thing was that the various formations we had visited in Wiltshire during July had always looked and seemed vastly superior in dynamism and strength to those we had encountered at Cheesefoot Head in Hampshire. The corridors and rings of these examples were much weaker, and the small formation we had visited at Longwood Warren could easily have been a hoax.

Yet, in a way, it made no difference whether the two men had made two or two hundred crop circles, the media would now pull away the carpet from beneath the feet of the whole circles debate. It would begin a landslide of hoaxers crawling out of the woodwork claiming responsibility, without a shred of evidence, for this circle or that formation. Doug and Dave had attained instant national notoriety, and now you too could do the same. In a few short hours the story would be carried across the globe by newspapers and television stations under headlines such as—*THE CROP CIRCLE MYSTERY SOLVED—TWO MEN OWN UP TO HOAXING THE WORLD.* All scientific support would cease. The media would pack up and go home, and the general public would conclude that it had *all* been just a hoax, and now it was over.

Doubts were even creeping into my mind. What if they were *all* hoaxes, and we had been fooling ourselves all along.

I needed to know more. The calls exchanged between primary circles researchers the previous day were obviously those passing between Pat Delgado, Colin Andrews, George Wingfield, and God knows who else. Perhaps the Beckhampton group of circles enthusiasts, who met regularly at the Waggon and Horses pub, just down the road from Silbury Hill and Avebury, would convene that evening for a crisis meeting. Maybe they would know more.

Solemn-faced, I drove from Somerset out to Wiltshire. On wooden posts marking the outer limits of the gravel-floored car park to Silbury Hill I saw felt-tipped images of two dolphin formations that had appeared locally, showing how quickly these designs had become meaningful symbolism to some New Ager, at least. Still, they were probably hoaxes, anyway.

Ascending the spiraling path to the flattened summit of the 4,500-year-old mound, I scanned the surrounding landscape and caught sight of a welcoming omen. Upon a sloping field of dry stubble a mile or so away was the perfect imprint of a massive pictogram in what seemed to be green grass. It was the East Kennet formation that had appeared in standing corn on Friday, July 26. Obviously, the sunlight raining down upon the fallen crop had allowed new shoots to take root and grow, thus reversing out the formation as a green negative after the wheat had been harvested.

It was a tranquil, yet compelling addition to the otherwise lifeless field. It had to be visited, and, after finding a garage selling camera film, I navigated the tiny country lanes and then left the car for the brisk walk across spiky stubble to the mammoth pictogram.

Its image was still dominated by a huge three-pronged key at one end of a long central corridor that included a massive flat ring and three other circles. The combine harvester's cutting blades had failed to pick up the fallen wheat, so it was still there on the ground.

I took several photographs across towards the omnipotent image of

Silbury Hill, towards which the formation was aligned. Alone there, without the hustle and bustle of circle enthusiasts pouring into the formation was a peculiar sensation. I just could not imagine anyone hoaxing this particular pictogram. On the other hand, perhaps this was all just wishful thinking—a vague hope that something might be salvaged from what had just become the most maligned mystery of our time.

20

Redeemed from Oblivion?

Saturday, January 18, 1992. In the months that followed the *Today* newspaper's revelations about the nocturnal exploits of Doug Bower and Dave Chorley, my interest in the crop circle phenomenon waned drastically. Various books I had intended reading on all aspects of orgone energy, quantum physics, and natural sources of energy were all returned to the library, unopened. I couldn't really be bothered anymore.

The Doug and Dave scandal had, as predicted, killed off much of the general public's enthusiasm for the subject. There had been further embarrassment when *Today* ran additional features on the claims of the two elderly gentlemen. Circles researchers had attempted to counter these claims, particularly George Wingfield, who vehemently supported the authenticity of a great many of the circles and formations supposedly hoaxed by the pair. Certainly, the sample formation that Doug and Dave had made for the cameras the week their original revelations had hit the headlines was a complete mess and unlike any of the majestically swirled, combed, and layered circles that normally appeared in the Wessex landscape. Still, the wheat used for the display that late in the season was so brittle that damaging the stalks was that much easier.

There were, however, further nails in the coffin of respectability for the circles phenomenon on Sunday, October 27, when Channel Four Television screened an *Equinox* program on the subject. Despite giving a balanced view of the possible causes of circles in the first half, part two focused on the hoaxing element, citing Doug and Dave's exploits before making fools of circle researchers Terence Meaden and Busty Taylor. Within a field near Marlborough, members of a group calling themselves the Wessex Skeptics showed how easy it was to fool the experts by creating a large circle with complicated floor patterns, surrounded by three "satellite" circles.

After Dr. Meaden was seen to pronounce the formation genuine, citing it as a prime example of his plasma vortex theory, he was told off screen that the Wessex Skeptics had made the circle. Upon returning to camera you could see he was visibly shaken by the blatant deception orchestrated by the program's production team, whom he had no doubt grown to trust during the period of filming.

I felt genuinely sorry for him.

The program's redeeming features were few. Time was given over to the extraordinary work on ball lightning by Dr. Yoshi-Hiko Ohtsuki, Professor of Physics at the Waseda University in Tokyo. He was shown arriving in Britain with a number of colleagues to meet Terence Meaden, whose plasma vortex concept was being seen by the Japanese physicist as indicative of "plasma fire," his name for ball lightning. Dr. Ohtsuki's successful experiment to create ball lightning in a laboratory using microwave energy was also shown, as were the perfect circular marks that appeared in aluminum dust placed on a tray left inside the special apparatus.

The program also featured footage of eyewitness accounts of circles forming, including the testimony of Westbury farmer Ray Barnes. Unfortunately, it also gave time over to a psychic lady drawing a space alien she had seen in a crop circle.

No conclusions were drawn, but the overwhelming feeling left at the finish was one of delusion and politics on the part of the researchers in both the scientific and parascientific camps. The titles rolled, and I could not help but feel that the main issues of the circles phenomenon were now being clouded by extraneous influences.

The Cornference in Glastonbury had brought me in contact with the Essex branch of the CCCS, under the direction of Neil Durant and Nicole

East. They asked me whether I would like to put across my views on the subject in a lecture. So, in the back room of The Swan public house in Rayne, Braintree, during late November, I appraised that eventful crop circle weekend in July, without mentioning orgone energy. However, the topic did crop up in conversation, with the result being a letter from Neil in early January 1992. It enclosed a copy of an article published in *The Circular*, the official journal of the CCCS. Dated January 1991 and written by someone named Simon Burton, it bore the title "Organic Energy—A Theoretical Energy Model for Cereology." For a few brief hours I took the date to infer it had been published that very month, provoking me to kick myself for not having published on the matter myself.

The lengthy piece detailed the author's belief that orgone, or "organic energy," as he referred to it, was the "model of an energy form" behind the creation of crop circles. To my knowledge Simon Burton had been the first person to link orgone with the circles phenomenon since Trevor James Constable's book *The Cosmic Pulse of Life* (later renamed *Sky Creatures*) was published in 1976.

News came also that month of a fresh batch of crop circles in Australia. Only in the last month a Mallee wheat grower named Ken Price of Hopetoun, Victoria, had stumbled upon six perfectly swirled circles when out harvesting a wheat paddock on his property. Each one varied in size from 2 to 3.5 meters in diameter, and completing the set was an ellipse some 6.5 meters in length found in an adjoining paddock. Mr. Price contacted his neighbors—the Jolly family of Speed, who lived just 20 kilometers away. They, as we have seen, had discovered a number of circles on their 9,000-hectare property in December 1989, and so could sympathize greatly with his predicament.

Ken Price is an experienced wheat grower and knows the genuine item when he sees it. In his mind there was no way these crop circles were hoaxes. Indeed, he was heard to pronounce to a local newspaper: "If anyone calls me a prankster, I'll punch them on the nose." And on the authenticity of the circles he had just this to say: "I assure you it's fair dinkum."[1]

My enthusiasm for crop circles was returning. Suddenly, ideas from all sorts of diverse directions were tending to suggest that Doug and Dave had not ripped out the heart of the circles phenomenon. No, it was still beating at a steady pace, and I was beginning to feel that same pulse rising within me once more.

21

Nuked Nodes and Crispy Crop

Tuesday, January 21st, 1992. Unbeknown to the general public during the great Doug and Dave debacle was that dramatic discoveries were being made in association with crop and soil samples taken from circle sites across Britain. News of these findings had been rippling through research groups and specialist publications during the autumn months of 1991. Montague Keen—a farmer of 20 years and the CCCS's resident agronomist—had outlined these discoveries to the organization's Essex branch the previous week, during an evening devoted to research preparations for the coming summer season, but, without pen or tape recorder handy, this information had simply gone over my head. He had, however, promised to go into greater detail during a planned lecture the following Tuesday evening at The Bull Hotel in Long Melford, Suffolk.

The capacity audience for this introduction lecture to the crop circle enigma was almost exclusively local farmers who had become bemused by the growing reports of circles not just in Wessex, but also to a lesser degree in the fields of East Anglia. From the intrigued smiles on many of their faces, as the agronomist ran through a selection of slides showing different formations, I could see they were finding the whole thing amusing, if nothing else.

Quickly, Montague Keen turned his attentions to the real news of the day—the analysis of plants and soil taken from within the circles.

" What I am about to reveal is the evidence as it stands at the moment," he wished to point out. "Our information is being updated all the time, and only in the past forty-eight hours there have been new developments."

Montague Keen spoke first of the dedicated work of circles pioneer Pat Delgado, who had responded to the requests of an American biophysicist named Dr. W.C. Levengood for crop samples. He specialized in plant analysis at the Pinelandia Biophysical Laboratory at Grass Lake, Michigan, and, having read Delgado and Andrews' 1989 book *Circular Evidence*, had expressed a wish to microscopically examine plants found inside crop formations.

Wheat samples were duly collected and dispatched, and it took Dr. Levengood only a short while to establish that clear and quite disturbing changes were taking place in plants extracted from circle sites. His first discovery involved rare and highly unusual genetic malformation or aberrations in the husk or seed cases he studied. These took the form of polyembryony—the multiplication of the embryos within the seed glume. Not only was this an astonishing and quite rare disorder, but it also hinted at the presence of an ionizing radiation at the moment of the circle's formation.

In further samples collected during the 1991 season from a formation in Cornwall and the Alton Priors pictogram of July 19, Dr. Levengood found a distinctive blackening on one side of sample seed heads and leaves. This blackening had not been caused by normal oxidization of the sort that takes place through burning but by a process known as reduction, a term describing the reducing of living matter to carbon without the presence of oxygen. Even stranger was his discovery that only the top three or four cells of the seed heads had been blackened in this way. Those underneath were completely unaffected. To Dr. Levengood this suggested that the wheat in question had been subjected to a short, sharp fusion of intense heat energy in a nonoxidizing environment, and the only scientifically accepted cause of such effects was lightning—the most common atmospheric, plasma-related phenomenon.

In crop samples taken from a formation at Newton St. Loe, near Bath, Avon, Dr. Levengood had been baffled to find abnormal swellings of the cell pits in the growth nodes on the main stems. Microphotographs revealed unusual stretch marks spreading out from the cell pits, clearly showing a rapid expansion of the cell walls. Samples collected from the formation we visited at Lockeridge Dene on July 20, 1991, were also found to possess particularly swollen nodes, a feature characteristic in many of the plants examined by Dr. Levengood. He felt these swollen nodes were the result of a sudden heating of the cellular moisture, and in an attempt to replicate these effects, Dr. Levengood placed crop samples inside a microwave oven for 30 seconds and obtained similar results.

If all possible mundane explanations for Dr. Levengood's findings could be eliminated, including the possibility that the nodes of young shoots are disturbed or even "popped" during the human circle-making process, then they were of enormous importance to the crop circle enigma. What is more, similar work was being done by another laboratory, this time in England.

During the 1991 season an artist and biologist named Kay Larsen of Luxulyan in Cornwall, microscopically examined barley samples collected from a circle near Newquay by CCCS member Barbara Davies. Photomicrographs showed a rapid weakening of the cellulose cell walls in the growth nodes, like those independently discerned by Dr. Levengood. This weakening had forced the nodes to rupture instantaneously and swell on one side before solidifying again, during which time the stalks had been bent to fall with the crop. Also in keeping with his American counterpart, Kay Larsen found that the cells in the swollen growth nodes gave the appearance of having been "exploded" by the sudden entry of a powerful energy, described as "short-lived intense heat."[1]

The results had led Kay Larsen to suggest that other scientists should try using a range of radiations upon growth nodes to see if similar effects could be generated under laboratory conditions.

Yet, by far, the most extraordinary and controversial scientific work carried out during the 1991 season was the analysis of soil removed from circle sites by an American named Michael Chorost. He had temporarily left his post at Duke University in North Carolina to work alongside Montague Keen, studying British crop circles on behalf of MUFON—the Mutual UFO Network—one of the United State's most respected UFO research bodies. Relying on the good will of circles enthusiasts, he had visited one formation after another, spending long hours examining the floor patterns, taking measurements and, more importantly, collecting soil for analysis back in the States. The main formations he chose for his test sites were the dolphin designs, to be found at Beckhampton and Lockeridge in early August, and the Barbury Castle formation of July 17.

As a UFO researcher, Michael Chorost had been trained to take samples from alleged landing sites, so that tests might be carried out in order to look for any radioactive trace elements present in the soil. It was quite obviously with this in mind that Chorost carefully packaged off the Wessex earth and, at the end of the summer season, teamed up with a graduate of the University of Tennessee named Marshall Dudley for the intended soil analysis. He designed sophisticated radiation detection systems for the Tennelec/Nucleus laboratory at Oak Ridge, Tennessee, and was in an ideal position to take on the job.

Cursory tests for radioactivity had already been conducted at various British circle sites using Geiger counters, but no abnormalities had ever been found. So it was not expected that the Americans would do any better. However, the Tennelec/Nucleus equipment had already revealed baffling inconsistencies in soil samples taken from a crop circle found at Dandridge, Tennessee, on May 17, 1991, but these findings were now to be eclipsed by what they discovered in the samples collected from Britain.

At levels too low to have been detected on a standard Geiger counter, the two American radiation experts were able to pinpoint anomalous levels of alpha and beta emissions in soil from various crop formations, including the Barbury Castle design. One increase in alpha radiation was registered at 198% above the control. In each case beta radiation was always slightly lower than the alpha emissions. Other readings were more curious, indicating an obvious *drop* in radioactivity within a sample taken from inside the formation. Confusing results of this nature were also obtained by Paul Devereux and his colleagues at megalithic sites during the Dragon Project in the early 1980s.[2]

More specific experiments on behalf of Chorost and Dudley were conducted at the Tennelec/Nucleus laboratory on a sample taken from The Firs farm dolphin formation of August 1, 1991. A so-called "gamma spectroscopy printout," designed to register low-level radioactive emissions, unexpectedly revealed the presence of no less than 11 inexplicable isotopes.

Now I'm not one for advanced physics, but, in simple terms, an isotope or radion–nuclide is a variation of an element, where the electrons have remained constant, but the nuclei have changed in number. Isotopes also possess different atomic weights as in 235, 238, or 239 for Uranium and are usually formed by the bombardment of external radiation. Each one gives off radioactive emissions for a set period of time before it loses its strength and becomes inactive, and these half–lives, as they are known, can vary in duration from a millisecond to billions of years. With such low levels of radioactivity, the formation concerned would never have posed any real threat to visitors, although it is possible that other, more lethal isotopes with shorter half–lives may have been present for a limited duration after the formation of the design.

Each and every one of these 11 radion–nuclides had but one factor in common—they were all "daughter" isotopes of deuterium—so–called heavy hydrogen. I understand deuterium to be the second isotope of hydrogen—the third being tritium—and that only one in every 6,500 hydrogen atoms is a deuterium atom. When combined with oxygen, hydrogen forms water, and the "water" oxide of deuterium is heavy water, used in the nuclear industry.

In the minds of Michael Chorost and Marshall Dudley, who studied the printout in sheer astonishment, the presence of the anomalous isotopes looked as if they were the result of deuterium nuclei bombarding stable trace elements in the soil to produce unstable, radioactive versions of the same atoms. How or why exactly, they could not be sure.

Curiously, deuterium is utilized in plasma physics to create high-temperature pulsed plasma streams (a form of ion energy) found in plasma generators. Deuterium plasma features also in particle acceleration to create emissions of high–energy ions through plasma discharges. On top of all this, deuterium plasma is employed as a working model in experiments to determine the nature of plasma emissions from deep space objects, such as neutron stars and dwarf stars. Thus in the knowledge that some UFOs are likely to be plasma constructs, and plasma has been linked to crop circle manufacture, Chorost and Dudley's discovery of deuterium–derived isotopes in British crop circles was highly significant. On a more mundane note, and bringing us back down to earth with a bang however, was the fact that deuterium is known to be one of several environmental isotopes found in surface soil.

Having played this full hand of cards at the farmers' meeting in Long

Melford that evening, Montague then produced a joker and tossed it into the crowd, for only in the past 48 hours, drastic reappraisals of the evidence had been made by the two American researchers. It seemed that due to "sloppy laboratory practice" on the parts of the technicians at Oak Ridge, and the delicate nature of the evidence presented, they were restudying the validity of the gamma spectroscopy printout to decide whether any of the traces indicating the presence of isotopes were, in fact, background interference from the sensitive instrumentation used in the analysis. It was being suggested that only some four out of the original 11 isotopes would stand up to further scrutiny. Quite clearly new tests needed to be conducted under highly controlled conditions, and this would involve further time and fresh samples.

Fall-out from the Chernobyl nuclear disaster had already been rejected as the possible cause of the radiation anomalies, as had crop fertilizer. However, some skeptical circles researchers were suggesting that the radiation could have stemmed from airborne sources. They were also complaining that not enough samples had been taken from control areas of lodging—the wind damage so often seen in the fields of Wessex during the 1991 summer season—which may have produced similar results.

Despite these obvious setbacks, it did seem that plant and soil analysis at laboratories in Britain and the United States were coming up with compelling evidence that the plants caught up in the circle-making process repeatedly underwent severe changes either at the time or afterwards.

Not only was this redeeming evidence for the circles phenomenon, but it also vindicated the findings of those researchers and scientists who had conducted extensive tests on UFO nests during the 1960s. This included the plant analysis carried out by horticultural consultant John Stuart-Menzies on the bleached manuka (tea-tree) leaves removed from the first North Island, New Zealand, nests of 1969. In *Laser Beams from Star Cities?*, Robin Collyns quoted Stuart-Menzies as saying: "Every ounce of moisture in the plant had been instantaneously vaporized, leaving them unusually dry and brittle," adding that: "The cells in the medullary rays were burst by the sudden vaporization of the cell sap." Stuart-Menzies attributed these effects to "some kind of high-frequency radiation" that cooked the material from the inside out, as in the process of "infrared cooking," i.e. microwaves, on "an enormous scale." Dr. Levengood came to similar conclusions about the "blown out" cells of the growth nodes in samples taken from British crop circles. Kay Larsen said the rupturing and swelling of cells on one side of the growth nodes he studied were consistent with "the rapid vaporization of the water in the stem" by a swift, powerful energy, acting as a "short-lived intense heat."[3]

Levengood described the polyembryony in the seed glumes and the expansion of the growth nodes as the result of a short, sharp fusion of intense heat energy. J. Allen Hynek noted after his investigation of the circle of damaged soybean found at Van Horne, Iowa, in July 1969 that the leaves of each plant were hanging wilted from their stalks. He suggested that the plants in the devastated circle had been subjected to a close range intense heat originating from above ground level.

Dr. Levengood found a blackening of surface cells upon the seed heads and leaves studied and concluded this effect to be the result of carbonization. Stuart-Menzies, studying the manuka samples taken from the first North Island UFO nest, felt that ." . . the energy received has reduced the pith to black carbon, without the outside showing any signs of burning . . ." As in the samples analyzed by Dr. Levengood, this is likely to have been the result of carbon reduction.

In 1969 Stuart-Menzies found "the presence of such extraneous matter as radioactive isotopes of Strontium-90 and Uranium-235" in the manuka, as well as traces of the metals silver and titanium. Similar isotopes might well have been found in a British crop formation by the Tennelec/Nucleus laboratory at Oak Ridge, Tennessee.

The relationship between UFO nests and modern-day crop circles was becoming blatantly clear. The cause of the plant damage in all cases involved the entry of an intense but brief burst of energy—its properties being likened to lightning (Levengood), microwave radiation (Larsen, Levengood, Stuart-Menzies), and radiation bombardment (Chorost, Dudley, Levengood, Stuart-Menzies). I felt it possible that at least some of these circular traces were the by-product of an exotic plasma form discharging energy through the medium of the electromagnetic spectrum upon contact with the ground.

A quick word with Montague Keen after he came offstage was followed by the brief company of a farmer who reached into his jacket pocket and slowly removed a ruffled photograph of a single crop circle. It had appeared in one of his fields, just 300 yards from a housing estate. "I kept it to myself," he admitted, in his mild Suffolk accent. "I told Montague, didn't I?" He looked towards the agronomist for a nod of approval. "But I just couldn't have people trample across them fields. And when I came to harvest it, I left it to the driver of the other combine harvester."

Why was that?

"Never went into the circle at all—not once. Call it superstition, but there's no way I was going in that circle." His head shook. "I just felt I should leave it be."

Wise words, for even though the great changes discovered in the plant and soil samples were helping to redeem the circles phenomenon from total oblivion, many more stringent tests would have to take place before the true nature and potency of the Circlemakers were understood.

PART FOUR
The Jump

22

The Light of Consciousness

Sunday, January 26, 1992. A major difference between the plasma vortex and orgone theories to the crop circle enigma is that the former cannot accept an intelligence behind what causes them, a matter I believe to be crucial if we are fully to comprehend the true source behind the Circlemakers. The seeming intelligence of exotic light forms was first recognized by Paul Devereux during his earthlights research. He cited examples where lights seen often appeared to possess minds of their own, responding to human thought in an almost playful manner, as a dolphin might respond to a swimmer or small boat.

During Project Hessdalen, one of the greatest sky watches of all time, there were unprecedented examples of "light consciousness," as Devereux refers to it. Hessdalen is the name of a remote and desolate valley in Norway where, since 1981, literally thousands of mysterious aerial lights have been reported by both local villagers *and* trained observers brought in to watch the skies. The project was set up in 1984 with the co-operation of UFO groups from Norway, Sweden, and Finland, and the results in the first year alone were quite simply astounding. Some 188 sightings were made of unidentified luminosities, and many photographs were taken.

Of more significance, however, was the manner in which the Hessdalen lights would appear to play with the project observers during their long nighttime vigils in the freezing temperatures. For instance, on February 12, 1984, a slow moving light, flashing rhythmically, was seen crossing the sky. A laser was trained on it, and immediately the light changed its flashing sequence. Once the laser was switched off, it returned to its original rhythmic pattern. The experiment was repeated four times by the observers, and on each occasion the light responded in the same way.

Project director Leif Havik became acutely aware of the playful character of the lights after a small red globe unexpectedly spun around his feet upon leaving the caravan HQ one evening in February 1984. He also discovered that observers would invariably see unidentified lights when they were caught off guard, usually with their cameras out of reach (something that F.W. "Fred" Holiday found occurred at Loch Ness to monster watchers there). For this reason he gave up taking a camera around with him, knowing it would invite a better response from the phenomenon.

Worse still was the way the aerial lights appeared to be mocking them, for on some occasions the light configurations would cluster to form the obvious appearance of earthly imagery. Once they formed themselves into a Christmas tree pattern, and during another aerial spectacle a cluster of lights formed into a clear representation of Marilyn Monroe in her classic billowing dress pose from the film *Seven Year Itch*.

There are many other cases where mysterious lights have appeared to respond to human interaction (and these I cite in my sequel to *The Circlemakers*, entitled *Alien Energy*, published in 1994). Could it really be possible that some component of the aerial lights responds to the emotions and thoughts of human consciousness?

"But how can earthlights as packets of exotic energy explain the structured craft, the humanoids, the abductions?" was the question poised by Paul Devereux in his ground-breaking book *Earth Lights Revelation*.[1] How indeed?

Pondering deeply upon this problem with long time colleague and friend, John Merron, in the lounge of my home in Leigh-on-Sea, Essex, that afternoon, in the wake of a raucous and rather over indulgent party the previous night to celebrate my 35th birthday, I received a few rare moments of insight, which I hastily scribbled down and later wrote up to form the basis of this chapter. John, it must be pointed out, worked alongside Paul Devereux and geologist Paul McCartney as part of the Dragon Project in the early 1980s. It was John who helped initiate the rock crushing experiments quoted in *Earth Lights Revelation*, whereby the team was able to photograph tiny spheres of light escaping from granite cores just moments before they shattered into pieces.

Yet my thoughts were now on a very important UFO event that occurred in West Essex in 1974. The date was Sunday, October 27, and the time was around ten o'clock in the evening when a white Vauxhall Victor left the town of Hornchurch and turned east on to the secluded country lanes of Rainham and Aveley. In the driving seat was a 29-year-old man named John Day, a joiner by trade and a warm and friendly character of East London descent. Next to him was his wife, Sue, and in the back seat were the couple's three young children, two of whom were curled up, fast asleep. The normal 20-minute journey from Sue's parents in Harold Hill to their home in nearby Aveley was being paced as there was a play on television John wanted to see, and there were no videoplayers in those days.

The quiet country lane was bordered on either side by intermittent hedgerow, broken only by a few, more welcoming features, such as the public house they had passed some minutes before, and the odd terraced cottage, here and there. Quite unexpectedly Kevin, aged just seven, caught sight of a roughly oval mass of electric-blue light moving across their line of vision at some height in front of the car. It passed overhead at an angle that necessitated John craning his head to watch the light disappear from view. As the sighting occurred, Kevin rose excitedly to a standing position and grabbed hold of the two front seats to support himself. On either side, his sister, aged eight, and his younger brother, aged four, lay curled up asleep, totally oblivious to the commotion going on in their midst.

The fateful journey continued for another mile with Kevin still standing up and looking out for the strange light, before the vehicle turned a right-hand corner, marked by a row of four terraced houses lying back from the road. Suddenly the car began to act oddly as John and Sue saw in front of them a thick bank of luminous green mist, filling the road from one side to the other. A sense of unreality overwhelmed the interior of their vehicle as simultaneously the engine died, the lights failed, and the car radio crackled, smoked, and faded, causing John to wrench out its wires to prevent a fire. A dreamy silence followed, without even

36. The road in West Essex where, on October 27, 1974, the Day family lost three hours of their lives.

37. Sketch of the luminous green mist engulfing the road at Aveley, West Essex, as drawn by John Day in 1977.

the sound of the tires rolling over the road being heard, before the car glided helplessly into the dense wall of glowing green fog.

The family's recollection of what happened next is a little vague. Whether still moving or not, both John and Sue experienced a tingling sensation as if their hair was standing on end, and then they can remember nothing.

The next thing John recalled was the car juddering, as if the engine had restarted, and finding that they were driving past White Post Wood, some half a mile on from where they had encountered the inexplicable green mist. Sue, on the other hand, could recall the journey only as they crossed a small humpback bridge over a stream by Running Water Wood, a quarter of a mile further on from where John had first picked up the journey again. For some reason, the interior light was on, and Kevin still stood with his hands gripping the two front seats. Both John and Sue recalled feeling distinctly nauseous, weak, and decidedly tired.

"Is everybody here?" Sue remembers asking, but no more was said until after they reached their home in the small town of Aveley, several minutes later.

Switching on the television to watch the play he wanted to see, John found the channel lifeless. A little confused, he turned the tuner but found there were no programs on at all. A clock in the kitchen was consulted, but this just added to his rising anguish. It claimed the time was well past one o'clock, which just had to be wrong. However, a telephone call to the Speaking Clock confirmed that the time was accurate. Suddenly a disconcerting realization befell John and Sue as they stood there in the lounge—three hours were missing from their lives.[2]

The encounter was shut out of their minds—no one talked about it at all. Okay, so there may have been a direct link between their encounter with the glowing green fog and the lost hours, but no way was it going to be discussed. Its implications were too unnerving, so they simply let the matter drop.

Yet, in the months and then years that followed, the whole family began to change dramatically. All but the youngest son suddenly gave up eating meat. Indeed, the two young children became vegetarians *before* their parents. John, a smoker of 60 to 70 cigarettes a day, screwed up his last cigarette packet and gave up completely. The same thing happened with alcoholic drinks. John, who had previously "liked a good drink," found he could no longer enjoy the taste of beer or any other sort of alcoholic beverage.

The two adults began changing in themselves, as well. From a happy-go-lucky Jack-the-lad, John became environmentally conscious, went to college to learn art and sculpture, and suddenly found he possessed an unshakable affinity with the mysteries of the past. Stone circles, ancient places of power, and the subject of ley lines and earth energies dominated his personal beliefs and interests.

Sue changed in slightly different ways. She found an affinity with the ancient magic and wisdom of our past heritage, and, as soon as the children were old enough, she became first a nurse and then a midwife, later going on to use her talents in Iraq during the first Gulf War of 1991. Both Sue and John also developed marked psychic abilities, which, although present before the encounter, seemed greatly enhanced afterwards.

Many strange events plagued the Day's Aveley home. They included poltergeist activity, spectral figures seen in the half-light of rooms, and bursts of light that were occasionally caught flitting across open spaces before vanishing from view.

Most curious of all were the incomprehensible nightmares that recurred, without explanation from 1974 onwards. They involved memories of tall figures in gray-white one-piece suits, visions of a bright room like an operating theater, and lying on a table like that found in a morgue. By now they realized that only outside help might begin to explain what was happening to them. So, in August 1977, after reading a feature in a local newspaper on my work as a UFO investigator, John Day introduced himself.

Investigations got under way, and, even though Spielberg's *Close Encounters of the Third Kind* was still a year away, I immediately concluded that these sincere, credible people might have been abducted aboard an alien spacecraft. There was no other answer in those days. Hypnotic regression sessions with distinguished London hypnotherapist Leonard Wilder followed, and in these John revealed a fantastic account of the car being lifted upwards. The rest of the story concerned a full blown abduction event on board some kind of unearthly "craft" in which there were tall alien figures wearing skintight suits with face- and head-masks. Also present were smaller, uglier characters with batlike heads and medical gowns. They were examiners of some sort.

Both John and Sue gradually pieced together their own separate ac-

38. John Day, whose family lost three hours after entering a glowing bank of green mist in the quiet lanes of West Essex in 1974.

counts of what had happened, and much of it tallied with the other's recall. John would not allow Kevin to be regressed due to his tender age, although he has since vindicated much of his parents' own accounts.

As a young and, sometimes, naïve UFO researcher who had read volumes of pulp paperbacks on the UFO phenomenon, I openly accepted the alien abduction answer to the Day family's missing time experience. This was not just because the family seemed sincere and honest but also because I desperately wanted to believe in extraterrestrial intelligences visiting our planet. Despite this desire, neither John nor Sue could recall actually seeing a "nuts and bolts" spacecraft and readily pointed this out to investigators. What's more, John retained a

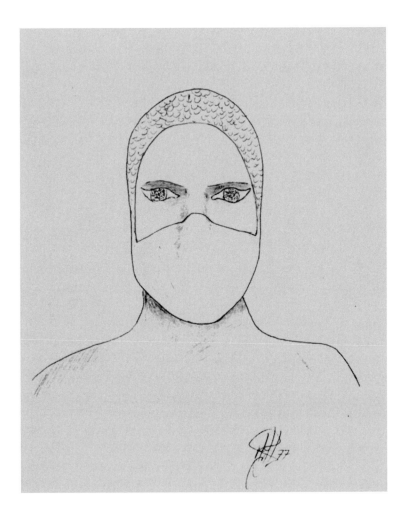

39. Face of one of the Watchers supposedly responsible for abducting the Day family in the lanes of West Essex in October 1974.

contradictory memory of looking down upon himself and his family slumped unconscious inside their own vehicle after entering the mist. Admittedly, he saw this scene in association with the interior of some kind of "craft," but even John realized that the whole event might well have been an out-of-the-body experience—for which reason he readily questioned the actual tangibility of its otherworldly interior, believing that it could have been a construct utilized for their purposes. Despite this belief, he became convinced of the absolute reality of the alien intelligence encountered during the abduction. He referred to the abductors as the Watchers and came to believe that they could communicate with him during dreams and other forms of mind contact. More curious still was John's statement, under hypnosis on Sunday, October 2, 1977, that the Watchers "need us . . . as hosts, and they know how, and they . . . and they are us."

What exactly was this supposed to mean?

In the years that followed I became good friends with John and Sue, witnessing strange phenomena in their home on several occasions. This included further poltergeist activity and the appearance, on one occasion, of a tall, silhouetted figure accompanied by a pungent smell of sulfur after first light one quiet morning in late 1977. I found I could even speak to the supposed outside intelligence behind the Day's abduction through the vocal chords of both John *and* Sue, using hypnosis.

40. Extraordinary sculpture entitled "The Quicksands of Kether" created by John Day following his abduction experience.

Through his mental contact with the Watchers, John was able to learn a considerable amount of information about many matters previously unknown to him. This information included a number of examples of what might be described as future technology, based on its apparent use by the family's abductors, including an ion drive system, which supposedly powered the "craft," as well as various mechanical or computer-like games shown to him by the Watchers.

Through visionary experiences and further dreams, John also came to believe that the Watchers had interacted with the human race in prehistoric times and that some people were their descendants, a concept that led John to refer to them as the Forefathers. Even more obscure was that Sue retained a memory of asking one of the tall figures his name, to which he had replied "I am Ceres." Ceres, as all crop watchers will know, is the classical goddess of corn and the harvest as well as an unwritten patroness of the crop circle enigma. The role played by this alien Ceres was, it seemed, to create the music of the spheres.

As completely absurd as this situation may now seem to the outsider, the Aveley couple were decent and honest people who possessed great wisdom and a profound understanding of life. Yet, somehow, they seemed linked through mental processes with an exterior intelligence connected in some way to the UFO phenomenon. For example, John, in particular, was able to predict UFO events—not to order, but with an uncanny accuracy on occasions. One night in 1978 John felt that the Watchers would make a return visit to the same location as their original encounter in 1974. Sure enough, driving along that very same stretch of road a few nights later, both he and Sue witnessed a dense mass of blue-white light on the ground, close to a small reservoir encircled by trees. There was at least one independent witness to this event.

In spite of this confirmatory evidence of his contactee claims, John remained happy to accept that he never actually boarded a physical spacecraft, but instead underwent a subjective, though truly alien contact in some form of astral domain. This was a very bold statement from someone whose memory clearly held the vivid recall of a full-blown abduction experience.

In the light of our new knowledge concerning orgone energy, plasma-based exotic light forms, and the crop circle enigma, the Day family's encounter with the luminous green mist, their loss of three hours, the changes in their life pattern, and the contactee experiences can all, I feel, be viewed from a revolutionary new perspective. Indeed, I would not be the first to suggest such a possibility, for in their 1989 book *Crop Circles: A Mystery Solved*, Jenny Randles and Paul Fuller said virtually the same thing about the Aveley Abduction, as the case became known, when they suggested: "There is no doubt that these people were completely sincere . . . (So) Why not work on the premise that the family encountered some sort of atmospheric vortex and suffered unconsciousness after driving off the road?"[3] While agreeing with their sentiments, I would question their conclusion.

Instead, let us suppose that the Day family encountered a fully manifested plasma–based construct on the open road near their Essex home. To them it appeared initially as an aerial blue oval mass and then, afterwards, as a dense green wall of luminosity upon the ground (or there were two quite separate objects—one blue, the other green). Whether it was of atmospheric or terrestrial origin is difficult to establish, although a number of mysterious lights have been reported in the area over the years.

Close encounters with this sort of intense light form are known to inflict severe effects upon both percipients and the surrounding environment. These encounters have almost always been likened to the resultant effects of exposure to a powerful electromagnetic field. Ufologists in the past have, therefore, suggested that such fields are perhaps a by-product of the near proximity of the UFO. More recently, Terence Meaden, Jenny Randles, and Paul Fuller have argued that such electromagnetic effects are the result of a circle–making plasma vortex, but today they might easily be seen as an outward manifestation of orgone— "the medium in which light moves and electromagnetic and gravitational fields exert force," or so Reich believed.[4]

In the case of the Day family, the direct effects of encountering such a powerful electromagnetic field produced by the exotic light form were, I would suspect, the vehicle's engine cutting out, the car headlights and radio dying, and the sense of unreality, as if entering a fantasy realm (the so–called "oz factor" as Jenny Randles has termed it). As with so many other cases of this nature, the closer they came to the light form, the worse the situation became.

When the car coasted into the green mist at an estimated speed of 30 mph, the physiological effects began with a distinct tingling sensation, followed immediately by a total blackout and then, finally, as the journey recommenced, nausea, weakness, and acute tiredness.

So far the Aveley case parallels exactly the expected sequence of electromagnetic effects generally associated with UFO close encounters, as proposed by the Canadians Michael Persinger and Gyslaine Lafrenière in 1983. They suggest that, at first, the observer will encounter only a simple light manifestation. But then, on moving in closer, he/she will begin to make out detail, such as shape, structure, and design. Even closer and he/she will enter into the powerful field of electromagnetism emitted by what they term the "space–time transient." What results are physical effects such as a tingling sensation and goose bumps, before these progress to hair–raising and intense feelings of pressure. Still closer and the observer experiences more severe effects such as eyes watering, skin reddening or tanning, violent nausea, a severe headache, and, then, finally, as in the Aveley case, loss of consciousness. Indeed, many of these physical effects were reported by the Day family following their own encounter with the exotic light form.

At the same time the enormous electromagnetic field emanating from the light form would, so Persinger and Lafrenière believe, stimulate body organisms and affect electrically sensitive regions of the brain, in particular the temporal lobe cortex. Apparently, two areas of the temporal cortex, the hippocampus and the amygdala, are so sensitive that electrically stimulated malfunctions over short or long periods of time can induce changed or modified memory, as well as visionary states similar to drug influenced hallucinations. Persinger and Lafrenière believe the effects of this stimulation can include altered states of consciousness, distortions of time and space, supernatural visitations, meaningful messages, and a drastic updating of post–memory recall to accommodate the dramatic effects produced by such altered states. It might also result in out-of-body experiences. Similar effects have been produced under laboratory conditions by artificially stimulating the hippocampus and amygdala. Near–death experiences are also considered by Persinger and Lafrenière to trigger such responses. It also seems realistic to suggest that those persons of a more sensitive, psychic nature might be affected far sooner than nonpsychics.

Similar resultant effects can be induced in psychics through direct contact with intense concentrations of energy, possibly orgone based, at places of ancient power. This is what happened to Bernard when he climbed the Wormwood Hill mound on the Gog Magog Hills in Cambridgeshire. At first he saw only bright bands of light but then came a rising tonal note, a headache, metallic taste, intense pressure, nausea, and dizziness, following which he twice experienced the first stages of an out-of-body experience as well as visionary glimpses of saffron-robed priests approaching in a ceremonial fashion. Bernard later said that, if he had not been helped away from the site, then he would have fallen unconscious to the ground and entered a vivid astral projection experience.

So what really did happen to the Day family out in the secluded country lanes of West Essex in 1974? Did they encounter a powerful electromagnetic field produced by a plasma-based light construct? Did they enter an altered state of consciousness, experience astral projection, and then take part in a subjective, though shared "alien" vision that their memory sculpted into a full abduction experience through dreams, hypnosis, and conscious recall? It is extremely likely, but that cannot possibly account for certain important elements of their story. Under hypnosis John recalled seeing himself and his family slumped unconscious in the car below. If this was part of his real, yet distorted, memory, then what happened to the family and the car during the three hours they lost from their lives? I do not believe they brought the car to a halt without crashing, before passing out and remaining slumped in their seats for three hours. The Aveley road may be quiet, but someone driving past would have seen the parked car and stopped to find out whether or not they were all right.

To add to the mystery, the very first thing the family recalled after the encounter was the vehicle juddering back to life as if being released from the effects of the electromagnetic field. They then became aware of driving along the same road, yet a full half a mile on from the position they encountered the luminous green mist (three-quarters of a mile further on in Sue's case). Their eldest son, Kevin, was still standing up in front of the rear seat, his hands on the front seats for support, and the two other children were still curled up asleep, again in the same positions they had been earlier on in the journey. It was as if the missing time had passed instantaneously without any break between entering the mist and coming out again further along the same stretch of road. If we are to accept their word as genuine, then this is the only logical solution available.

Even accepting the temporal cortex hypothesis, there are still a great many aspects of close encounters that defy explanation, such as the objective reality of many UFOs and their occupants. There exist many cases where light forms have mimicked human thought, like the example of Norway's Hessdalen lights taking on a life of their own and converging to form obvious earthly symbols such as a Christmas tree and Marilyn Monroe. Similar shape-shifting abilities have been accredited to the Will-o'-the-Wisps said to transform themselves into the desires and wishes of the lone traveler, whether it be a beautiful young girl or a crock of gold, in an attempt to lure them into the quagmire. On still other occasions, mysterious lights have guided to safety people who are lost, either after intense mists have come down, or when they have become disorientated in woodland (see my book *Alien Energy* for various examples of this phenomena).

Earthlight consciousness is most probably the result of a process called nonlocality, or quantum entanglement, which holds that a particle, if it splits, can still communicate information to its twin, even if it goes to the opposite end of the universe. If one half does one thing, the other will respond in the same way. If, then, you can imagine an infinite amount of particle twins doing this everywhere, it allows for the instant transfer of information data across any distance (the matter is being looked at today by scientists as a means of instant data transfer in quantum computing processes). Indeed, it is the only theory that makes senses of everything from telepathy to psychokinesis and even the teleportation of matter from one place to another. Quantum entanglement exists, and, in doing so, provides a means of linking our own neurological functions with the essence of exotic light forms.

As we have seen, such energy constructs, which by day might be described as metallic or milky-white disks or spheres and as mysterious lights at night, seem to be able to replicate and then rebroadcast the subconscious thought patterns of percipients. However, it remains unclear whether this process occurs individually or through the collective unconscious. This last theory, devised by distinguished Swiss psychiatrist and freethinker Carl Jung (1875-1961), states that everyone in the Western World is subject to universal, unconscious archetypes and symbols created through art, architecture, religion, mythology, and philosophy. For instance, to a devout Catholic the accepted image of the Blessed Virgin Mary is a beautiful young lady wearing a white robe with a blue wimple and over-robe. In real life, as a Jewish woman living in Palestine during the first century AD, she would never have looked this way, and yet this is our conceptual image of her after nearly 2,000 years of artistic and religious tradition, and this is the way she most often appears in visions. Similar archetypes feature again and again in UFO lore—each being slightly updated from one decade to the next as our technology steadily advances. It was a trend predicted by Jung himself in the 1950s within a ground-breaking book entitled *Flying Saucers: A Modern Myth of Things Seen in the Skies* (1959)[5] and explored later by earth mysteries guru John Michell in his book *Flying Saucer Vision* (1967).[6] Archetypes appear to act as an accepted means of direct communication between the human mind and any perceived external intelligence, whatever its origin or nature.[7]

The closer a percipient comes to a buoyant plasma light form, the stronger the nonlocality process takes hold. This, I now believe, enables the light source to transmogrify into archetypal forms reflecting the acceptance levels of the person or persons concerned. It can actually remold and transform itself into anything from a Christmas tree to Marilyn Monroe, pretty girls, crocks of gold, visions of the Virgin Mary, signs of the saints, alien spaceships, or little green men, whatever the unconscious human mind believes it is feasible to see and experience under such circumstances. These encounters will have an objective and often–physical reality that will last only for the duration of the interaction. The archetypal forms, projected by the plasma form, will afterwards either dissipate or withdraw back into the higher reaches of the electromagnetic spectrum—the only evidence for its temporary existence being whatever physical traces are left behind following the close encounter.

In our technological age these tangible visions have taken the form of encounters with aliens traveling inside spacecraft. However, the subconscious of an individual will reflect differing archetypes depending upon his or her own social or religious upbringing. In some cases these images will be accompanied with warnings of doom and destruction if mankind does not mend its wicked ways. The strange thing is that visions of the Virgin Mary say exactly the same thing as the Space People.

Taking the matter one step further, I now feel that if a percipient physically encounters a plasma–based light construct at zero distance—as the Day family would seem to have done in 1974—he or she will, through the altered states induced by temporal cortex stimulation, take an active role in this temporary environment, which I feel must encompass a five-dimensional continuum, instead of the usual four-dimensional environment on which space-time operates in the physical universe. If this assumption is correct, then it will result in noticeable distortions both of space and time, as would appear to have occurred in the Aveley case, and, indeed, in so many other reported cases of missing time and close encounter situations.

It seems that, by interacting with an exotic light form, a percipient enters into his or her own personally induced mystical experience, while at the same time temporarily breaking free from the space–time continuum. Here reside forms of life that we cannot even comprehend at this stage of human development, and their existence might well be explained by the intelligent nature of earthlights and UFOs, and the actions of alien entities seen in connection with such powerful sources of electromagnetic energy. This explanation might sound a little fantastic, but it must be remembered that orgone, as the fabric behind plasma manifestation, is not simply a low–level energy, a waveform, or a radiation; it is a building block that brings into focus other dynamic forces, such as light, electromagnetism, and gravity. It is through their manifestation that we can perceive and measure orgone, for it exists in part beyond the four dimensions of the space–time governed by the General Relativity Theory of Einstein.

In metaphysics, orgone is the fifth element, ether, but, in physics, it may be seen as the Fifth Force, the much sought–after superforce. Physicists have shown it to exist through the equations that constantly add up to a missing link in the interplay between the forces that govern the space–time continuum. As early as 1922, equations were put forward by the German mathematician Theodor Kaluza that unified electromagnetism with gravity, simply by showing they were both manifestations of a fifth–dimensional superforce. In 1926 a Swedish physicist named Oscar Klein was able to incorporate Kaluza's ideas into a quantum theory.

Re-evaluations of these so–called Kaluza–Klein or Unified Field theories by quantum physicists in the 1980s have strongly supported the concept of a superforce, but not one existing in five dimensions as conceived by Kaluza—one embracing eleven different dimensions—no more, no less. To these people, the universe was created in an eleven-dimensional state with no distinction between matter and force, only a pure ultra–dimensional energy source. Once this energy had started to disperse after the Big Bang, some of the dimensions curled into themselves, leaving only four—three of space and one of time—to create the physical universe.

This is a currently held view concerning the construction and mechanics of *our* universe. So can this eleven-dimensional, or fifth-dimensional (i.e. multi-dimensional), superforce really be the structure behind the bioenergy named by Reich as orgone—the same mass-free energy arguably behind the creation of genuine crop circles and "saucer nests"? Is this also responsible for the distortions in space-time experienced during missing time experiences?

Orgone exists in different forms throughout the universe and is the only force that is consistent in all dimensions—those we know and those we'll never know. We will only ever be aware of its echoes, and these we will perceive in terms of supernatural phenomena and mystical experiences.

Yet, aside from the alien abduction scenario, I have the feeling that these multi-dimensional experiences may also be the answer to another age-old enigma—the stories of people encountering the fairy folk. Many such cases are recorded in folklore and usually tell of a person in a grassy knoll entering an illuminated door that has never before been seen. Inside, they find the elven folk singing and dancing in a magic circle and serving all kinds of exotic food and drink. When, after what seems like only a few hours, they leave the mound and return home, many days, weeks, even years are found to have mysteriously gone by. Respected French UFO author Jacques Vallee was the first to note the obvious comparisons between encounters with the fairy folk and UFO occupant cases in his landmark book *Passport to Magonia* (1968).

American writer Washington Irving's classic story of Rip Van Winkle (1819), who encounters strangely dressed men that offer him some of their liquor, following which he falls asleep against a tree and wakes up 20 years later without having aged a day, could well have been based on an Orcadian folk story. It tells of a drunken fiddler from Stenness in the Scottish Orkney Isles who hears strange music coming from a mound, actually a barrow called Salt Knowe, near the Ring of Brodgar stone circle. Inside he finds *trowes* (trolls) in revelry, and so he plays his fiddle for two hours before returning home, only to find that he has been missing for 70 years and that everyone he used to know is now dead. Washington Irving's father came from the Orkney Isles, and so there is every possibility that he had heard this story when in his youth.

John Aubrey's account of the "shepherd of Winterbourne Basset," who encounters fairies on Hackpen Hill in Wiltshire should also be recalled here. He approached a "Fairy Hill," from which strange music emanated.

41. Painting of an elf created by fantasy artist Brian Froud in 1976.

The ground then opened up, and the shepherd was taken "strange places" underground where the fairies played on "viols and lutes." It was said that he "got no good" of his visit to fairyland "for never any after-wards enjoy themselves." So, did the poor fellow, in fact, encounter a plasma–based construct out on Hackpen Hill that induced within him a mystical experience that was truly out of this world? That it was said to have taken place within a "Fairy Hill," a Bronze Age round barrow most probably, suggests that the power source behind this manifestation was the orgone potential of the mound itself, as was most likely the case with Bernard's otherworldly experience on the Wormwood Hill mound in Cambridgeshire. All of these episodes derive from the same root cause.

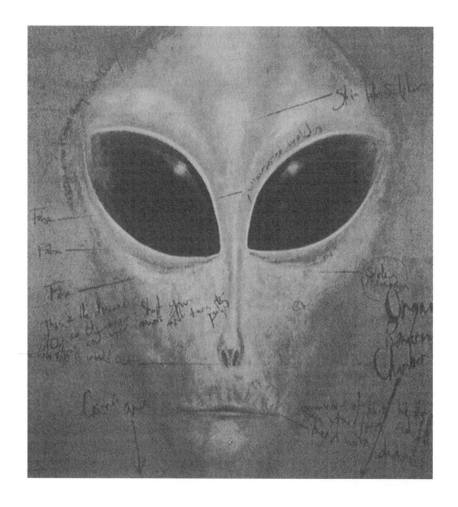

42. Crop artist Rod Dickinson's interpretation of an alien gray.

Linking this story directly with the UFO phenomenon is the fact that, in 1977, witnesses from Haverford West in Dyfed, South Wales, watched as a "round flat disk, whitish in color," seemed to travel out to sea and "crash" into an offshore rocky outcrop named Stack Rocks. Moving in to take a closer look, the gathered crowd saw two small silver-clad humanoids walking about on the uneven surface of the rock, even though the object seen earlier had now disappeared. What happened next is bizarre, for they then saw "a door opening and shutting fairly rapidly on the right-hand side of the rock face," around which there appeared to be a "shimmering haze." One of the entities repeatedly entered inside the opening, the size of a household door, and seemed to walk up and down unseen steps actually within the rock. Eventually, both the humanoids and the mysterious door entrance vanished abruptly.[8]

If I am not mistaken, this imaginary door in Stack Rocks with its "shimmering haze" parallels almost exactly the very similar mysterious doors that appear out of nowhere on the sides of fairy mounds, when previously none had been seen. These doors, remember, are said to lead down to the neverworld, the realm of fairy.

Another perfect example of a UFO looking like a fairy hill is recorded by Carl Jung in his book *Flying Saucers: A Modern Myth of Things Seen in the Sky*.[9] The case concerns a flying saucer contactee named Orfeo Angelucci, author of a book entitled *The Secret of the Saucers* (1955).[10] Following a trigger sighting in 1946 and an initial close encounter in May 1952, Angelucci—a mechanic with Lockheed Aircraft Corporation at Burbank, California—felt unwell one day two months later and so made the decision to take a day off work. The date was July 23, 1952, and Angelucci decided to go for a walk. On the way home, at an isolated spot, the same strange sensations that had overwhelmed him during his first close encounter suddenly returned. With these sensations came "the dulling of consciousness I had noted on that other occasion," i.e. a state of awareness, a precondition of what Jung referred to as "the occurrence of spontaneous psychic phenomena." I shall leave Jung's words to describe what happened next:

> Suddenly he saw a luminous object on the ground before him, like an "igloo" or a "huge, misty soap bubble." This object visibly increased in solidity, and he saw something like a doorway leading into a brightly lit interior. He stepped inside, and found himself in a vaulted room, about eighteen feet in diameter. The walls were made of some "ethereal mother-of-pearl stuff."[11]

What followed was an onboard experience in which, after the closure of the door, Angelucci was supposedly whisked into orbit around

the planet and told by an etheric voice that hate, selfishness, and cru-
elty "rise from many parts of it like a dark mist." The vehicle then climbed
into deep space, and he saw out of a porthole a crystalline UFO about
1000 feet long and 90 feet thick from which emanated a sweet music
that brought "visions of harmoniously revolving planets and galaxies."
He was told also that, because of his physical weakness, he had "spiritual gifts," the reason why "heavenly beings could enter into communication with him." It was due to the presence of the second UFO,
Angelucci was informed, that he could not only experience the music
but also hear the voice.

After further visions, in which he saw his life lie clear before his eyes
and thought that he was about to die, Angelucci "came to himself once
again" and was borne back to earth. On alighting from the strange object, which was where he had encountered it originally, it "suddenly
vanished without trace." Later, he noticed a burning sensation on the
left side of his chest and found a stigma the size of a 25¢ coin, "an
enflamed circle with a dot in the middle." This, he interpreted, as a "symbol for the hydrogen atom." Following the encounter Angelucci's life
changed forever, as he became a contactee preaching the gospel of the
saucers.

Others might doubt the authenticity of such an encounter with a
grounded lightform, that was simply a 1950s model of the fairy hill. Yet,
for me, this account has all the hallmarks of a classic encounter with a
plasma construct—its etheric nature, the visions and sweet music, and
the downloads of wisdom and knowledge. Although I have little doubt
that the experience was real, I do not believe for one second that the
object took off and went into deep space. The whole thing occurred on
the ground where Angelucci entered within the construct, which, in
accordance with flying saucer lore of that period, became a space vehicle that could journey into space. Why he interpreted his stigmatic
mark as a "symbol for the hydrogen atom" is baffling, although such
statements are typical of the strange pseudoscience preached by
contactees following close encounters of this kind.

Going back to southern England, what about Aubrey's schoolmaster,
Mr. Hart, who encountered a "fairy dance" on the downs beyond Yatton
Keynell? What happened to him? He said that "pigmies," or "very small
people," had "pinch'd him all over" and were making "all maner of small
noyses." Did he, too, encounter a plasma energy construct and suffer

visionary experiences based on his own era's comprehension of such unique interactions with fifth–dimensional environments? Remember, his experience had lasted nonstop from "neere darke" through until the sun rose the following morning, which even around midsummer's eve, the shortest night of the year, would suggest a period of at least six hours.

In British folklore fairy rings were thought to be not only where elves and fairies gathered and danced their merry *roundelays* ('fairy circles'), but also gateways into the elfin kingdom, which is why it was ill advisable to step inside one, lest you be spirited away to the fairy realm. Although the terms "fairy ring" or "fairy dance" were usually applied to rings of dark discoloration in grassy areas caused by fungi, we know from the account of Gwen Horrigan that in the English Cotswolds as late as the 1940s the name was applied also to crop circles. How fitting, therefore, that the crop circles of yesteryear were thought of as portals into the fairy kingdom? I am sure that many circles enthusiasts would consider modern circles as potential sites for UFO experiences, and, if the orgone solution to at least some of their number is correct, then the connection is not without foundation.

43. Poor fellow plucked from a fairy ring just before his final abduction by fairies.

There appears to be little difference between the fairy encounters of the past and the alien abduction scenario of today—we have simply updated our expectations of the phenomenon. But now we are able to view these profound human experiences as much more than just the delusions of weak-minded people. No, they are far more important than we could have ever imagined.[12]

An understanding of exotic light forms as plasma constructs, similar to Constable's vision of his "critters," or orgone "bioforms," not only offers an explanation for the appearance of crop circles and UFOs, but it also takes us closer to comprehending the abduction experience, both in the past and in the present day. More than this, it opens up the possibility of time distortions, time lapses, and episodes occurring outside of normal space–time since orgone exists across all dimensions, not simply in our own space–time.

Yet, even though sentience and intelligence have been accredited to plasma constructs and exotic light forms, are they really alive? Trevor James Constable, in assigning them the name "bioforms," implies that they are manifestations of biological life in their own right. Yet this cannot be right, as the term "biological" refers only to organic life that has evolved from the chemical proteins that come together to form DNA and RNA, the building blocks of life on earth. If exotic energy constructs are really sentient life forms, then we must look for evidence of "life" of a quite different kind—one that can inhabit a plasma-based environment. As we shall see in the next chapter, written in July 2008, nearly 17 years after writing the one you have just read, this is exactly what scientists are now discovering in the first decade of the twenty-first century.

44. Fairy lights would take on whatever form necessary to lure victims into the quagmire.

23

Plasma Life
and the Fifth Dimension

Life may exist outside the standard carbon model—that is the opinion of V.N. Tsytovich of the General Physics Institute at the Russian Academy of Science in Moscow. Working alongside colleagues from the Max-Planck Institute for Extraterrestrial Physics in Garching, Germany, and the University of Sydney, Australia, he has determined that under certain conditions nonorganic substances, essentially microscopic dust, can combine to form complex mixtures that bear distinct evidence of self-organization. Normally, physicists might see such structures as simply random, but Tsytovich and his colleagues have noted that microscopic strands of these solid particles seem to twist into corkscrew shapes, or helical structures, which, because they are electrically charged, become attracted to each other. Not only do these strands appear intuitively to organize themselves, like to like, but they can change in a manner reminiscent of biological molecules, such as DNA proteins, the building blocks of carbon-based life.

These inorganic self-organizing strands are able also to divide, or bifurcate, making copies of themselves. They, in turn, interact with other strands to form new structures able to induce changes in their neighbors and even evolve into more complex structures, leaving less able

189

ones to dissolve, or break down, like some kind of natural order in which only the fittest survive, an act reminiscent of biological life. Thus, it becomes conceivable that under certain conditions, this self–organization of inorganic matter constitutes evidence for the existence of new types of life outside of the carbon–based model.

In themselves these findings are incredible, since it was under very similar circumstances that biological life on earth came about some 3.65 billion years ago. Yet, there is one important additional fact about the existence of these self–organizing strands of inorganic matter important to this debate—they can exist only in plasma, the fourth state of matter, something which might need some explanation. Solid objects constitute the first state of matter, and, when they are heated, they become liquid, the second state of matter. When liquid is heated, it becomes gas, which is the third state of matter. All three coexist together in the universe and can shift from one to the other with relative ease, most obviously through heat and compression. However, there is a fourth state of matter, and this is plasma, the very stuff making up everything from lightning, to ball lightning, exotic light forms, even the flame of a fire, if through heat it becomes hot enough. In essence, plasma is simply ionized gas (which is composed of ions—that is atoms where an electron has broken free to leave behind a positively charged atom—as well as free electrons and neutral particles).

According to Tsytovich: "These complex, self–organized plasma structures exhibit all the necessary properties to qualify them as candidates for inorganic living matter . . . they are autonomous, they reproduce, and they evolve." He notes that the ideal plasma environments necessary to create these helical structures are most common in outer space. Thus it is possible that, within deep space, plasma–based life could well exist.

Much of the light we see coming from stars, nebula, and supernovae is plasma, while the sun itself is a 1.5–million–kilometer (932,060 miles) ball of plasma, heated by nuclear fusion. In its superheated state, plasma is also produced by collapsed stars such as black holes and neutron stars. Not only does plasma make up the accretion rings of ionized gas that surround them, but it also forms the great jets or particle beams, which shoot out along their lines of axis at close to the speed of light, causing energy releases across the electromagnetic spectrum (including ultra–high–energy cosmic rays). It has been theorized that the core of a neutron star—created when a regular star that has used up its nuclear

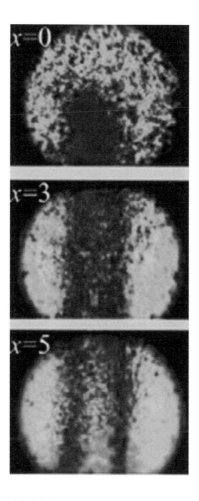

45. Helix patterns created by microscopic dust in a plasma environment.

fuels collapses to form a compact object no larger than 6–7.5 miles in diameter—consists of a special type of plasma known as quark–gluon plasma. Indeed, neutron stars are the most likely place to find quark–gluon plasma, which is thought to have filled the universe shortly after the Big Bang.

All these facts may lead to speculation that deep space objects, neu-

tron stars in particular, are a major source of plasma–based life forms
and might even be intelligent life forms in their own right. It is a theory
I have contemplated for some time now. It is one that also begs the
question of whether plasma life, if it exists, might be considered a living, thinking entity, accessible to sympathetic mental communication
with the likes of us.

Tsytovich points out that plasma can be created at the point of a
lightning strike, and since the self–organizing inorganic structures that
form in plasma—"plasmons" as Tsytovich now calls them—are so close
to the nature of biological molecules, then, perhaps, they enabled the
creation of templates for the first organic molecules, which went on to
create life on Earth. In other words, plasma life existed first and actually
caused the organization of the chemical proteins that produced the first
biological life, either here on earth or out in space. As forward thinking
as such ideas might seem, it flies in the face of the so–called exobiologi-
cal origin of life, which suggests that life came to Earth on an extraterrestrial vehicle, most probably a meteor, asteroid, or comet. This is the
so–called theory of panspermia, literally life everywhere. This said, there
is nothing to stop life that evolved from plasmons elsewhere in the
cosmos hitching a ride to Earth.[1]

Many exotic light forms, UFOs, are now believed to be plasma constructs either created in the upper atmosphere or within the earth. This
was certainly the conclusion of Norway's Project Hessdalen with respect to many of the sightings reported in the Hessdalen area in its first
year of operation.[2] Moreover, it is now known that in 1997 Britain's
Ministry of Defense (MoD) commissioned a major study—code-named
Condign—to assess the nature of UAPs ("unidentified atmospheric phenomena") and any possible threat they might pose to national security.
Following the examination of some 3,000 cases made to the MoD between 1987 and 1997, an official report was completed in 2000. It came
to 465 pages and was released to the public finally in 2006 through the
Freedom of Information Act. Its conclusion was that, although UFOs
pose no obvious threat to national security, those UFO reports that
could not be dismissed as the misinterpretation of mundane phenomena, such as the planet Venus, odd–looking clouds, aircraft lights, satellites, meteors, fireballs, etc., were most likely "buoyant plasmas," i.e.
exotic plasma constructs held together by electromagnetic fields.[3]

Even though the British MoD saw no threat posed by UFOs to
Britain's air defenses, other than any problems that might arise from

them appearing in the proximity of aircraft and helicopters during take-offs and landings, they failed to consider the likely sentience of these "buoyant plasmas." In many instances, exotic light forms have responded to observers, appeared on command, or acted in a manner suggesting intuitive thinking. As mentioned before, mysterious lights have even guided people who are lost to safety, and this activity strongly suggests a form of sentient intelligence. Some of these cases might be explained in terms of unconscious telekinetic manipulation on the part of the witnesses involved, yet was it remotely possible that the newly found plasmons are the basis of a more complex life force existing within exotic light forms? Might plasma constructs be able to act in an intelligent manner, communicate and relate to each other, and even interact with us?

As we have seen, powerful electromagnetic fields of the sort thought to be generated by exotic light forms can seriously affect the brain, causing strong physiological effects, such as nausea, black outs, and radiation sickness as well as serious psychological effects, such as hallucinations, delusions, and near-death experiences. Moreover, the closer you get to these light forms, the more space-time becomes distorted before finally ceasing to function in a normal manner. Today there really is good evidence that such warps in space-time are associated with plasma environments.

Quantum scientists and particle physicists have been attempting to confirm the existence of multiple dimensions since the coming together of the Kaluza–Klein or Unified Field theory of quantum physicists in the 1980s and the construction of billion–dollar particle accelerators such as the Large Hadron Collider (LHC) in Geneva, which will aid us in detecting echoes of the fifth dimension if it really exists. However, in 2007 a team of Hungarian researchers announced that, in their opinion, deep space might already provide the strongest evidence not just for the existence of the fifth dimension, but also its suspected effects on space-time, with the key being the extreme gravity existing within certain deep space objects.

Scientists at the Research Institute for Particle and Nuclear Physics in Budapest are focusing their attentions on a strange star system known as Cygnus X-3, composed of a collapsed compact star, thought to be a neutron star or a so-called strange quark star, in a tight orbit with a large, bloated main sequence star, like our own sun. The former steals, or accretes, helium gas from the surface of the latter, which is then superheats to create an accretion disk of super hot plasma (ionized gas) around its equator. Excess matter is sporadically ejected from the compact star along its line of axis as powerful particle jets that penetrate deep space, reaching out to distances of up to tens of light years.

Gergely Gabor Barnaföldi and collaborators P. Levai and B. Lukacs, the Hungarian research team involved in the work, investigated whether a state of extreme gravity exists through the tension caused by the close proximity of the two individual components of Cygnus X–3. With the working hypothesis that it does, they surmised that this gravitational field would be strong enough to force an interplay between the normally inactive fifth dimension and the quark–gluon plasma forming the core of the neutron star. The result is the production of exotic forms of subatomic particles known as strange quarks. These quarks then penetrate through the surface of the object and collide with other types of subatomic particles produced in normal space–time, creating ultra-high–energy cosmic particles with unique characteristics called "cygnets." These particles, seemingly, have been detected hitting the earth and penetrating deep underground.[4]

Barnafoldi and his collaborators consider that extreme gravity enables the fifth dimension, which exists normally as curled up "rings" or "folds," to uncurl and come into play within our own space–time. In the physical universe, the fifth dimension is not known to affect matter, but, where strange quark stars are concerned, normal quarks are made to behave like strange quarks, which are forced to move more slowly through 4D space–time, since they need to curl around the folds of fifth-dimensional space. This activity actually produces a certain stability within the star.[5]

If a fifth-dimensional state does exist within deep space objects, such as the suspected neutron star Cygnus X–3, and such environments are also ripe for plasma-based life, then it is possible that a very similar environment might exist within some buoyant plasmas, i.e. exotic light forms of the sort that exist in our skies. How might this be possible? The answer is the manner in which these object's powerful electromagnetic fields exert themselves on the core of the plasma construct, which may cause gravitational distortions that, in turn, uncurl fifth-dimensional environments. Thus, anyone or any object actually entering or coming into contact with plasma constructs of this type will enter a fifth-dimensional environment and suffer the consequences.

It is possible, therefore, that, in addition to being nonbiological, sentient life forms in their own right, the exotic light forms can warp space-time through the presence inside them of fifth–dimensional environments. If missing time abduction experiences, like that experienced by the Day family in Essex during 1974, are real, then the only explanation *is* that both the car and its occupants were, quite literally, temporarily removed from normal space-time, after entering a fifth dimensional realm, and then released from this hold after having lost three hours of their life and half a mile of their journey. In other words, the time for them passed instantly, even though they were missing from normal space-time for three whole hours.

In many cases of missing time, what the percipient or percipients recall bears no relation to the length of time that goes missing from their lives. For instance, the book *The Missing Seven Hours* (1978) by American writer David Haisell recounts the story of a "repeater" UFO witness named Gerry Armstrong (pseudonym). He had moved from the United Kingdom to Jackson Point, Canada, in 1967, where he settled down with his wife Susan. Here he experienced various UFO sightings, which brought him into contact with investigator David Haisell in 1973—a meeting that eventually led to the writing of the book.

It is, however, Armstrong's first UFO encounter that is of relevance here. It took place at the age of twelve, when he lived with his family in Sydenham on the outskirts of southeast London. According to him, in July 1953 he attended a summer camp with teachers and other children at an undisclosed location in the county of Kent. On one of the days he, a teacher, and around 30 to 40 other children went on a field trip. The party crossed fields, valley, woods, and forests, and around one in the afternoon they came upon an old, disused quarry. A game of hide-and-seek was organized, enabling Armstrong to sneak off on his own. He found a suitable tree, which provided shade from the sunlight, and here opened a pack of five cigarettes. Slipping one out, he lit it, and then something odd occurred. As he recalled to David Haisell: "And then nothing. Blackness. Dark. Very very dark. Voices. 'Over here,' was the first thing I heard. 'Over here Mr. Rice. Found him, sir. Put that cigarette out, Gerry. Rice is coming.' And this is the crazy thing. I had my cigarette and it was still burning, and I still had four in the pack."[5]

On their arrival at the scene, the school teacher and the other children questioned Armstrong as to where he had been, for he was quickly informed that he had been missing for seven hours. The time was now nine o'clock, and it was almost dark. The twelve-year-old had absolutely no recall of what had happened, since for him no time at all had passed. His story completely baffled everyone, for apparently they had made a thorough search of the location soon after they realized he was missing, but he simply was not there.

Armstrong was helped back to the camp and later examined by a doctor who found that he had dilated eyes and an unaccountable sore on his neck. The symptoms, however, were diagnosed as the result of sunstroke. All Armstrong recalls at the time was being in a dreamlike state and so simply accepted the doctor's prognosis. Finally, he was allowed to return to the dormitory, where he quickly fell into a deep sleep. The next day he felt much better and rejoined the other children for regular activities.

Thinking nothing more of the incident, Armstrong carried on with his life but soon began experiencing UFO sightings on a fairly frequent basis. He also suffered a recurring dream which implied that his missing seven hours were due to an abduction scenario, and that, before he blacked out, some kind of alien entity had approached him as he leaned against the tree smoking the cigarette.

This is obviously a curious story, without any ready answers. Yet, for me, the most important facet of the case is the cigarette itself, for Armstrong seemed sure that the one he was smoking when the darkness came was the same one he was smoking seven hours earlier, when his friend called for him to stub it out as the teacher was on his way. Thus, if we can take Armstrong's testimony at face value, then it clearly implies that the seven hours went missing instantaneously, and that he was thrust from one moment to the next without actually spending the intervening time at the actual location of the incident. This conclusion is substantiated by the fact that the disused quarry was searched during the intervening seven hours.

This episode was the same as what happened to the Day family in 1974—the time had gone missing instantaneously, strongly suggesting that, in some abduction scenarios, the percipient or percipients involved are quite literally removed from the earth plane and then replaced back as if they had been shunted from one moment in time to the next, evidenced from the fact that they had "disappeared" from the place of their abduction during the intervening period. If this is correct, then such encounters might last anything from a few hours to a few days, or perhaps even a number of years if fairy encounters are to be believed, during which time the percipients will, quite frankly, cease to exist in normal space–time. Moreover, it becomes clear that should plasma life exist, then just maybe there is a very real intelligence at the core of such "abduction" experiences. Plasma life becomes the true face of genuine alien encounters, which through the process of quantum entanglement can interact with us by creating believable fifth–dimensional environments that our minds can accept as feasible under such extreme circumstances.

I think that, should it exist, plasma life is more than simply a disparate sentience within each individual light construct. I suspect that its individual intelligence might well be linked through quantum entanglement, not just with that of other plasma light forms but also plasma environments in deep space, such as the cores of neutron stars. Through nonlocal processes, individual sentience can be transmitted from one plasma cluster to another, meaning that a plasma construct encountered here on earth might contain or be linked with plasma life elsewhere in the galaxy, the universe, or even in parallel universes. It might even be possible that plasma constructs serve as portals, or warps in the fabric of space–time, transferring matter from one plasma environment to another, allowing for the possibility that some UFOs and aliens might well be able to take on a temporarily physical existence in this world.

Thus percipients involved either in close encounter or full–blown abduction experiences, when entering inside the fifth–dimensional realm of the light construct, become part of a two–way communication process with plasma life, which I feel is truly alien in every sense, since they are not of this earth and are not organic, carbon–based life forms. Yet, since their building blocks, the "plasmons" of V.N. Tsytovich, are so similar to the natural organization of our own building blocks of life and the two might even share a common origin, there is a clear relationship between the two, quite separate, forms of life. In other words, we are related in some obscure manner with plasma life, one of the reasons why perhaps it seems so interested in our evolution.

Once again, the processes of quantum entanglement would come into play to enable this interplay to take place, both in surviving our entry and exit into the fifth–dimensional environment, which is, I suspect, like a form of instant matter transfer, or teleportation, and the processes allowing our brains to link entirely with the world created for the duration of the abduction encounter. In most modern cases, this world will be the interior of a technologically advanced space craft, the sort of thing we would expect any advanced interstellar race to possess. Yet, in reality, it is a fake, formed, and constrained simply for the purposes of the two-way interaction to take place.

Thus, what we perceive to be alien beings, or indeed any other type of communicating being, is most likely the collective "mind" of plasma life forms, broadcast into our brains during extreme close encounters—the appearances of such entities dictated by earthly preconceptions of otherworldly contact, which in the modern day is perceived as space aliens. In the past it was, of course, fairies, angels, divinities, or perhaps even ancestor spirits that we would expect to see under such circumstances. Tomorrow, with our advances in understanding alien contact, the mask worn by plasma life forms could well be something else. Perhaps it will be based around the very valid idea that alien intelligences come not from outer space, but via inner space, the space between spaces, a concept very brilliantly aired at the end of the fourth, Spielberg-directed Indiana Jones film "Indiana Jones and the Kingdom of the Crystal Skull" (2008).

Have you noticed how the exterior and interior details of flying saucers have changed from those reported in connection with the earliest contactee cases in the late 1940s, early 1950s, progressively through to the vehicles involved in alien abductions in the 1980s and 1990s? Have you noticed how the computers and control panels of the earliest flying saucers are simply ridiculous looking today when compared against our own advanced technology? This is because those individual details in the flying saucers never really existed—they were thought constructs, temporarily physical in some instances, created to impress the contactees of the time, based on conceivable future technology at the time. Remember, in the nineteenth and early twentieth century, the unidentified aerial vehicles were dirigibles complete with propellers, under slung cockpits, and entities looking like the earliest airmen. The phenomenon updates according to how we currently perceive future technology and advanced intelligence.

So I ask again, in 2008, what really happened to the Day family back in 1974? In my opinion, the closer their vehicle got to the glowing green mist, the more the family was affected by a powerful electromagnetic field (shown by the nausea and unreality of the situation, the so-called "Oz factor") emanating from the manifested plasma light source. It caused a form of astral detachment from their physical bodies, similar to a near-death experience, evidenced by John momentarily glimpsing himself slumped over the wheel of the car, his wife next to him. The onboard experience was quite simply out of this world—the whole thing taking place in a created construct and ending only with the gradual breakdown of the plasma light form. This breakdown severed the link with the construct's fifth-dimensional state and the plasma-based alien intelligence existing in this environment—the consequences being three hours missing from the family's lives, their car being thrust outside of space-time, and deep changes within them that gradually evolved their world thereafter.

Such experiences are going to leave the witnesses' heads with such a powerful view of alternative dimensions that the brain almost certainly blocks it out for sanity reasons. We also cannot rule out the possibility that the truly alien intelligence behind the experience initiated this loss of memory. These are all just thoughts and opinions. However, everything I have proposed is all quite feasible through our ever-advancing knowledge of quantum physics, astrophysics, and the subatomic world. There is nothing here which is entirely outside the realms of scientific understanding. This is not to say I don't believe in physical aliens and UFOs, only that to try and understand the mechanics of such experiences we need first to look at what we do know as opposed to what we don't. I urge ufologists and crop circle enthusiasts to embrace some of these ideas and work with them. I also advocate a better understanding of plasma physics, which I strongly sense holds the key not just to alien interaction and the UFO phenomenon but also to teleportation across inner space.

And why is orgone so important? I sense that it is, in fact, the only medium that is constant across multiple dimensions, even though we do not become aware of its direct presence until its potential is registered within the known ranges of the electromagnetic spectrum. Free-thinkers and even science writers have linked it with little understood power sources such as zero-point energy and, more recently, dark energy—both being little understood components of the physical universe. Yet, in all honesty, orgone is as enigmatic now as it was when Wilhelm Reich first started to notice its effects upon our world in 1939.

No one can really define its nature, and for most scientists it simply does not exist. I view it as the multi–dimensional framework, the constant medium, that holds together the core of the plasma construct, whether manifest or not.

Alien abductions are not as straight forward as most people like to think. Seeing them all as purely physical experiences relating to flesh and blood extraterrestrials and "nuts and bolts" spacecraft is, in my opinion, naive. Only by investigating revolutionary new concepts such as the possibility of plasma life, fifth–dimensional environments, and their relationship to life on earth can we hope to truly understand what is going on out there.

24

Blowing Out the Brains

Direct interaction with a plasma–based light form has more serious effects upon the percipient or percipients involved than what has so far even been considered within these pages. I suspect that exposure to life forms existing within a fifth–dimensional environment leaves you with more than just a headache or a bad case of nausea after the event. The evidence points towards the disturbing fact that close encounters and abductions brought on by such multi–dimensional interactions rearranges and reprograms certain neurological functions in the brain's temporal lobe cortex to create lasting changes. It is what might be referred to in religion as "seeing the light" or enlightenment. In other words the percipient or percipients involved can be quite literally rewired, "illuminated."

Blowing out the brains in the manner suggested could explain the dramatic changes in lifestyles and spiritual beliefs experienced by the Day family following their encounter with the oval blue light and glowing green fog in the lanes of West Essex in 1974, for they, too, literally "saw the light." It also seems likely that exposure to buoyant plasma's strong electromagnetic field produces one further, very important alteration in the temporal lobe cortex—it sets up an open channel between plasma–based life and the observer, which is then maintained through quantum entanglement. It is a situation that gives the percipient the overwhelming impression that he or she possesses a telepathic link with the alien intelligence responsible for their UFO encounter.

As the human mind would find it difficult to comprehend the idea that it has suddenly gained a mental link with sentient exotic energy, it seems to continue to use a belief and expectation in archetypes to communicate new information gained from the life forms existing within the plasma constructs. The unfortunate, though necessary, result of such blatant rewriting by the unconscious mind will be downloads of information, which can be either meaningful or utter drivel. It will either supply the keys to quantum mechanics, future technology, and inner dimensions of existence or it will provide you with the dimensions of the mother ship orbiting the earth or the reasons why the alien nations are not making open contact with humanity quite yet.

In the case of UFO contactees, I have found that, time after time, despite the dubious identity of their communicators, they can accurately predict the appearance of unidentified aerial light phenomena. They can also supply information on the nature of UFOs and many other related paranormal events, much to their own surprise on occasions.

I have spoken already of the mass meetings in the Californian desert where flying saucer contactee George Van Tassel would channel the Space People and accurately predict the appearances of unidentified aerial lights. Do remember here that it was Van Tassel who first suggested to Trevor James Constable that the upper atmosphere was full of invisible life forms science knew nothing about. Yet Van Tassel *still believed in his own flying saucer contacts.*

John Day has been able to predict the appearances of strange lights in the same vicinity as his original 1974 encounter. He has also attained a remarkable volume of creative material on everything from future game designs to the nature of earth energies at ancient sites and even how the Watchers interfered with human evolution in the past. Under hypnosis in October 1977, John also claimed that UFOs utilized magnetic lines of force, what we might now call ley lines, for navigation and mapping purposes. Also curious was the answer John gave under hypnosis in 1977 to a question from Leonard Wilder concerning the nature of the UFOs' propulsion system, for he responded: "Very complicated, but the words I remember was ion magnetic . . . they spun, they created

. . . they spin vor . . . vortex." Was he talking about an alien spacecraft, a plasma vortex, a thought construct, or all three?

Barry King, the UFO investigator who helped investigate the Aveley case, was a good friend of mine as well as an alleged abductee himself. After three close encounters *before* he met John Day, I used hypnosis on Barry in early 1978, which helped him recall his supposed onboard experiences. Yet it also did something else. As was the case with John and Sue Day, he found that the apparent entities responsible for his experiences could take control of his conscious mind and speak to me using his vocal chords, a process similar to the trance mediumship of spiritualism. They claimed to be from a planet revolving around the star Merak, in the constellation of the Big Dipper, part of the Great Bear. Regularly, Barry and I would arrange hypnotic sessions, either at his home or mine, where he would fall into a trance and allow the Merak to speak through him. These sessions were during the very same period that I was speaking in a similar manner to the Watchers through the unconscious bodies of both John and/or Sue Day, and, yes, it did get confusing at times as one alien source tended to contradict the other. Almost all of the Merak material passed to Barry was, in retrospect, real crazy-man stuff. There were, however, just a few pearls of wisdom among the background din.

One significant event, which showed that Barry King's mind was in touch with an external influence connected in some manner with unidentified aerial phenomena, was very revealing indeed. It began during the evening of Wednesday, March 22, 1978, with Barry lying down in a state of hypnosis induced by me. The Merak were speaking through him in their usual stern manner, and, after relating certain other-worldly matters, I asked if they could prove their existence in the form of a UFO sighting. The assertive voice responded that they would indeed do this. I asked when, and after a few moments of prolonged silence, the Merak came back and said that the sighting would take place in exactly two weeks' time, i.e. during the evening of Wednesday, April 5. On asking where this sighting would take place, there was another pause, before the voice said, simply, "Stamford." This was the name of a town in the county of Northamptonshire, over 100 miles away from Barry's home in Dagenham, Essex. It was also somewhere we had never visited and, prior to this time, had no interest in whatsoever.

Over the next few days Barry received a clairvoyant image of where in Stamford we should be at the appointed time—it was a field out in the country somewhere, next to a stone bridge. Why there is anybody's guess. Still, the description of the site was crosschecked against an Ordnance Survey map, and sure enough there was a bridge in the exact position indicated by Barry. In addition to this information, he was told that the sighting on April 5 would take place between nine and ten o'clock, which was the same hour that the original pronouncement had been made on May 22. So confident were we that something of importance would occur between nine and ten o'clock on April 5, that I contacted the Nottingham UFO Investigation Society to tell them what was going on, and they agreed to send along sky watchers to witness the event.

The big day came, and the location near Stamford, seen only in vision by Barry, was reached by early evening. It was exactly as Barry had described beforehand. Members of the Nottingham UFO group turned up with their binoculars and cameras ready for the expected light display.

Barry and I waited as the hour in question approached and then watched as it passed by without incident. The Merak came through Barry as he rested in the back seat of the car and apologized profusely, saying that the "force of the earth" had prevented them from manifesting at the selected location. However, they insisted that they had not let us down, as would be shown in good time.

Despondent and somewhat embarrassed, the two of us returned to Essex, without realizing until later that an event of great magnitude *had* taken place between nine and ten o'clock that night. Already sighting reports were being phoned through to my parents' home at Wickford in Essex, and the following day's national newspapers were full of accounts of strange lights that had been seen in the skies over England precisely *between nine and ten o'clock that evening*. Nothing like this had been featured in the British national press for some while, highlighting the uniqueness of the situation. Yet confusing the issue somewhat was the discovery that most of the 30 or so sightings reported that night were, in fact, a bright fireball, a plasma-based meteor of considerable brilliance that had streaked across the sky that very same hour. Despite this discovery, at least some of the reports, including one photograph of a strange aerial light, were clearly not the fireball.

There were other similar events predicted by Barry King's Merak, but this one has stuck in my mind the most. Years later, when I gave up believing that I had been speaking directly to spacemen through the likes of Barry King and the Day family, I still accepted that something clearly associated with the UFO phenomenon had been influencing their minds.

I have become convinced that, due to the complexities and inadequacies of the human mind, it needs to use appropriate archetypal forms to enable recognizable communication with the raw consciousness behind exotic plasma light forms. As we have seen, since 1947 these archetypes have tended to show themselves as aliens visiting our planet in space vehicles that we see as "flying saucers" and UFOs. So, in theory, these "alien" archetypes are our creations, produced by our own social conceptions, wishes, desires, fears, and anxieties, for it is the spirit of the age.

The very same disjointed communication process is happening today in the crop circle community with psychics such as Rita Goold and Isabelle Kingston, the clairvoyant and medium who communicates with the Circlemakers under the name of "the Watchers." Whether these are the same communicators as those involved with the Day family's abduction is difficult to say, although there are many similarities in the information offered by the two quite separate sources.

In 1987 Isabelle received a message from the Watchers compelling her to move from her house in Reading, Berkshire, to a new home in the Marlborough area of Wiltshire. With her son and mother, Isabelle began a new life, and it was then that she received further psychic communications. She was told that Silbury Hill was a very important place to the Watchers and that, within a year, a sign would be seen here that would reveal to her why she had been brought to Wessex. A year later, almost to the day, during the late evening of Wednesday, July 13, 1988, a lady named Mary Freeman from Marlborough was driving through Avebury, along the road that follows the Kennet Avenue of standing stones, towards the junction with the A4 Marlborough Road. Unexpectedly, she became aware of a huge amber-colored light moving through the clouds. From its base came a tube-like beam of bright white light that struck the ground south of Silbury Hill.[1]

Mary Freeman had recently become acquainted with Isabelle Kingston and was able to convey details of this incident to her that same night.[2] A day or so later, Richard Martin, a reporter from the *Marlborough Times*, received a telephone call to say that a quintuplet set of crop circles had been found at first light in the field to the south of Silbury Hill. For Isabelle, this was her promised sign. Within eight weeks of this first crop circle event at Silbury Hill, no less than 51 crop indentations were to appear within seven miles of this area, the greatest manmade orgone accumulator in Europe. Not only did these incidents reveal why she had been drawn to the region, but they also showed the undeniable link between ancient sites, crop circles, UFOs, and the human mind.

Interestingly, John Day had also singled out Silbury Hill as a location important to the Watchers. He was shown scenes of some kind of foundation ceremony in which a sacred stone, like a shivalingam of Hindu tradition, was rested upon the apex of a protoform of the mound prior to its completion. Further layers of earth were then brought in to build up the structure, the sacred stone being removed via a small tunnel before its final completion. Exactly why he was shown this imagery was not made clear, although John came to believe that those responsible for the construction of Silbury Hill had been inspired, as he had, by direct communication with the Watchers.

At the commencement of the 1990 summer season, Isabelle Kingston was asked by psychic researcher John Haddington to recommend a likely location for a crop watch. Psychic information from the Watchers—or the Elohim as they have also referred to themselves—indicated that the fields at Alton Barnes, below the long barrow upon Walker's Hill known as Adam's Grave, should be watched, as circles would appear here. At the time this area had seemed unlikely as the nearest circle to date had been two miles away, and yet it was the only site that was specified. For several nights the fields in question were watched without success, but then, just a month later, during the night of July 12, Alton Barnes became host to the most dramatic pictogram to date. To cap it all, on that very same day a second remarkable formation was discovered above the white horse on Milk Hill, only a mile or so northwest of Adam's Grave.

During the early hours of Sunday, June 18, 1989, Rita Goold followed the written instructions of the Circlemakers and led a party of cerealogists into an already formed circle at Cheesefoot Head. It was on this occasion that they were to experience and record the sound and motions of the now famous trilling noise. At the same time a luminous object shaped like "a pair of horns" was seen high above the field in question by an observer on a nearby road, who had also heard the trilling noise.[3]

That observer was Ron Jones, a keen circles researcher from Andover in Hampshire. He later accompanied Colin Andrews and George Wingfield in their pursuit of the noise following Rita and her husband Steve's departure around 2:30 a.m.[4] The three men found themselves crossing darkened fields as they tried to trace the source of the still audible sound. At one point Ron Jones, who was trailing behind, became disturbed when he heard an inexplicable crackling noise coming from a dark silhouetted hedge by his side. Quickly he caught up with the other two and spoke of his anxiety. Some minutes later the party came to a halt some 20 to 30 yards from a clump of long grass and bushes. The trilling noise appeared to be emanating from this very position, although, for some reason, they were reluctant to go any further, deciding instead to return to their car.

After sunup a ringed circle was discovered at Cheesefoot Head, just 500 or so yards from the earlier circle where the six had sat and listened to the trilling noise. It was the first to have appeared in the whole of Britain for a period of eight days.

Precisely one week later, during the early hours of Sunday, June 25, Ron Jones retired to bed and suddenly became aware of the trilling noise once more. It was the same as before, but this time it seemed to be with him in his room. He sat up and listened as the sound spun around and around his head. The next thing he recalled was astrally projecting back to the spot beyond Cheesefoot Head where he had experienced the loud crackling noise coming from the hedge.[5]

What happened next is of paramount importance to the circles debate, for, glancing around, Ron saw a series of horizontal bands of light rotating and pulsing up–and–down above the sea of standing crop. After what seemed like an eternity in this strange state of bilocation, Ron found himself back in bed. The experience ended after he clearly heard three separate tonal notes that appeared to permeate the air around him.

What Ron did not know at the time was that a new circle with a long curved spur (giving it the appearance of a tadpole), had formed overnight at the exact position he had seen the horizontal bands of light above the standing wheat at Cheesefoot Head.

Since that time, Ron Jones has been inspired to follow some diverse, yet quite astounding lines of enquiry concerning the nature of the circles phenomenon, which I am sure he will reveal in time.

Ron's link with the phenomenon had been heightened dramatically the night he saw the luminous object, heard the trilling noise, and experienced the crackling sounds at Cheesefoot Head. This enhancement allowed a direct mental empathy with the very source of the Circlemakers through the process of nonlocality. A week later this link was strong enough to pull his consciousness to the spot where some form of exotic light source, perhaps a buoyant plasma, was discharging energy into the ground. The pulsing motion of the bands of light and, more importantly, the triple tone heard by Ron are clear indications that this was indeed the case, for they are similar indeed to the effects experienced by Bernard on the Wormwood Hill tumulus in Cambridgeshire during 1981. I now firmly believe that this contact with an ultraterrestrial intelligence enabled Ron Jones to attune to the circles phenomenon and, in doing so, provided him with an insight into the very nature of the Circlemakers.

Cut through the clichés, and you will find that psychic communication works—there really are people attuned to the very source of the phenomenon. And even more important is that these individuals act as catalysts, triggering exotic light forms into manifestation, often without realizing it themselves.

These life forms exist as alien intelligences, just as they were once the fairy folk of former times, and both identities are generated, programmed, and updated by us. Yet, even if this is so, some hybrid archetypes regurgitated by our deep subconscious mind recur time and time again in UFO encounters and dream recalls of supposed superior intelligences. In the western hemisphere the most dominant dark memory bred by abduction experiences is obviously the gray, famously popularized by Whitley Strieber on the cover, and within the contents, of his international bestseller *Communion* (1987), about his own abduction experiences at the hands of "the Visitors," as he calls them. Their faces dominate UFO lore today, although formally it had been that of the tall, long-haired albino with angular facial features, piercing eyes, and long slender fingers. Collectively these slender aliens are referred to in UFO literature as "Nordics," but to John Day and his family, and to Isabelle Kingston, they are the Watchers, whose role on earth as wisdom bringers is recorded in Judeo-Christian texts such as the book of Enoch, the earliest versions of which have been found among the Dead Sea Scrolls and date to the first century BC.

The description given of the earthly Watchers matches exactly their alien counterparts—extremely tall, pale skin, strange eyes, and long white hair—indeed, the classic description of an albino. How is this possible? It either means that the Enochian Watchers were actually space aliens or that their earthly likeness and name were stolen by the alien intelligences behind close UFO encounter and abduction experiences. If so, then why choose this mythical identity? Why choose to imitate the Watchers (known also as the Elohim, the "sons of God"), who in Judeo-Christian tradition are classified as angels, both the heavenly and fallen?

In my books,[6] I have proposed that the Enochian Watchers were a powerful priestly elite who some 12,000 years ago masterminded the Neolithic revolution in the Near East. They built circles of beautifully carved and decorated standing stones and other cult buildings at places such as Göbekli Tepe and Nevali Çori in southeast Turkey, where the earliest advances in human civilization took place. Everything from the first domesticated crop to the earliest clay figurines, pottery, metalwork, eye liner, beer, wine, stone carving, and rectilinear buildings came from this same region of the globe, a fact which can be put down to the priestly or shamanic elite that masterminded the creation of the earliest human settlements here. Indeed, the circular stone structures, the earliest form of megaliths anywhere in the world, around which these settlements most likely arose, are collectively viewed as the oldest temple in the world. What is more, it is precisely all these firsts that the earthly Watchers are accredited as having given to humankind in the book of Enoch, set in the biblical land of Eden, which can be shown to have been located where the Tigris and Euphrates rivers take their course in the same region as Göbekli Tepe.

Yet, if this shamanic elite at places such as Göbekli Tepe, in the mountains above the city of Şanlıurfa (ancient Edessa), provided all these firsts for mankind, then just who were they and where did they gain such profound knowledge and wisdom?

As to who they were, I suspect that they were multi-talented individuals who arrived in the Near East from another part of the ancient world in the midst of global catastrophes caused during that millennium by a comet impact. But from where exactly they came is still a matter of careful debate. As to where this knowledge and wisdom might have come from, the answer almost certainly is otherworldly journeys through shamanic flight, something clearly indicated by the astral nature of the art found at these proto-Neolithic cult centers. This art includes extraordinary sculptures and reliefs of animals, birds, humans, and hybrids, which Dr. Klaus Schmidt of the German Archaeological Institute (DAI), who heads the team currently uncovering the complex at Göbekli Tepe, sees in terms as the "watchman (*sic*) of the period," a term he uses for those responsible for the construction of these circular monuments. The word "watchman" is so close to "Watcher" that this cannot be coincidence.[7]

If these elite shamanistic "watchmen" were gaining their advanced knowledge and wisdom from otherworldly sources, then there is little question that they would have believed themselves to be in communication with the nonterrestrial intelligences that inhabited the sky world—the astral realms in which they moved during altered states of consciousness.

Is it possible that the Enochian Watchers, as the builders of the earliest megalithic monuments (something that John Day attempted to convey intuitively with regards to the origins of prehistoric monuments such as Silbury Hill), were, in fact, communicating with the very same transdimensional intelligences that have masqueraded in more modern times as, among other things, the Watchers encountered by the Day family during the Aveley abduction, and the grays or "Visitors" popularized by Whitley Strieber?

If correct, then this communication could help explain why the alien Watchers chose to manifest in the guise of the Watchers of Enochian tradition, for these shamanic elite, these "watchmen," were themselves in contact with the very same plasma–based life as we are today. This contact might additionally explain why so many stones circles and megalithic monuments were eventually built in areas associated with geological and geophysical anomalies, such as fault lines and places of powerful magnetic variation, which have been linked with the production of UFOs, earthlights, ghost lights, earthquake lights, etc. This I feel might have resulted from the fact that the Enochian Watchers, the earliest megalithic builders, become familiar themselves with the nonterrestrial intelligences behind the manifestation of mysterious light forms, which I sense existed in their world some 12,000 years ago when the earliest phases of Göbekli Tepe were being built.

No one can rightly say whether UFO encounters did, indeed, take place some 12,000 years ago in the rugged mountainous region where civilization began. Yet, what we *do* know is that Turkey's Şanlıurfa province certainly plays host to UFO activity today, with one of the country's most high profile cases in recent years occurring in its Karaköprü area around 4 a.m. one morning in October 2007. A witness, described as an "amateur videographer," filmed an object said to have been a "strange hexagonal ball of light" that hovered in the sky emitting red, green, and white lights, while at the same time moving quickly and erratically. It disappeared after some 15 minutes without leaving a trace.[8] Karaköprü is at the foot of the mountain range in which Göbekli Tepe is situated. Sightings like this are happening today, but were the human Watchers of Göbekli Tepe communing with the plasma intelligences behind very similar light constructs as much as 12,000 years ago? I think they were.

Books have been written by the likes of Zecharia Sitchin (*The Twelfth Planet*, 1977) and J. J. Hurtak (*The Book of Knowledge: The Keys of Enoch*, 1975) linking the Enochian Watchers with alien intelligences, but in these cases it is assumed that the Watchers themselves *are* aliens (a conclusion that might easily be drawn from the Day family's encounter with "the Watchers" of *their* abduction experience). Yet I believe the connection is more subtle than that. I believe it is possible that the Enochian Watchers were in communication with the same plasma intelligences responsible for UFO encounters such as the Aveley abduction, and only now is their nature being scientifically understood for the first time. I suspect that they might also have understood such multi-dimensional experiences, most likely in a manner which we are now at last beginning to comprehend ourselves. It was through such contact, and the lingering myth of such contact, that the Watchers' own archetypal form became encoded into the consciousness of the plasma constructs, ready to be used many thousands of years after the Watchers had disappeared from the face of the earth.

It is strange, also, that the original inhabitants of fairy land, the elven folk, were described not originally as "little people," or as imps and devils, but as humanlike albinos, the same description as both the Enochian *and* alien Watchers. Perhaps then this connection between the plasma-based intelligences, masquerading as Watchers, grays, fairies, etc., and humankind conveys a very deep resonation of such communications between the Enochian Watchers and plasma-based life forms.

If all of this is correct, then it is plausible that at least some of the knowledge and wisdom that the Enochian Watchers provided to catalyze humanity's first human civilization was derived from the same nonhuman intelligence responsible for changing the lives of the Day family during the Aveley abduction back in 1974. Just like so many other abductees worldwide, their brains were completely rewired through contact with this unknown force, which I propose is more prevalent, and perhaps even, more powerful in areas of extreme geophysical and geological anomalies. It enables these transient intelligences that come to us through inner space to gain communication with our minds, which are then downloaded with otherworldly knowledge and wisdom that updates the course not only of our lives, but also of those around us, i.e. our family, tribe, clan, or social group. Thus a kind of butterfly effect is set up, which has a knock-on impact across a much wider distance, as was the case with the spread of civilization catalyzed by the Watchers in southeast Turkey—the original Garden of Eden.

I suspect, also, that such contact is not a new thing. It has been going on for tens of thousands of years in one form or another. But how can we know for sure that alien intelligences *were* involved in human evolution? As we shall see in the final chapter, it is an enigma that only now are we in a position to unravel for the very first time.

25

Deep Space Consciousness

Wednesday, July 16, 2008. It is following a visit to an extraordinary new crop formation that appeared yesterday in a wheat field next to Avebury's prehistoric henge that I bring you this final chapter. As the book began with the bizarre presentation of Trevor James Constable's immortal *Sky Creatures*, which argues that UFOs are etheric lifeforms, "critters" as he calls them, I must close with the rediscovery of another crucial book to this debate.

Earlier that morning, July 16, I picked up and read *Space-Time Transients And Unusual Events* (1977) by cognitive neuroscience researcher and university professor Dr. Michael A. Persinger, and his research colleague Gyslaine Lafrenière. It was their later work that set out the physiological and psychological effects thought to be induced in a person when he or she comes too close to the electromagnetic fields of a close proximity UFO.

I quickly became interested in the results of the authors' analysis of patterns formed by anomalous events around the globe. These events included everything from UFO sightings to strange falls of objects from the sky, monster sightings, out-of-place appearances of animals, peculiar animal behavior—in fact everything of the type that anomalist writer

Charles Fort (1874–1932) recorded in works such as *The Book of the Damned* (1919) and *Lo!* (1931), and what we today refer to as "fortean" phenomena. Persinger and Lafrenière attempt to demonstrate that the appearance of such "space–time transients" have a clear relationship to areas of geophysical abnormalities, which include earthquakes, faulting, volcanoes, etc. This finding was independently confirmed by earth mysteries researcher and writer Paul Devereux.[1] Moreover, the two authors record that some of these quite diverse phenomena seem to peak coincident to each other across the months and years.

Persinger and Lafrenière also noted a coincident pattern between anomalous activity and recorded solar flare activity as well as stellar events, such as the appearance of new stars (nova) and supernovae. They proposed that the cause of these "stellar–fortean contiguities," as they called them, might well relate to the fact that stellar events, whether in our galaxy or even outside it, create huge bursts of electromagnetic (EM) radiation, which reach the solar system and are registered by us either as light rays (the appearance of nova and supernovae) or as effects on instrumentation directed at areas of the EM spectrum outside the visible light range, such as gamma rays, radio waves, microwaves, infrared radiation, and X–rays.

Stellar activity of this nature so many light years away from the solar system is unlikely to cause anomalous phenomena down here on Earth, but other previously ignored factors associated with such events might, indeed, play a role. Persinger and Lafrenière propose that accompanying these star bursts across the EM spectrum are what they refer to as a "gravity shock wave," a kind of pulse that can induce a gravitational tension on whatever lies in its path. They speculate that this tension would result in an "intense disturbance" within the fabric of space containing what they describe as the "neutrino sea" in which gravity occurs.

Although the theory of a "gravity shock wave" heralding major stellar events remains hypothetical and highly controversial, its implications, if correct, are immense. Such cosmic disturbances would create a shock wave that Persinger and Lafrenière say would ride ahead of the oncoming EM radiation, reaching the solar system first. Its arrival would most likely cause intense flaring in the sun as well as severe tectonic stress within the earth's crust, resulting in earthquakes, tsunamis, and possibly even volcanic activity. As a secondary effect of these tensions beneath the earth's surface, fault lines would be placed under immense pressure, which, in turn, would result in fortean anomalies—Persinger and Lafrenière's space-time transients—including a proliferation of UFO events in regions of the planet where geophysical anomalies are known to occur, i.e. in the vicinity of major faulting. As I have attempted to convey in previous chapters, such tensions within the earth and the resulting changes in the earth's natural magnetic fields create a medium in which plasma constructs—exotic light forms, UFOs—can manifest.

The work done in this field by Persinger and Lafrenière is itself quite extraordinary, for, if they are right, then it means that there could well be a direct relationship between stellar events occurring on the other side of our Milky Way galaxy and UFO events down here on earth. Yet, this is merely the beginning of a revelation that is going to shake to the core our understanding of alien contact, for Persinger and Lafrenière cite as the best example of this relationship between cosmic distur-bances and space-time transients the case of Cygnus X-3.

In the first week of August 1972 our sun produced the most intense period of solar flare activity ever recorded. As Persinger and Lafrenière state, it was "the most amazing display in solar history." Throughout that same month there were brilliant fireballs seen in the skies as well as a high incidence of meteors, and, more significantly, a wave of inex-plicable UFOs reports. "Fortean events approached a maximum," they wrote. Then, almost one month later, they said, "a radio outburst, un-precedented in the history of radio astronomy, struck the earth from Cygnus X-3."[2]

To Persinger and Lafrenière this event was seen as highly significant, leading them to conclude that the outburst of radio waves was linked with a gravity shock wave coming from the same source, i.e. Cygnus X-3, which was responsible, therefore, for the high incidence of space-time transients. Both the radio waves and the shock wave, they speculated, left Cygnus X-3 at the same time, yet the gravity shock wave then pulled ahead reaching the solar system around August 2, 1972, and causing the "greatest solar storm in 370 years of observation."[3]

Persinger and Lafrenière suggest that even the earth's spin might have been affected by the incoming shock wave, though this effect could perhaps have been put down to the solar flare activity. Then, finally, around one month after the shock wave, the incoming, although some-what slower, wave of radio radiation coming from Cygnus X-3 was fi-nally detected by radio telescopes. Since this binary system, with its active neutron (or strange quark) star alluded to in Chapter 23, lies around 30,000 light years from earth in astronomical terms, and there was a month's time delay between the arrival of the shock wave and the subsequent radio waves, Persinger and Lafrenière calculated an arrival delay of 0.5 miles per second between the two components. They thus estimated the velocity for the radio waves at 185,999.5 miles/second and that of the gravity shock at 186,000 miles/second, which is the speed of light itself.

Similar ideas regarding a gravitational "superwave" causing geophysical events on earth has long been championed by physician, science consultant, and writer Paul Laviolette, most popularly in his book *Earth Under Fire* (2005).[4] He, too, believes that a gravitational wave coming from a distant stellar source would travel faster than any EM radiation ejected at the same time. He has speculated that the Asian tsunami of December 26, 2004, could have been triggered by an incoming "superwave" arriving in advance of a powerful gamma–ray burst (GRB) from a distant stellar source named SGR 1806–20 some three days later on December 29.

This powerful GRB is thought to have been triggered when a type of neutron star known as a magnetar, just 12 miles (20 km) across yet with an extremely dense magnetic field, exploded around 50,000 light years away to produce more energy in 0.2 seconds than the sun does in 200,000 years. Astronomers have dismissed the idea that the GRB was in any way responsible for the Asian tsunami, citing as evidence the fact that it occurred three days *after* the great human tragedy. However, they have not taken into account the likelihood that the massive earthquake in the Indian Ocean that triggered the tsunami could have been exacerbated by a gravity "superwave" traveling ahead of the gamma–ray burst. This superwave could have arrived days, or even weeks, before the GRB, causing extreme tensions within the earth's crust, resulting finally in the powerful earthquake of December 26.

If such gravity shock waves do cause severe geological reactions beneath the earth's surface, then in areas, where faulting produces the highest incidence of geophysical anomalies, UFOs are going to proliferate, as are close encounters and abduction scenarios, where percipients would come into contact with nonterrestrial, plasma–based intelligences.

Amazingly, immediately prior to the Asian tsunami, there was, indeed, a wave of UFO sightings reported in areas affected, so much so that the inhabitants of these regions believed that the UFOs had come to warn them of the impending catastrophe, as is shown from the following news report from *India Daily* dated December 31, 2004:

> An enormous number of UFO sightings before Tsunami and earthquake in South and Southeast Asia—were they trying to warn?
>
> Was it a coincidence? Lots of people now from the tsunami and earthquake hit areas are reporting about strange Unidentified Flying Objects they saw a few days before the megaquake and tsunami. People in Indian state of Tamil Nadu, Andaman and Nicobar Island as well as many in Indonesia were reporting for some time about strange flying objects in the sky. Some even are conjecturing that this horrific Tsunami and earthquake may be some kind of experiment. In Port Blair, the capital city of Andaman Island of India, last week some tourists saw strange silent flying objects. In Sumatra, remote places also had similar experiences for quite some time. According to some UFO experts, UFOs always hover around the epicenter of major calamities. They somehow sense these coming natural disasters. Some believe that they try and communicate with us to warn. Some even believe these UFOs simulate natural disasters in the earth. India especially in the Himalayas, China, Indonesia were experiencing heavy UFO sightings in recent days. Remote areas of Bangladesh, Mayanmar, and Andaman Island, Sri Lanka have also recently reported such sightings.[5]

Clearly, many areas of the East Asian continent, not just those around the Sumatran epicenter of the tsunami earthquake, were experiencing a heavy spate of UFO sightings. Among these sightings would have been various close encounters and, arguably, even a few abduction scenarios. As we can see, some people saw the presence of UFOs prior to the tsunami as being some kind of secret "experiment," while others concluded that UFOs hang around places of impending calamities. Still others thought the UFOs could sense imminent natural disasters or that they might even have caused them. These interpretations are all very revealing psychology, although the single most compelling solution to this entire mystery is that both the UFO sightings as well as the earthquake and subsequent tsunami were triggered by a gravity shock wave that originated within a star some 50,000 light years from earth.

Such conclusions have incredible implications for human evolution, for, aside from the more obvious EM radiation and gravity shock waves presumed to be produced by neutron stars, such stellar events also create streams of cosmic radiation, or cosmic rays, which are the highest known energies in the EM spectrum. These rays are ejected from the star either during explosions or via intense jets of plasma that reach out for immense distances, sometimes up to tens of light years, destroying everything in their path. They are like cosmic gun barrels shooting out cosmic rays on a linear course that can and, frequently, do reach our solar system. On reaching the earth's upper atmosphere, the rays collide with oxygen and nitrogen atoms, destroying themselves in the process, but at the same time producing showers of secondary particles called muons. These particles usually rain down harmlessly on the earth's surface.

The point of origin of these cosmic rays is almost always scrambled due to the fact that, as charged particles, they are bounced around and generally knocked off course by powerful magnetic fields that permeate both the solar system and the galaxy, as a whole. Yet, occasionally strong burst of cosmic rays, if neutral in charge, can arrive directly from source, unaffected by any magnetic fields encountered. When unaffected cosmic rays arrive on Earth, their point of origin can more easily be determined.

By far the best candidate for a source of cosmic rays in our galaxy is Cygnus X-3, which, since its remarkable burst of radio waves recorded in August 1972, has periodically burst into life causing a heavy influx of radiation across the EM spectrum. This influx includes ultra-high frequency gamma rays, infrared radiation, X-rays, radio waves, and cosmic rays, which reach here with ease due most probably to the fact that its neutron star has been classified as the galaxy's first known microblazar. This type of star has one of its twin plasma jets spewing out stellar debris along the line of its axis, which is aimed directly at the solar system. Indeed, when our radio telescopes picked up Cygnus X-3's record-breaking burst of radio waves back in 1972, it would have been additionally pumping out bursts of EM radiation across the spectrum, including very powerful cosmic rays. However, it was not until a number of deep underground particle detectors went operational in the early

1980s that the truly unique nature of Cygnus X-3's cosmic rays was realized. Not only were they neutral with very little mass, but they were also able to penetrate rock to a depth a few hundred yards before finally breaking up to create secondary muons that were registered by the highly sensitive equipment set up to monitor the decay of a subatomic particle known as the proton. In fact *so* unique were these particles, which came in waves of 4.8 hours, the orbit time of Cygnus X-3's neutron star around its main sequence companion star, that they were given their own name—"cygnets," meaning "children of the swan."

Some of the greatest stellar events in our galaxy would have been marked by a notable rise in cosmic rays reaching earth, and their levels can be estimated today by examining the nuclear fallout left behind by disintegrating cosmic rays in the thick layers of ice at the two poles, the lowest of which are as much as 500,000 years old. Ice core samples reveal peaks of cosmic ray activity exactly when major advancements in human history took place—200,000 to 190,000 years ago, when modern humans emerged on to the scene; 70,000 to 60,000 years ago, when the first migrations out of Africa took place; around 40,000 to 35,000 years ago, when the earliest cave art began appearing in Western Europe, Australia, and Africa, and around 14,000 to 13,000 years ago, just prior to the emergence of the Neolithic revolution, as is evidenced from all the extraordinary advances that took place in the region of Göbekli Tepe around 12,000 years ago.[6]

In *The Cygnus Mystery* I championed the theory, proposed as early as 1973 by astronomer and science writer Carl Sagan, that cosmic rays have been essential to the evolution of humankind, due principally to the mutating effect of cosmic radiation on DNA, the building block of life. However, I now feel that there might have been additional stellar-based factors behind human evolution. For aside from diet, nutrition, and migration, it could well be that the suspected gravity shock waves that herald the arrival—from neutron stars in particular—of other forms of EM radiation, including cosmic rays, causes extreme tension beneath the earth's surface. This radiation leads not simply to geophysical events such as earthquakes, tsunamis, and volcanoes, but also to UFO sightings, close encounters, and abduction scenarios. This effect would have influenced Africa's Rift Valley, where some 200,000 years ago in the region of Lake Turkama, on the border between Kenya and Ethiopia, modern humans emerged for the first time, and where around 70,000 to 60,000

years ago, a time of extremely high cosmic ray activity, the first migrations out of Africa occurred. This area is riddled with faulting of the sort
that might easily have produced such anomalous phenomena, which in
turn caused sudden advancements in human intellect and creativity
that allowing the inhabitants of the region to pull ahead of their nearest
rivals to become our earliest ancestors. This advancement, I believe,
was due in part to their exposure to powerful plasma constructs where
fifth-dimensional environments and an alien mindset existed.

Our ancestors were changed in the same manner that the minds of
John Day and his family were following their own close encounter with
a plasma construct—what Constable would have referred to as an
orgone bioform—on the roads of West Essex back in 1974. Such contact
with nonterrestrial intelligences led to advances in human understanding that climaxed with the earliest migrations from this region into other
parts of the ancient world. With these migrations went an understanding of the subtle relationship that existed between humankind and nonhuman intelligences associated with mysterious lights, which we must
assume appeared in whatever guise was deemed acceptable to the different tribes' long-held beliefs in supernatural beings.

Our first ancestors are likely to have venerated primordial animal
forms such as the snake, which is currently humanity's oldest known
symbol of worship. This suspicion is evidenced by the discovery of a
ritual cave in Botswana's Tsodilo Hills, where excavations in 2006 revealed that the indigenous San bushmen have been coming here unin-
terrupted for up to 70,000 years in order to venerate the snake in the
form of a snakelike rock.[7] In San mythology humankind is descended
from a python, an unconscious expression perhaps of the serpentlike
DNA inside us all, which might just have evolved through a deep connection with plasma life forms of a nonterrestrial origin.

Cygnus X-3 is, by far, the best candidate for a source of cosmic rays
within our galaxy, and so there is every chance that at least some part of
the intense waves of cosmic radiation reaching earth since the dawn of
humankind originated inside this distant neutron star. If Persinger and
Lafrenière's findings regarding the influence of Cygnus X-3 on anomalous
events back in August 1972 are correct, then there is good reason to assume
that this distant star might also have played a role in human evolution.

In Chapter 23 I proposed that neutron or strange quark stars were
sentient, perhaps even conscious, plasma sources of immense power,

within which exist fifth–dimensional environments. I suggested also that, through the process of quantum entanglement, plasma life forms within such stellar sources might be able to transfer consciousness, or even physical matter, to plasma sources elsewhere in the universe, including plasma light constructs of the sort that I suspect humanity has been encountering since the dawn of time. If so, then there is a slim, but tantalizing, possibility that neutron stars such as Cygnus X–3 are consciously aware when sudden ejections of EM radiation, including cosmic rays, produce gravity shock waves that hit the earth causing the production of plasma lights and earth changes. This plasmatic medium of existence can then be used to transfer, or even teleport, some facet of the star's sentience across the vistas of space to inhabit this environment, and, by doing so, interact with emerging life on earth.

As sensational as such a theory is going to seem, there is some evidence that this might indeed be the case. John G. Cramer, a popular science writer and Professor of Physics at the University of Washington in Seattle, has proposed that microscopic wormholes, portals in space-time, can be projected through space by extraterrestrial intelligences to explore and provide connections to other places and existences. He asks: "if this wormhole transport is possible, shouldn't the technologically advanced civilizations of our galaxy already be sending tiny accelerated wormhole portals in our direction? Where are they?"

Where indeed . . . His answer is that perhaps they are already here. He cites the detection during the early 1980s of Cygnus X–3s "cygnets"[8] and goes on to say that cosmic–ray experts have assumed these unique particles are a natural phenomenon, not an artifact of some advanced civilization. Yet he goes on to say:

> But that assumption could be wrong. It is interesting to contemplate the possibility that some advanced civilization may be mapping the galaxy with accelerated wormhole portals, sending little time-dilated observation points out into the cosmos as peepholes for viewing the wonders of the universe. And perhaps, when a particularly promising or interesting scene comes into view, the peephole is halted and expanded into a portal through which a Visitor can pass.[9]

Thus, he is suggesting that the cygnets of Cygnus X–3 might contain microscopic wormholes, which can act as portals for some "advanced civilization" to survey the furthest reaches of time and space. However, we need not see such intelligent use of wormholes as deriving from an "advanced civilization," for it is more likely that the source of any kind of sentient utilization of these cygnets is the plasma source that sent them out in the first place—the neutron star at the heart of Cygnus X-3, and other similar such stellar bodies in deep space. If so, then it could mean that the suspected plasma intelligences at the heart of such stars can utilize these tiny wormholes quite literally as portals across space-time, to sense, see, and experience other worlds, other realities.

Perhaps this interpretation is why cruciform crop circles appearing today—such as the one that appeared at Charley Knoll, Leicestershire, in 1993[10] and the T-shaped formation of circles discovered at West Overton, near Avebury, in 2003—are being identified as Cygnus in its form as the Northern Cross. Is it also why psychics and mystics working in the field of crop circles are beginning to latch on to Cygnus as the source of a sublime signal that permeates through the void of inner space?

For instance, on July, 17, 2006, a visionary, who lives in Australia and goes by the name "Raphiem," experienced a vivid dream, which seems to have been more an OOBE—an out-of-body experience:

> I was hovering way up in space looking down on the Earth . . . I could see a huge brilliant luminescent shape—ultra-violet with magenta edges pulsing very far in the distance. The shape appeared to be like that of a cross (3 cross-bars) . . . Later the "blue" voice in my head said that this was a beam emanating from the Cygnus star cluster region, however not in this universe but a higher frequency in Universe 2. Same space-time coordinates as Cygnus but higher dimensions.

Two weeks later Raphiem experienced another powerful dream. This time he was flying over a wheat field in which there was a large crop formation that bore the appearance of a cereological figure of eight, quite serpent-like in appearance. Where the two halves met in the center was a three-dimensional cross, like the one seen in the previous dream, which was vibrating in a manner that made it emit brilliant lumines-cent colors. Raphiem's spirit guide, whom he refers to as "blue," told him that this was the "818 activation gateway . . . a thought to matter ampli-fier," and that this alluded to a coming event on October 17, 2006.

Through this dream, Raphiem came to believe that, on October 17, the world could expect a "cosmic trigger"—a huge burst of UV radiation from a powerful deep space source in the Cygnus region, operating on a higher dimensional level. Now, all of this should perhaps be dismissed as the outpourings of some well-meaning New Age channeler, without any consequence to our debate. However, its implications are enormous and far-reaching, for Raphiem, with the help of a network of online friends, organized a global attunement for October 17, 2006, which became known as the "1017 activation," using various forums, blogs, and internet sites. On that day, apparently, an estimated one million people tuned in, each one imagining a torch—a beam of violet-colored light—approximately twice the size of earth, approaching from Cygnus and synching with our world for a period of exactly 17 hours.

Other mass attunements were organized by those inspired by the success of the initial "cosmic trigger" of October 17, 2006. One, on July 17, 2007, called for a million "light workers" to take part in what it referred to as "firing the grid." Even though this figure might not have been reached, those promoting this activation did what they could to get no less than "2 billion" people to read about their intentions. Several other similar such events are planned between now and 2016.

Raphiem sees the crop circle enigma as expressing this activation process, involving a UV beam of radiation originating from the Cygnus region. He and his friends have separately linked these trigger events with what they call the "Cygnus-X region" and see it as the key to humanity moving on to the next stage of existence. They link these "activations" with specific numbers, such as 17, 71, 717, 1017, 1771, 818, and 1881. Strangely, I found that the same numbers—17, 71, 81, and 1881 in particular—had spontaneously figured in a sequence of events that in 2004 had first led me to investigate the idea that some kind of invisible pulse, or signal, from a deep space object in the Cygnus region was triggering advancements in human evolution.

Raphiem and his friends' perceived cosmic activations, involving specific key numbers, relate to an emerging process—one that features the crop circles, their symbolism, and the environment in which they appear (i.e. Alton Barnes, Avebury, Barbury Castle, Silbury Hill, etc). Remember also that it was at Avebury that our ancestors in the Neolithic Era created the largest stone circle complex in the world, as well as the biggest earthen mound in Europe (Silbury Hill), and there has to have been a good reason for these mammoth building projects. What did the original Circlemakers, the creators of the stone circles and circular henge monuments, know about this sacred landscape that we are only now waking up to for the first time? Has it anything to do with why those who built Avebury directed its central axis towards Deneb, Cygnus's brightest star? Or did it have anything to do with why, long ago, John Day singled out this same ritual landscape, and the construction of Silbury Hill in particular, as a foundation point for those he calls the Watchers, whether you see them as the founders of the Neolithic Revolution or simply as one of the many masks worn by the plasma–based life forms influencing life on earth?

Perhaps we are heading towards a culminating event in which the act of the *new* Circlemakers in creating crop formations is going to result in something earth changing in its implications. Is it possible that the crop circles are now acting as beacons, cereological sigils, drawing something truly alien into our midst? Is this being recognized, heralded even, by those of our communities who are the most intuitively aware, including the human Circlemakers who, in similarities with the surrealist painters of the nineteenth century, feel inspired to do what they do? If so, what is this coming event, and how might it affect our world? Is it really connected with a deep space source in the Cygnus constellation— arguably the neutron star, or strange quark star, Cygnus X–3, with its highly unique "cygnet" particles reaching earth and penetrating deep underground on a regular basis? If such a culminating event *is* in the cards, then it could happen soon. If not, then perhaps we might have to wait a lifetime, or many lifetimes, for this ongoing process to come to fruition. Yet to quote songstress Kate Bush from her poignant song "Cloudbusting"—about the tragic life of Wilhelm Reich—"just saying it could even make it happen."

Afterword

Contacting the Circlemakers—
A Crop Circle Meditation

The crop circle enigma is not going to go away. Year after year it gains in popularity, as more and more people take an active role in this modern-day mystery. Some are happy simply to visit formations in order to experience their atmosphere and ponder upon the wonders of their manufacture and origin. Others will wish to conduct on-site investigations or archive research, while still others will attempt to make contact with the Circlemakers through psychic processes, and below I offer a few simple guidelines on how this contact might be achieved.

Communion with the Circlemakers

The simplest plan of action in order to attempt communion with the Circlemakers (the name I shall use for what I see as the plasma intelligences behind exotic light forms) would be to find a circle or formation that you feel exudes a superior feel about it, not just in its construction, but also in its position in the landscape and feeling to you. This process has to be a personal thing, as what might seem important to one person could be dismissed by another. Once inside, find a position that feels comfortable and calming, and then wait for an opportunity to conduct a brief meditation. When this moment occurs, visualize a ball of light around head height out in front of you. See it gradually increase in size like a star shining brighter and brighter. Let this ball increase until it envelops both you and the entire circle or formation. Then see these energies beginning to turn like the spokes of a wheel, ideally in the same direction as the flow of the fallen crop.

Doing this meditation put something of your own energies into the site. This will activate the site's own inherent energies, setting it up as a beacon of light for any unseen intelligences that might just become aware of your call.

After this preparation, reach out with your mind towards whatever you conceive of as the true Circlemakers, and attempt to allow your consciousness to interact or become at one with them. Do this interaction with an open heart. If you feel they have become aware of you, ask them to provide you with some kind of sign of their presence. Ask for something you believe might feasibly take place—perhaps the manifestation of a mysterious light, or some kind of inner message in the form of words, images, or instructions to do something or go somewhere.

After you have given your mind long enough to freefall in order to pick up any extraneous thoughts and ideas, return to the radiant light you have sent out, and then draw the excess back to yourself by reversing the visualization. Bring it all back together as a radiant ball in front of you, and then see it become just a pinpoint of light that goes down into the ground and is lost from view. This visualization will leave a bit of you at the site and enable you to link with the place after you leave. This link might be important for dreams and meditations at a later date. If you like, you can conduct the whole meditation holding a crystal, into which you see the pinpoint of light enter at the very end. As to which type of crystal you might use, this is up to you. However, quartz works well as a place of storage for energies, and its so-called piezoelectric qualities have been linked by some researchers with the manifestation of earthlights.

Thereafter it is up to you to wait around long enough to experience anything unusual that might constitute the sign that you have asked for. You might have to be patient, and there is no guarantee that it will happen at the circle or formation. It might well be best to repair to some local vantage point and wait patiently there. But don't forget to watch the landscape as well as the sky, for a large number of earthlights actually manifest at ground level and would be missed if you have your eyes peeled to the sky.

Beyond this suggestion, simply use your own intuition and imagination, and watch your dreams. Yet, remember that the Circlemakers are more likely to interact with you if you address them directly. What you consider to be real out there starts with you. You must believe they are there and *can* manifest if it suits their purposes. Work also with known psychics, or mediums, who might well have a better means of direct communication. If you are in a group, then decide which one of you is the most psychic and look towards him/her for an empathic link with the phenomenon. This is very important, as we are not all super psychics! Good luck, and remember to try and record any strange incidents that might occur, either on handycams or by using a voice recorder. If you are using a handycam, make sure that it has a low light or zero lux setting, which will enable you to record in the darkness. Be on the look out all the time, and expect the unexpected.

Useful Websites:

Crop Circle Connector
www.cropcircleconnector.com

Temporary Temples
www.temporarytemples.co.uk

Useful Addresses:

Silent Circle
The White Horse,
Compton Bassett,
Wiltshire SN11 8RG
www.silentcircle.co.uk

Avebury Henge Shop
High Street,
Avebury,
Wiltshire SN8 1RF
www.hengeshop.com

The Barge Inn
Honeystreet,
Wiltshire SN9 5PS
www.the-barge-inn.com

If this Appendix has whetted your appetite for active involvement in UFO and crop circle research, then may I suggest you take a serious look at the titles included in the Bibliography. These listings will give you an ideal grounding in the different subjects allied to the phenomenon. Any information, anecdotes, press cuttings, or correspondence concerning the subject of this book should be addressed to Andrew Collins, PO Box 3242, Marlborough, Wiltshire SN8 1UZ, UK. Receive free issues of Andrew's regular e-newsletter *Earthquest News*, by logging on to www.andrewcollins.com, where you can read more about the author and his work in the fields of ancient and more-modern mysteries.

Notes and References

Preface 2008

1. Plot, *The Natural History of Staffordshire*, pp. 9–19, pl. opp. p. 28.
2. Spence, *The Myths of the North American Indians*, pp. 152–56.

Chapter 2—Girl on a Horse

1. Wingfield, "Towards an understanding of the nature of the circles," in Bartholomew, ed., *Crop Circles, Harbingers of World Change*, pp. 25–7.

Chapter 3—Diminishing Health

1. Wingfield, "Beyond the current paradigms," in Noyes and Taylor, eds., *The Crop Circle Enigma*, pp. 99–110.
2. Wingfield, "Towards an understanding of the nature of the circles," in Bartholomew, ed., *Crop Circles, Harbingers of World Change*, pp. 25–7.

Chapter 5—Rita's Return

1. Wingfield, "Beyond the current paradigms," in Noyes and Taylor, ed., *The Crop Circle Enigma*, p. 104.
2. In September 1990, Doug Bower and Dave Chorley claimed, without due evidence, that they hoaxed this circle found in 1989 during Operation White Crow. However, George Wingfield and many other circles researchers remain wholly unconvinced by this claim, knowing that information concerning its discovery was freely available in many published accounts.
3. Delgado and Andrews, *Circular Evidence*, pp. 65–6.
4. Delgado and Andrews, *Crop Circles the Latest Evidence*, p. 15.
5. Brown, "White Crow and Grasshopper Warbler," *The Cerealogist* 6 (Summer 1992), pp. 3–4.

Chapter 6—Why Warminster

1. Collins, BUFORA case 76-361 C4b. See also Shuttlewood, *UFO Magic in Motion*, pp. 192–5.
2. It is worth pointing out that on the morning we were at Upton Scudamore a huge pictogram was discovered in the fields nearby, although we saw nothing at the time.

Chapter 7—No Sleep Till Cheesefoot Head

1. Harris, "UFO and Silver-suited Entity seen near Winchester," *Flying*

Saucer Review 22:5, pp. 3–6.

Chapter 8—The Scientific Shaman
1. Lecture by Busty Taylor at Essex CCCS on Thursday, February 20, 1992, where the slide was also shown.
2. Delgado and Andrews, *Circular Evidence*, p. 35.
3. Randles and Fuller, *Crop Circles: A Mystery Solved*, pp. 84–5.
4. Constable, *Sky Creatures*, p. 232.

Chapter 9—The Return of the Ether Ships
1. Constable, *Sky Creatures*, p. 55.
2. Ibid., p. 192.
3. Randles and Whetnall, *Alien Contact—Window on Another World*, pp. 54–5.
4. Constable, p. 21.
5. Ibid., pp. 100–1.
6. Ibid., pp. 118.
7. Ibid., p. 119.
8. Ibid., p. 119.
9. Ibid., p. 123.
10. Ibid., p. 146.
11. "1966 Tully . . .," *Australian Flying Saucer Review*, Sydney edition, 9 (November 1966). The article on the Tully case in the May–June 1969 issue of *Flying Saucer Review* speaks of the swirl as anti-clockwise, therefore contradicting its Australian counterpart. I have taken the word of the earlier source since that article was compiled the same year as the event.
12. Basterfield, *Circles Down Under*. Five new circular areas were found in a lagoon area at Euramo, near Tully. They formed an arc and ranged from three to nearly five meters in diameter.
13. Constable, *Sky Creatures*, pp. 201–2.
14. Ibid., p. 202.
15. Kelley, "What is Orgone Energy?" *The Creative Process* 2:1.

Chapter 10—Nesting Habits
1. Constable, *Sky Creatures*, p. 172.
2. Delgado and Andrews, *Circular Evidence*, p. 44.
3. Hopper, "Corn Triangle is a Mystery," *East Anglian Daily Times*, July 24, 1991.
4. Basterfield, *Circles Down Under*.

5. Ibid., and the original news feature in the *Weekend Truth* newspaper of December 16th, 1989, speaks of five circles being initially found. Auchetti, "The Turriff Ground Ring Summary," *Australian UFO Bulletin*, VUFORS, 1990, pp. 11–20, speaks of only four circles being found.

6. Auchetti, pp. 11–20.

Chapter 11—Orgone Aftermath

1. Strainic, "Once Upon a Time in the Wheat," *The Circular* 3:1, pp. 6–7.
2 Constable, *Sky Creatures*, pp. 175–6.
3. Delgado and Andrews, *Circular Evidence*, p. 95.
4. Ibid., pp. 65–6.
5. Strainic, p. 6.
6. Reich, *The Orgone Energy Accumulator: Its Scientific and Medical Use*, pp. 16–20.

Chapter 12—Lights of the Damned

1. Randles and Fuller, *Crop Circles: A Mystery Solved*, p. 150.
2. Devereux, *Earth Lights Revelation*, p. 82.
3. Wingfield, "The English Crop Circles in 1988," in Good, ed., *The UFO Report 1990*, p. 57.
4. Aubrey, *Hypomnemata Antiquaria A* (Aubrey III, Bodleian Library), as quoted in Westwood, *Albion: A Guide to Legendary Britain*, p. 65; Grinsell, *Folklore of Prehistoric Sites in Britain*, p. 116; Briggs, "The fairies and the realms of the dead," *Folklore* 81 (1970), p. 89; Briggs, *The Anatomy of Puck*, pp. 34–5.
5. Halliwell–Phillipps, *Illustrations of the Fairy Mythology of Shakespeare of a Midsummer Night's Dream*, 1845, cf. the now lost volume "B" of Aubrey's *Hypomnemata Antiquaria*, as quoted in Briggs, *The Anatomy of Puck*, p. 33.

Chapter 14—Places of Power

1. Nelson, *My Trip to Mars, the Moon and Venus*.
2. See Michel, *UFOs and the Straight Line Mystery*.
3. Heselton, *Tony Wedd: New Age Pioneer*, p. 80.
4. Screeton, *Quicksilver Heritage*, pp. 140–8.
5. "Circumlibra" (Lockwood), "Etheric Centers," *The Ley Hunter* 2 (1969).
6. Casteret, *Ten Years Under the Earth*, pp. 187–8.
7. Collins, "Consciousness, Stones and Energies," *Earthquest News 6* (Spring 1983), pp. 5–16.
8. Delgado and Andrews, *Circular Evidence*, p. 29.

Chapter 15—Wild is the Wind

1. See Janet and Colin Bord's essential book *The Secret Country* for accounts of weather retribution in association with acts of disturbing ancient sites.
2. Graves, *Needles of Stone*, pp. 103–16.
3. Ibid., p. 106.
4. Collins, "Consciousness, Stones and Energies," *Earthquest News* 6 (Spring 1983), p. 15.
5. Wingfield, "The English Corn Circles in 1988," in Good, ed., *The UFO Report 1990*, pp. 62–5.
6. "Dust Whirls and Fairy Dances," *Monthly Weather Review* 27:3 (March 1899), p. 111.
7. Wingfield, p. 70.
8. Wingfield, "Ever Increasing Circles," in Good, ed., *The UFO Report 1991*, pp. 15–6.
9. Meaden, "Crop Circles and the Plasma Vortex," in Noyes and Taylor, eds., *The Crop Circle Enigma*, p. 77–9.
10. See Meaden, *The Circles Effects and its Mysteries*, for a full account of the plasma vortex hypothesis and its relationship to UFOs and crop circle creation.

Chapter 16—The Rainmakers

1. See Eisenman, *Maccabees, Zadokites, Christians and Qumran* for a full account of the *zadok* rainmakers and their relationship to Jesus, James, and John the Baptist.
2. Graves, *Needles of Stone*, p. 115.

Chapter 17—Earthlights Revelation!

1. Phillips and Collins, "The Deeper Mysteries of Loch Ness," *Why? A Television Documentary Series*, 1980. The story was recounted to me personally by an elderly resident of Inverness, whom we tracked down after being alerted to the legend's existence by a local investigator.
2. See Persinger and Lafrenière, *Space-Time Transients and Unusual Events*.
3. Devereux, *Earth Lights Revelation*, pp. 49–50.

Chapter 18—The Cornference

1. Holiday, *The Dragon and the Disc*, p. 198.
2. Davis, "The Cambridgeshire Mandelbrot," *The Cerealogist* 5 (Winter 1991), pp. 7–8.

3. Michell, "Geometry and Symbolism at Barbury Castle," *The Cerealogist* 4 (Summer 1991), pp. 24-5.

Chapter 20—Redemption from Oblivion?
1. MacLean, "Reluctant recruit to the circle of crop circle watchers," *Melbourne Age*, county edition, December 31, 1991.

Chapter 21—Nuked Nodes and Crispy Crop
1. Keen, *Scientific Evidence for the Crop Circle Phenomenon*, p. 11.
2. Devereux, *Places of Power, Secret Energies at Ancient Sites*, pp. 83-4.
3. Keen, p. 11.

Chapter 22—The Light of Consciousness
1. Devereux, *Earth Lights Revelation*, p. 204.
2. Collins, "The Aveley Abduction, Part One," *Flying Saucer Review* 23:6, pp. 13-25, and Collins, "The Aveley Abduction, Part Two," *Flying Saucer Review* 24:1, pp. 5-15.
3. Randles and Fuller, *Crop Circles: A Mystery Solved*, pp. 211-2.
4. Kelley, "What Is Orgone Energy?" *The Creative Process* 2:1, pp. 58-80.
5. Jung, *Flying Saucers: A Modern Myth of Things Seen in the Skies*.
6. Michell, *Flying Saucer Vision*.
7. Similar ideas are conveyed also in the works of Dr. Gregory Little. See *The Archetype Experience* (1984), *People of the Web* (1990) and especially *Grand Illusions* (1994).
8. Jones Pugh, "Stack Rocks Humanoid Display," *Flying Saucer Review* 23:6 (April 1978), pp. 7-8.
9. Jung, pp. 154-66.
10. Angelucci, *The Secret of the Saucers*.
11. Jung, p. 157.
12. For a deeper consideration of the relationship between fairies and the UFO phenomenon, see Graham Hancock's remarkable book *Supernatural: Meetings with the Ancient Teachers of Mankind* (2005).

Chapter 23—Plasma Life and the Fifth Dimension
1. For the original story on the discovery of plasmons, see "It might be life Jim . . .," physicists discover inorganic dust with life-like qualities," *Physorg.com*, August 9th, 2007 at http://physorg.com/news105869123.html. For the scientific paper see Tsytovich *et al*, "From plasma crystals and helical structures towards inorganic living matter," *New Journal of*

Physics 9 (2007) 263.

2. Strand, *Project Hessdalen 1984: Final Technical Report*, 1984, pp. 19–20.
3. For scans of the Condign report go the website "Flying Saucery—The Real UFO Report," at http://www.uk-ufo.org/condign/condscan.htm.
4. See Collins, *The Cygnus Mystery* (2006), and his online article "Cygnus X-3 and the Cosmic Ray Mystery," at http://www.andrewcollins.com/page/articles/thecygnusmystery_cygnusx3.htm.
5. For the original story see "Look to quark stars for fifth dimension" NS 194:2609, June 23, 2007, p. 12. Go to http://www.newscientist.com/data/pdf/press/2609/260912.pdf, while Barnaföldi's paper was published in *Astronomische Nachrichten* AN999, 88:789–792 (2006). Available at http://arxiv.org/pdf/0706.0378.
6. Haisell, *The Missing Seven Hours*, p. 29.

Chapter 24—Blowing out the Brains

1. Delgado and Andrews, *Circular Evidence*, pp. 115.
2. Personal conversation with Isabelle Kingston.
3. Wingfield, "Ever Increasing Circles," in Good, ed., *The UFO Report 1991*, p. 21.
4. Ibid., p. 23.
5. Ibid., pp. 25–6, and personal conversation with Ron Jones at Essex CCCS meeting on Thursday, February 20, 1992.
6. See Collins, *From the Ashes of Angels* and *Gods of Eden*.
7. "Neolithic human, animal figures unearthed in southeastern Turkey," People's Daily Online, source: xinhua, at http://english.people.com.cn/200610/10/eng20061010_310385.html.
8. Zahir, "Close encounters of the Turkish kind," Asia Times Online, at http://www.atimes.com/atimes/Middle_East/IJ31Ak02.html.

Chapter 25—Deep Space Consciousness

1. See Devereux, *Places of Power*.
2. Persinger and Lafrenière, *Space-Time Transients and Unusual Events*, p. 184.
3. Ibid., p. 186.
4. Laviolette, *Earth Under Fire*.
5. "An enormous number of UFO sightings before Tsunami and earthquake in South and Southeast Asia—were they trying to warn?" *India Daily*, December 31, 2004, at http://www.indiadaily.com/editorial/12-31h-04.asp.
6. See Little, "Has Andrew Collins Solved the Greatest Mystery of Our

Times? The Cygnus Constellation and Human Evolution," *Atlantis Rising*, to be published, for a full account of the spikes in cosmic ray activity over the last 200,000 years, and its relationship to mtDNA mutations.

7. Doyle, "Botswana 'snake rock' may show Stone Age religion," *Reuters*, November 30, 2006, at http://www.alertnet.org/thenews/newsdesk/L30693310.htm.

8. Cramer, John G, "Children of the Swan," *Analog: Alternative View Column AV-12* (March 1986), at http://www.npl.washington.edu/AV/altvw12.html.

9. Cramer, John G, "More about Wormholes—To the Stars in No Time," *Analog*: Alternative column AV–39 (May 1990), at http://www.npl.washington.edu/AV/altvw39.html.

10. See Douglas, *Charley Knoll: An Archetypal Crop Circle Adventure*, which links the 1993 formation with the Cygnus stars.

Bibliography

NB: If the entry consulted was not a first edition, then the date of first publication is given after the title, but before publication details.

"1966 Tully. . . ," *Australian Flying Saucer Review* (UFOIC edition), 9 (November 1966).

Angelucci, Orfeo, *The Secret of the Saucers: How UFOs Work*, Amherst Press, Amherst, WI, 1955.

Aubrey, John, *Hypomnemata Antiquaria A* (Aubrey III, Bodleian MS), ed. Sir Thomas Phillipps: A pt. I, *Aubrey's Collections for Wilts*, 1821; A pt. II, *An Essay Towards the Description*, etc., 1838.

Auchetti, John W., "The Turriff Ground Ring Summary," *Australian UFO Bulletin*, VUFORS, 1990.

Barnaföldi, G.G., P. Lévai and B. Lukáes, "Searching Extra Dimensions in Compact Stars," *Astronomische Nachrichten* 999:88 (2006), pp. 789–792. Available at http://arxiv.org/pdf/0706.0378.

Bartholomew, Alick, ed., *Crop Circles, Harbingers of World Change*, Gateway Books, Bath, 1991.

Basterfield, Keith, *Circles Down Under*, UFO Research Australia, January 1992.

Bastian, H. Charlton, *The Beginnings of Life*, 2 vols., Macmillan, London, 1872.

Bord, Janet and Colin, *The Secret Country*, 1978, Paladin, London, 1979.

Briggs, K.M., *The Anatomy of Puck*, Routledge, London, 1959.

Briggs, K.M., "The fairies and the realms of the dead," *Folklore* 81 (1970), pp. 81–96.

Broadhurst, Paul, *The Sun and the Serpent*, Pendragon Press, Launceston, Cornwall, 1989.

Brown, K., "White Crow and Grasshopper Warbler," *The Cerealogist* 6 (Summer 1992), pp. 3–4.

Burton, Simon, "Organic Energy—A Theoretical Energy Model for Cereology," *The Circular* 1:2 (January 1991).

Casteret, Norbet, *Ten Years Under the Earth*, J. M. Dent, London, 1939.

Chapman, Robert, *UFO—Flying Saucers over Britain*, 1968, Mayflower, London, 1976.

"Circumlibra" (Frank Lockwood), "Etheric Centers," *The Ley Hunter* 2, 1969.

Collins, Andrew, *Alien Energy*, 1994, Eagle-Wing Books, Memphis, TN, 2004.

Collins, Andrew, BUFORA case 76-361 C4b.

Collins, Andrew, "Consciousness, Stones and Energies," *Earthquest News* 6 (Spring 1983), pp. 5-16.

Collins, Andrew, *From the Ashes of Angels*, 1996, Bear and Company, Rochester, VT, 2001.

Collins, Andrew, *Gods of Eden*, 1998, Bear and Company, Rochester, VT, 2002.

Collins, Andrew, "The Aveley Abduction, Part One," *Flying Saucer Review* 23:6, pp. 13-25.

Collins, Andrew, "The Aveley Abduction, Part Two," *Flying Saucer Review* 24:1, pp. 5-15.

Collins, Andrew, *The Cygnus Mystery*, Watkins, London, 2006.

Collyns, Robin, *Laser Beams from Star Cities?*, Pelham Books, London, 1975.

Constable, Trevor James, *The Cosmic Pulse of Life*, 1976, Neville Spearman, Sudbury, Suffolk, 1977. Republished as *Sky Creatures: Living UFOs*, Pocket, New York, NY, 1978.

Davis, B., "The Cambridgeshire Mandelbrot," *The Cerealogist* 5 (Winter 1991), pp. 7-8.

Defence Intelligence Analysis Staff, "Unidentified Aerial Phenomena in the UK Air Defence Region: Executive Summary, Scientific & Technical Memorandum (The Condign Report)", December 2000 (55/2/00), available at http://www.uk-ufo.org/condign/condscan/htm.

Delgado, Pat, and Colin Andrews, *Circular Evidence*, Bloomsbury, London, 1989.

Delgado, Pat, and Colin Andrews, *Crop Circles the Latest Evidence*, Bloomsbury, London, 1989.

Devereux, Paul, and Paul McCartney, *Earth Lights*, Turnstone Press, Wellingborough, Northants, 1982.

Devereux, Paul, and David Clarke, Andy Roberts and Paul McCartney, *Earth Lights Revelation*, Blandford Press, Poole, Dorset, 1989.

Devereux, *Places of Power, Secret Energies at Ancient Sites*, Blandford Press, Poole, Dorset, 1990.

Douglas, Karen, *Charley Knoll: An Archetypal Crop Circle Adventure*, Temporary Temples Press, Gosport, Hants, 2004.

"Dust Whirls and Fairy Dances," *Monthly Weather Review* 27: 3 (March 1899), p. 111.

Eisenman, Robert, *Maccabees, Zadokites, Christians and Qumran*, E.J. Brill, Leiden, Holland, 1983.

Field, John, *English Field Names, A Dictionary*, 1921, Alan Sutton, Gloucester, 1989.

Gerish, W.B., ed., *The Mowing Devil etc.*, privately published, 1913.

Gerish, W.B., *Hertfordshire Folk Lore*, S. R. Publishers, East Ardsley, Herts., 1970.

Good, Timothy, ed., *The UFO Report 1990*, Sidgwick and Jackson, London, 1989.

Good, Timothy, ed., *The UFO Report 1991*, Sidgwick and Jackson, London, 1990.

Graves, Needles of Stone, Granada, London, 1978.

Grinsell, Leslie V., *Folklore of Prehistoric Sites in Britain*, David and Charles, Newton Abbott/London, 1976.

Grinsell, L.V., *The Ancient Burial-Mounds of England*, Methuen, London, 1935.

Guieu, Jimmy, *Flying Saucers Come from Another World*, Hutchinson, London, 1956.

Haisell, David, The Missing Seven Hours, Paperjacks, Ontario, Canada, 1978

Halliwell-Phillipps, J.O., *Illustrations of the Fairy Mythology of Shakespeare of a Midsummer Night's Dream, 1845*, AMS Press, New York, NY, 1970.

Hancock, Graham, *Supernatural: Meetings with the Ancient Teachers of Mankind*, Century, London, 2005.

Harris, L., "UFO & Silver-suited Entity seen near Winchester," *Flying Saucer Review* 22:5, pp. 3–6.

Heselton, Phillip, *The Elements of Earth Mysteries*, Element Books, Shaftesbury, Dorset, 1991.

Heselton, Phillip, *Tony Wedd: New Age Pioneer*, Northern Earth Mysteries, Hull 1986.

Holiday, F.W., *The Dragon and the Disc*, Sidgwick and Jackson, London, 1973.

Hopper, P., "Corn Triangle is a Mystery," *East Anglian Daily Times*, July 24th, 1991.

Hurtak, J.J., *The Book of Knowledge: The Keys of Enoch*, Academy for Future Science, Las Gotes, CA, 1975.

Hynek, J. Allen, *The UFO Experience*, Abelard–Schuman, London, 1972

Jones Pugh, Randall, "Stack Rocks Humanoid Display," *Flying Saucer Review* 23:6 (April 1978), pp. 7–8.

Jung, C.G., *Flying Saucers: A Modern Myth of Things Seen in the Skies*, Harcourt, Brace and Co, New York, NY, 1959.

Keen, Montague, *Scientific Evidence for the Crop Circle Phenomenon*, Elvery Dowers, Norwich, Norfolk, 1991.

Kelley, C.R., "What is Orgone Energy?" *The Creative Process* 2:1.

Laviolette, Paul, *Earth Under Fire*, Inner Traditions, Rochester, VT, 2005.

Lehrs, Ernest, *Man or Matter*, Harper and Row, New York, NY, 1958.

Little, Gregory L., *Grand Illusions: The Spectral Reality Underlying Sexual UFO Abductions, Crashed Saucers, Afterlife Experiences, Sacred Ancient Sites, and Other Enigmas*, White Buffalo Books, Memphis, TN, 1994.

Little, Gregory L., "Has Andrew Collins Solved the Greatest Mystery of Our Times? The Cygnus Constellation and Human Evolution," *Atlantis Rising*, to be published.

Little, Gregory L., *People of the Web*, White Buffalo Books, Memphis, TN, 1990.

Little, Gregory L., *The Archetype Experience, Resolving the UFO Mystery and the Riddle of Biblical Prophecy using C.G. Jung's Concept of Synchronicity*, Rainbow Books, Moore Haven, FL, 1984.

MacLean, S., "Reluctant recruit to the circle of crop circle watchers," *Melbourne Age*, county edition, December 31, 1991.

Meaden, George Terence, *The Circles Effects and its Mysteries*, Artetech, Bradford–on–Avon, Wilts., 1990.

Meaden, George Terence, "Crop Circles and the Plasma Vortex," in Noyes and Taylor, *The Crop Circle Enigma*, pp. 78–9.

Michel, Aimé, *UFOs and the Straight Line Mystery*, S.G. Phillips, New York, NY, 1958.

Michell, John, *Crooked Soley: A Crop Circle Revelation*, Roundhill Press, Brighton, Sussex, 2005.

Michell, John, *Flying Saucer Vision*, Sidgwick and Jackson, London, 1967.

Michell, John, "Geometry and Symbolism at Barbury Castle," *The Cerealogist* 4 (Summer 1991), pp. 24–5.

Morris, Ronald W. B., *Prehistoric Rock Art of Southern Scotland*, B.A.R. British Series 86. B.A.R., Oxford, 1981.

Nelson, Buck, *My Trip to Mars, the Moon and Venus*, Quill Press, West Plains, MO, 1956.

Noyes, Ralph, and Busty Taylor, eds., *The Crop Circle Enigma*, Gateway Books, Bath, 1990.

Oldfield, Harry, *Dark Side of the Brain*, Element Books, Shaftesbury, Dorset, 1988.

Persinger, Michael, and Gyslaine Lafrenière, *Space-Time Transients and Unusual Events*, Nelson–Hall, Chicago, IL, 1977.

Phillips, Graham, and Andrew Collins, "The Deeper Mysteries of Loch Ness," *Why? A Television Documentary Series*, privately published, 1980.

Plot, Robert, *The Natural History of Staffordshire*, 1686, E.J. Morton, Didsbury, Manchester, 1973.

Randles, Jenny, and Paul Fuller, *Crop Circles: A Mystery Solved*, Robert Hale, London, 1990.

Randles, Jenny, and Paul Whetnall, *Alien Contact—Window on Another World*, Neville Spearman, Sudbury, Suffolk, 1981.

Reich, Wilhelm, *Contact with Space—Oranur, Second Report,1951-56*, Core Pilot Press, Rangeley, ME, 1957.

Reich, Wilhelm, *Oranur Experiment: First Report, 1947-51*, Wilhelm Reich Foundation, Rangeley, ME, 1951.

Reich, Wilhelm, *The Function of the Orgasm*, 1942, Orgone Institute Press, New York, NY, 1948.

Reich, Wilhelm, *The Orgone Energy Accumulator: Its Scientific and Medical Use*, The Wilhelm Reich Foundation, Rangeley, ME, 1951.

Screeton, Paul, *Quicksilver Heritage: The Mystic Leys Their Legacy of Ancient Wisdom*, Thorsons, Wellingborough, Northants, 1974.

Shuttlewood, Arthur, *The Flying Saucerers*, Sphere Books, London, 1976.

Shuttlewood, Arthur, *The Warminster Mystery*, Neville Spearman, Sudbury, Suffolk, 1967.

Shuttlewood, Arthur, *UFO Magic in Motion*, Sphere Books, London, 1979.

Shuttlewood, Arthur, *UFOs—Key to the New Age*, Regency Press, London, 1971.

Sikes, Wirt, *British Goblins: Welsh Folk-lore, Fairy Mythology, Legends and Tradi-

tions, Low, Marston, Searle and Rivington, London, 1880.

Sitchin, Zecharia, *The Twelfth Planet*, 1977, Inner Traditions, Rochester, VT, 1991.

Smith, A. H., *English Place-Name Elements*, 2 vols., Cambridge Univ. Press, 1956.

Spence, Lewis, *The Myths of the North American Indians*, Harrap, London, 1916.

Strand, Erling, *Project Hessdalen 1984: Final Technical Report*, Project Hessdalen, 1984.

Strainic, M., "Once Upon a Time in the Wheat," *The Circular* 3:1 (1991), pp. 6–7.

Strieber, Whitley, *Communion*, Wm. Morrow, New York, NY, 1987.

Tsytovich, V.N., G.E. Morfill, V.E. Fortov, N.G. Gusein-Zade1, B.A. Klumov and S.V. Vladimirov, "From plasma crystals and helical structures towards inorganic living matter," *New Journal of Physics* 9 (2007) 263.

Vallee, Jacques, *Passport to Magonia*, Regnery, New York, NY, 1968.

Westwood, Jennifer, *Albion: A Guide to Legendary Britain*, Granada, London, 1985.

Wingfield, George, "Beyond the current paradigms," in Noyes and Taylor, pp. 99–110.

Wingfield, George, "Ever Increasing Circles," in Good, ed., *The UFO Report 1991*, pp. 15–6.

Wingfield, George, "The English Crop Circles in 1988," in Good, ed., *The UFO Report 1990*.

Wingfield, George, "Towards an understanding of the nature of the circles," in Bartholomew, pp. 25–7.

Online

"An enormous number of UFO sightings before Tsunami and earthquake in South and Southeast Asia—were they trying to warn?" *India Daily*, December 31, 2004, at http://www.indiadaily.com/editorial/12-31h-04.asp.

Collins, Andrew, "Cygnus X-3 and the Cosmic Ray Mystery," at http://www.andrewcollins.com/page/articles/thecygnusmystery_cygnusx3.htm.

Cramer, John G, "Children of the Swan," *Analog: Alternative View Column AV-12* (March 1986), at http://www.npl.washington.edu/AV/

altvw12.html.

Cramer, John G, "More about Wormholes—To the Stars in No Time," *Analog*: Alternative column AV-39 (May 1990), at http://www.npl.washington.edu/AV/altvw39.html.

Doyle, Alister, "Botswana 'snake rock' may show Stone Age religion," *Reuters*, November 30, 2006, at http://www.alertnet.org/thenews/newsdesk/L30693310.htm.

"It might be life Jim . . . ', physicists discover inorganic dust with life–like qualities," *Physorg.com*, August 9th 2007 at http://physorg.com/news105869123.html.

"Look to quark stars for fifth dimension," *New Scientist* 194:2609, June 23, 2007, p. 12, at http://www.newscientist.com/data/pdf/press/2609/260912.pdf

"Neolithic human, animal figures unearthed in southeastern Turkey," *People's Daily Online*, source: xinhua, at http://english.people.com.cn/200610/10/eng20061010_310385.html.

Zahir, Fazile, "Close encounters of the Turkish kind," *Asia Times Online*, at http://www.atimes.com/atimes/Middle_East/IJ31Ak02.html.

Videos

Crop Circle Communiqué, CircleVision Production, 1991.

Index

fairy folk, 90–91, 106;
Kennet Avenue, 140, 205;
megalithic complex, Wilts., xvii, 6, 103, 116, 132, 213, 224;
super ley line, 145
Avebury Trusloe, Wilts., UK, dumbbell, 26, 138;
Roy Lucas, 116
Aveley, Essex, UK, Day abduction site, 167–170, 177
Aveley abduction case, 174–176, 180, 203, 210–212

B

Ball lightning, 118–119, 129, 153, 190
Bangladesh, 217
Barbury Castle, Wilts., UK, formation, xvii, 6–8, 14–15, 77, 84, 96, 109, 138, 144–145, 149, 158, 223;
hill fort, 6, 8, 12, 14, 16, 19, 96;
lights, 9
Barnaföldi, Gergely Gabor, 194
Barnes, Ray, 118–120, 153
Barrows,
ancient monuments, 6, 17, 27, 94, 96, 99, 128;
chalk image, 13;
crop circles, 145, 182;
fairy/troll activity, 181, 182;
geomagnetic anomalies, 78;
nodal points, 128;
orgone accumulators, 106–107, 126;
power sites, 86, 99, 102;
weather control, 113–114, 126
Basidiomycota (fungus), 85
Basterfield, Keith, 70
Bastian, H. Charlton, 38–39
Beaker People, 26
Beckhampton, Wilts., UK, 9;
crop circles, 10, 23, 26, 77, 138, 158;
crop circle group, 150;
lights, 132;
Waggon and Horses ph., 150
Beginnings of Life, The (Bastian), 39
Bell, Melvyn, 116
Bernard, Essex psychic, 105, 107, 176–177, 182, 208
Big Bang, the, 180, 191
Big cat sightings, 128
Big Dipper, the, 203
Bio–energetic beacon, 50
Bioforms,
creation of, 3;
crop circle creation, 109;
effects of contact with, 60;

film images, 50, 53;
orgone/plasma constructs, 59, 93, 109, 187, 220;
water, 59–60
Biological ether, 38
Bions, 38–39, 123
Bion vesicles, 38–39, 60, 129
Biophysics, 36
Bioplasmic energy, 49
Bishop's Canning, Wilts., UK, 97
Black darts, 51–52
Black holes, 190
Black's Meadow, Windsor Hill, Bucks., UK, xix–xx
Blackbird, Operation, Bratton, Wilts., UK, 27
Blackmore, Charles, 68
Blind springs, 107–108
Bloy, Colin, 146
Book of Knowledge: The Keys of Enoch, The (Hurtak), 211
Borderland Sciences Research Foundation, 55
Boreham Wood, Wilts., UK, dolphin formation, 139
Botswana, 220
Bouffioulx, Belgium, 72, 74
Bower, Doug, xvii, 147, 152
Bowles, Joyce, 31, 132
Brain, human, effects of electromagnetism, 130, 176, 193;
plasma life forms, 198–199;
reprogramming the temporal cortex, 201, 212;
teleportation, 198
Brain, the, crop formation, Chilton Foliat, Berks., UK, 140–141
Braintree, The Swan ph., Rayne, Essex, UK, 154
Bratton, Wilts., UK, xxi, 27
Bratton Castle, Wilts., UK, 27
Brief History of Time, A (Hawking), 143
British Broadcasting Corporation (BBC), 5, 23
British UFO Research association (BUFORA), xix, xx, 46
Broadhurst, Paul, 145
Bronze Age culture, and art, 13, 16, 94, 96, 137;
earthen mounds, 90, 99, 107, 182;
weather control, 113–114
Brown, Old Ambrose, 90
Brown, Ken, 23
Brownite, 45–47
Burderop Down, Wilts., UK, 6
Burford, Oxon., UK, 87

beams of radiation, 222, 223
Cygnus-X region, 223

D

DAI, *see* German Archaeological Institute, 210
Daily Star, The (newspaper), 5
Dandridge, Tennessee, USA, 158
Dark energy, 199
Dark Gods, The (Roberts), 147
Davies, Barbara, 157
Day family, 167–174
Day, John, 167–174, 203, 206, 210;
    abduction experience, 167–173;
    effects of the experience, 169–170;
    predictions by John, 202–203;
    Rollright Stones, 104;
    Silbury Hill, 206, 210;
    Watchers, 206, 208, 210, 224;
    West Essex, 167, 171–172, 177, 201, 220
Day, Kevin, 167, 169, 171, 177
Day, Sue, 167, 169–171, 173–174, 177, 203
Daylesford Hill Farm, Oxon., UK, 85
Daytime Live (television program), 23, 77
Dead Sea, Israel, 125
Dead Sea Scrolls, 125, 208
Deadly Orgone Radiation (DOR), 42–45, 60, 65, 68, 78–80, 98–99
Deetken, Chad, 82
Delgado, Pat, 22–23, 69, 77, 109, 137, 148–150, 156
Department of Scientific and Industrial Research (DSIR), NZ, 67, 69
Deuterium, 159
Devereux, Paul,
    Dragon Project, 87, 103–104, 158, 167;
    earthlights, 128–129, 131–132, 165–166;
    geophysical anomalies, 214
Devil, 88, 211
Devizes, Wilts., UK, xvi, 27, 116, 138;
    four ring circle, 14
Dexter, Adrian, 146
DNA, 140, 187, 189, 219–220
Dolphin, whale formations, 139–140, 150, 158
Dolmen, 78, 94, 99, 103, 105
Dorset, 13
Dowsers, 99, 103, 104, 107–109, 113, 114, 123, 145, 146
Dragon and the Disc, The (F.W. Holiday), 96, 139
Dragon Project, The, 82, 87, 103–105, 158, 167
Dragons, origins of, 96, 102

Dragon symbol, 98–99
Dream communications, 173, 174, 177, 196, 208, 222, 223, 226, 227
Dudley, Marshall, 158–159, 161
Duke University, North Carolina, USA, 157
Durant, Neil, 153

E

Ea, Reich's UFOs, 43
Early British Trackways (Watkins), 100
Earth energies, xvii, 10, 82, 99, 101, 103–104, 107, 126, 170, 202
Earthlights, 129–133, 165–166, 180, 210;
    and light consciousness, 165–166;
    and light phenomena, 10, 59, 87, 131, 132, 202;
    piezoelectric properties, 129–130,
    at Warminster, Wilts., 132–133
Earth Lights, (Devereux and McCartney), 129
Earth Lights Revelation (Devereux), 87, 129, 166–167
Earth mysteries, xxii, 78, 100–104, 113, 126, 128, 179, 214
Earthquakes, 129, 214, 219
Earthquake lights, 129, 210
Earthquest, 114–115
Earthquest News (journal), xxi, 104, 115
Earth Under Fire (Laviolette), 216
East Field, Alton Barnes, Wilts., UK, xxi, xxii, 17–19, 21, 23, 96
East Kennet, Wilts., UK, barrow, 6, 96;
    formation, 150
East, Nicole, 153–154
Eastbourne, Sussex, UK, 13
Eden, biblical land, 209, 212
Eden, Bill, 105
Edessa, Turkey, 209
Edwards, Bill, 86–87
Egypt, 96
Einstein, Albert, 41, 180
Eisenman, Robert, 125
Elders, Elder race, 137
Electromagnetic anomalies, at ancient sites, xi, xxi
Electromagnetic fields, 57, 65, 117–118, 130–131, 175–177, 192–194, 201, 213
Electromagnetic spectrum, 3, 51, 53, 161, 179, 190, 199
Electromagnetism, 41, 176, 180
    see also EM radiation and EM spectrum
Electronic sparrow, 23
Elements of Earth Mysteries, The (Heselton), 101

249

Overtown Farm, Wilts., UK, 8
Oxford University, Oxford, UK, xii
Oxfordshire, circles 1939–1946, 69, 87, 133
"Oz factor," 175, 199

P

Paeroa, North Island, NZ, 67
Palestine, 120, 178
Palmer, Ray, 56
Panspermia, theory of, 192
Particle beams, 190
Passport to Magonia (Vallee), 181
Pasteur, Louis, 38–38
Peak–Garland, Heather, 132
Pedley, George, 57–58
Peebles, Ohio, serpent mound, 139
Peggie with th' Lantern, 86
Pennisi, Albert, 58
Persinger, Dr. Michael,
    anomalous activity and recorded
        solar flares, 215;
    anomalous events and human evo-
        lution, 220;
    electromagnetic fields' effects on the
        human brain, 130, 176, 214;
    gravity shock wave, 214–216;
    paranormal events and electromag-
        netic fields, 130, 176;
    space–time transients and geophysi-
        cal abnormalities, 132, 213–215;
    stellar–fortean contiguities, 215;
    strange light phenomena, 131;
    UFO encounters, 176
Peru, xvii
Phillips, Graham, 127
Phillips, Ken, xix
Phinehas, 125
Physics, *see* individual entries for
    astrophysics;
    biophysics;
    etherian physics;
    metaphysics;
    quantum physics;
    plasma physics
Pillinger, Ian, 14
Pinelandia Biophysical Laboratory,
    Grass Lake, Michigan, USA, 156
Pink blancmange, 46
Pinket, 86
Places of power, 78, 170, 210;
    discussion of, 98–110
Places of Power, Secret Energies at Ancient Sites
    (Devereux), 104
Plasma, 59–60, 65, 74, 116–18, 129, 190;

aspects of,
    balls, 129;
    discharges, 159, 161;
    earthquake lights 129, 210
    earthlights, *see* under Earthlights;
    fire, 129, 153;
    intelligences, 199, 211, 216, 222, 225;
    jets, 218–219;
    light forms, 174, 177, 187, 197, 199, 210, 205; 221;
    lightning, 156;
    meteor, 204;
    stars, 190;
    streams, 159;
    super hot, 194, 218;
    UFOs, *see* UFOs;
buoyant plasmas, 179, 192–194, 201, 208;
constructs, xvii, 57, 129, 159, 175, 177, 182, 185, 187, 192, 194, 197, 200, 202–203, 211, 215, 220;
deuterium plasma, 159;
environments, xviii, 130, 187, 190–191, 193, 197;
fifth dimension, 220;
fourth state of matter, 190;
generators, 159;
manifestation, 180;
plasma vortex, Meaden vortex, xii, xxi, 19, 109, 118, 120, 129, 153, 165, 175, 203;
plasma–based life, 189–202, 210, 211, 220, 221, 224;
plasma physics, 159, 199;
plasma source, 220–222;
plasmons, 192;
quark–gluon, 191, 194;
self–organization, 189, 190, 192;
state, 3, 60;
Plasma physics, 159, 199
Plot, Robert, xii
Poltergeist activity, 69, 170, 173
Port Blair, Andaman Island, India, 217
Potter, Clive, 46
Prana, 100
Pratt, Edward "Ted," 32, 132
Preshute Down, Wilts., UK, Temple
    Farm formation 7.19.91, 15, 18, 81
Prestatyn, North Wales, 52–54
Price, Ken, 154
Probe Report, The (Mrzyglod), xxi
Project Blue Book, 63
Project Hessdalen, Norway, 165–166, 192
Psychics, 1;
    as communicators with the

256

S

Sagan, Carl, 219
St. Catherine's Hill, Winchester, Hants., UK, 31-32
St. Michael Line, Cornwall to Norfolk coast, UK, 145
Salisbury, Wilts., UK, 31, 116
Salt Knowe barrow, Orkney Isles, Scotland, 181
Samhain, 114
San culture and bushmen, 220
San Diego, California, USA, 55
Sand gardens, in *zen* tradition, 123
Sand paintings, in Amerindian tradition, 123
Şanlıurfa, Turkey, 209-210
Saucer nests, 116;
  animal reactions to, 109;
  Australia, xx, 57-59;
  crop circles, 120, 181;
  fairy folk, 116;
  North Island, New Zealand, 65, 67-68, 160;
  precursors of crop circles, xiii-xiv, 47, 75-76, 83;
  UFOs, 57, 59-60, 65, 84, 131, 160-161
Schmidt, Dr. Klaus, 210
Schrödinger, Erwin, xv
Schrödinger's Cat, xv
Screeton, Paul, 101-103
Secret arrows, in *feng-shui* tradition, 100
Secret of the Saucers, The, (Angelucci), 184
Self-organization of inorganic matter, 189, 190
Seven Stars, The, Alton Barnes, Wilts., UK, 21
Seven Year Itch (movie), 166
SGR 1806 - 20, 216
Sha, 98-99
Shaman and his practices, 37, 100, 121-122, 124-126, 209-210
Shepherd of Winterbourne Basset, 90, 181
Shipton-under-Wychwood, Oxon., UK, 87
Shivalingam, 206
Shuttlewood, Arthur, 28-30, 63
Silbury Hill, Wilts., UK, 24-25, 27-28, 90, 106, 132, 150-151, 205-206, 210, 223-224
Sitchin, Zecharia, 211
Sky creatures, 3, 50, 51
Sky Creatures; Living UFOs (Constable), 3-4, 15, 37, 48, 50, 56, 59, 65, 154, 213
Smoke at sites, 73, 116-117

Snailwell, Cambs., UK, 142
Snake worship, 220
Solar flare activity, 214, 215
Sounds, unusual,
  at ancient sites, 104;
  at Barbury Castle, 109;
  at Cheesefoot Head, 22, 208;
  at Chilcomb Down, 33;
  "electronic sparrow" at Kimpton, Hants., 23;
  in association with circles, 1, 10, 118;
  infrasound/ultrasound, 81;
  trilling noise, 22-23, 30, 206-208;
Southend-on-Sea, Essex, UK, 85
Space Brothers, 48-49
Space People (Van Tassel), 61, 100, 101 179, 202
Spacecraft from Beyond Three Dimensions (Allen), 55
Space-Time Transients And Unusual Events (Persinger and Lafrenière), 214
Space-time, 179-181, 187, 193-195, 197, 199, 222
Space-time transients, 130, 132, 176, 214-215
Spare, Austin Osman, xvi
Speed, Victoria, Australia, 70, 154
Spence, Lewis, xii-xiii
Spielberg, Stephen, 63, 170, 198
Spirit Guide "Blue," 222
Spunkie, 86
Sri Lanka, 217
Stack Rocks, Dyfed, South Wales, UK, 183-184
Stamford, Lincs., UK, 203-204
Stanton Moor, Derbys., UK, 114
Star Fellowship (Tony Wedd), 100
Star-country, xiii-xiv
Star-maiden, xii-xiv
Stars,
  black holes, 190;
  collapsed, 190, 193;
  cygnets, 194, 219, 221-222, 224;
  dwarf, 159;
  magnetar, 216;
  microblazar, 218;
  nebula, 190;
  neutron, 159, 190-191, 193-194, 197, 216, 218-222, 224;
  nova (new), 214;
  quarks, 193-194, 216, 220, 224;
  supernovae, 190, 214
Starch, 45, 47
Stenness, Orkney Isles, Scotland, 181
Steiner, Rudolph, 49-50
Still, Ernie, 46

258

Stone circles, 78, 82, 94, 99, 102–103, 113, 170, 223–224;
    as orgone accumulators, 113;
    Avebury. xvii, 6;
    Nine Ladies, 114–116;
Stonehenge, see individual entry;
    Ring of Brodgar, 181;
    Rollright Stones, 86
Stonehenge, Wilts., UK, 8, 28, 96, 103, 138, 141, 145, 149
Strieber, Whitley, 208, 210
Strontium–90, (isotope), 67, 161
Stuart-Menzies, John, 65, 67–69, 160–161
Stump, Bedfellow (ca. 1633), 93
Sumatra, Indonesia, 217
Sun and the Serpent, The (Broadhurst), 145
Sunday Telegraph, The, (newspaper), 143
Sunderland, Gaynor, 52–53
Sunderland, Marion, 52
Superforce, 180–181
Superwave, 216
Sweden, 165
Sydenham, outskirts of London, UK, 195
Symbolism, xvi, 125, 150, 223

T

1017 Activation, 223
Takapuna, North Island, NZ, 67
Talmudic tradition, 125
Tamil Nadu, India, 217
Taupo, North Island, NZ, 65
Taylor, Busty, xxii, 5, 78;
    1987 Chilcomb Down black darts picture, 51–52;
    Circlemakers at Cheesefoot Head, 22;
    Crop Cirle Enigma, The, 13;
    duping of, 153;
    white jelly at 1985 Goodworth Clatford circle, 45
Telegraph Hill, Hants., UK, 31
Teleportation, 178, 197, 199
Temple Farm formation, 15
Temporal lobe cortex, 176, 201
Tennelec/Nucleus laboratory, Oak Ridge, TN, USA, 158, 161
Tetzlaf, Roy, 78
Thing, The (Shuttlewood), 63
Thomas, Franklin, 49
Tichit, Germain, 59
Tigris River, Middle East, 209
Today (newspaper), 147–148, 152
Tom at East Field, Alton Barnes, Wilts., UK, 23–24

Tomas, Andrew, 2
Tony Wedd: New Age Pioneer (Heselton), 101
Tornado and Storm Research Organization (TORRO), xxi
trowes (trolls), 181
Tsodilo Hills, Botswana, 220
Tsunamis, 214, 216–218, 219
Tsytovich, V.N., 189–190, 192, 197
Tucson, Arizona, Little Orgonon, Reich Institute, 44, 79
Tully, Queensland, Australia, 57–59, 68, 70, 148
Turkey, 149, 209, 210, 212
Turriff, Victoria, Australia, 70
Twelfth Planet, The (Sitchin), 211
Twigg, Alan, 45

U

Uffington, Berks., UK, white horse, xvii, 6, 27, 145
UFO Experience: A Scientific Inquiry, The, (Hynek), 63
UFO-Flying Saucers over Britain (Chapman), 62
UFOs, (see individual entries for more specific details), intro., xi, xvi–xviii;
    Africa's Rift Valley, 219;
    Angelucci, 184–185;
    archetypes and archetypal forms, 178, 179, 202, 205, 208;
    Armstrong, Gerry, 195–196;
    as bioforms/"critters," 3, 15, 187, 213;
    as multidimensional experiences, 181, 211;
    as physical effects on humans, 60, 131, 176;
    Asian tsunami, 217–218;
    Black's Meadow, Windsor Hill, Bucks., UK, xix–xx;
    Bronze Age culture, 96;
    BUFORA, see individual entry;
    Chilcomb, Hants., UK, 31, 133;
    communication with, 48–49, 171–174, 202–206, 210;
    Constable, T. J., summary of work, 48–54, 57;
    crop circles, xxi, 29, 37, 63, 96, 133, 161, 187;
    Day abduction, 167–174;
    earthlights, 129–130, 133, 180;
    electromagnetic effects, 130–131;
    fairy folk, see individual entry;
    fault lines, 128–129, 217;
    film images, 51–54, 65, 72, 131, 211;

259

Wickford, Essex, UK, 204
Wilcot Road, Alton Barnes, Wilts., UK, 18
Wilder, Leonard, 170, 202
Will-o'-the-Wisp, 29, 85, 129, 178
Wiltshire Times (newspaper), xx, 84
Winchester, Hants., UK, 22, 31, 146, 148
Windmill Hill, Wilts., UK, 26
Windsor Hill, Bucks., UK, xix
Wingfield, George,
    Cornference, 138, 141;
    Doug and Dave scandal, 150, 152;
    formations at
        Alton Barnes, 51–52;
        Cheesefoot Head, 22, 207;
        Devizes, 14;
    Ickleton, 142
Winterbourne Basset, Wilts., UK, 90, 181
Wintle, Richard, 8
Wisley, Surrey, UK, 46
Witches, 86, 113–114, 126, 128

Wooburn Green, Bucks., UK, 84
    Black's Meadow circles, xix
Wood, Ethel, 87
Woods, Jim, 50–51
Wormholes, 221–222
Wormwood Hill, Cambs., UK, 105, 107, 176, 182, 208
Wroughton, Wilts., UK, airfield, 8

Y

Yatton Keynell, Wilts., UK, 92–93, 185
Yucca Valley, California, USA, 50

Z

Zadoks, 125–126
Zero–point energy, 199
Zen, 123–124
Zohar, 125

ANDREW COLLINS

Andrew Collins was born in 1957 and, after being adopted at a tender age, was brought up by loving parents in the Essex town of Wickford. As a teenager he became a UFO investigator and was quickly drawn to the apparent psychic connection between witnesses and what they see. In 1977 he investigated the first ever missing time abduction case reported in the UK that took place at Aveley, West Esssex. It was an investigation that changed his life. In 1979 he became a journalist with the magazine *Strange Phenomena* and openly sought the help of psychics in an attempt to better understand the relationship between UFOs, prehistoric sites, earth energies, and the human mind. This work resulted in two books: *The Circlemakers* in 1992 and *Alien Energy* in 1994.

As a science and history writer, Andrew is the author of various books that challenge the way we perceive the past. These publications include *From the Ashes of Angels* (1996), which shows that the Watchers of the book of Enoch were human angels as well as the bringers of civilization, and that their homeland—the biblical land of Eden—was situated in southeast Turkey, where the Neolithic revolution began; *Gods of Eden* (1998), which shows that Egyptian civilization is thousands of years older than is conventionally believed; *Gateway to Atlantis* (2000), which demonstrates that Plato's Atlantis was located in Cuba and the Bahamas, and *The Cygnus Mystery* (2006), which argues that cosmic rays from the Cygnus constellation were responsible for advances in human evolution as well as the origin of the earliest sky religions, including that of ancient Egypt. Andrew lives near Marlborough, Wiltshire, in the heart of crop circle country, with his wife Sue.

For more information on books and current research by Andrew Collins, go to his website at www.andrewcollins.com.

EDGAR CAYCE'S A.R.E.

What Is A.R.E.?

The Association for Research and Enlightenment, Inc., (A.R.E.®) was founded in 1931 to research and make available information on psychic development, dreams, holistic health, meditation, and life after death. As an open–membership research organization, the A.R.E. continues to study and publish such information, to initiate research, and to promote conferences, distance learning, and regional events. Edgar Cayce, the most documented psychic of our time, was the moving force in the establishment of A.R.E.

Who Was Edgar Cayce?

Edgar Cayce (1877–1945) was born on a farm near Hopkinsville, Ky. He was an average individual in most respects. Yet, throughout his life, he manifested one of the most remarkable psychic talents of all time. As a young man, he found that he was able to enter into a self–induced trance state, which enabled him to place his mind in contact with an unlimited source of information. While asleep, he could answer questions or give accurate discourses on any topic. These discourses, more than 14,000 in number, were transcribed as he spoke and are called "readings."

Given the name and location of an individual anywhere in the world, he could correctly describe a person's condition and outline a regimen of treatment. The consistent accuracy of his diagnoses and the effectiveness of the treatments he prescribed made him a medical phenomenon, and he came to be called the "father of holistic medicine."

Eventually, the scope of Cayce's readings expanded to include such subjects as world religions, philosophy, psychology, parapsychology, dreams, history, the missing years of Jesus, ancient civilizations, soul growth, psychic development, prophecy, and reincarnation.

A.R.E. Membership

People from all walks of life have discovered meaningful and life–transforming insights through membership in A.R.E. To learn more about Edgar Cayce's A.R.E. and how membership in the A.R.E. can enhance your life, visit our Web site at EdgarCayce.org, or call us toll-free at 800-333-4499.

Edgar Cayce's A.R.E.
215 67th Street
Virginia Beach, VA 23451–2061

EDGARCAYCE.ORG

2012 In Your Pocket
by Geoff Stray

Everything you ever wanted to know about 2012 is packed into this handy little guidebook by 2012 expert Geoff Stray. With illustrations, diagrams, and concise text, Stray takes us on a journey from our past to our future with Mayan prophecies, hints from ancient Egypt, Shamanism, solar cycles, the Galactic alignment, and so much more.

Learn how our past is speaking to us about what lies ahead. What will the world be like after December 21, 2012? This pocket–sized guide gives the answers. A must–have for enthusiasts of ancient mysteries and prophecies, as well as anyone who plans to be alive in 2012!

From 4th Dimension Press

"This book is a rich and intriguing reading delight. I loved it!"
—Caroline Myss, Ph.D

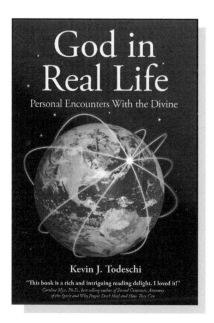

God in Real Life
by Kevin J. Todeschi
CEO of Edgar Cayce's A.R.E.

What if it was truly understood that individuals can have real encounters with the Divine, even in this modern world? What might happen to our collective worldview if we suddenly realized that, in truth, there is a caring God very much concerned about each and every one of us? Presented here are personal accounts from people of all ages, races, and religions who have one thing in common: an experience with the Divine. Their stories suggest that the time has come for our 21st century world to acknowledge that there is much more to us than a simple physical body. Perhaps the time has come to acknowledge that we are never really alone.